THE LETTER OF PETER TO PHILIP

SOCIETY
OF BIBLICAL
LITERATURE

DISSERTATION SERIES

Howard C. Kee, Editor

Number 53

THE LETTER OF PETER TO PHILIP

Text, Translation, and Commentary
by Marvin W. Meyer

Marvin W. Meyer

THE LETTER OF PETER TO PHILIP

TEXT, TRANSLATION, AND COMMENTARY

Scholars Press

Distributed by
Scholars Press
101 Salem Street
Chico, California 95926

THE LETTER OF PETER TO PHILIP

TEXT, TRANSLATION, AND COMMENTARY

Marvin W. Meyer

BT
1390
.L3813

1981

Library of Congress Cataloging in Publication Data

Letter of Peter to Philip. English & Coptic.
   The letter of Peter to Philip.

   (Dissertation series ; no. 53)
   Text of the letter in Coptic and English.
   Originally presented as the author's thesis.
   Bibliography: p.
   Includes index.
   1. Letter of Peter to Philip. 2. Gnosticism.
I. Meyer, Marvin W. II. Series: Society of Biblical
Literature. Dissertation series ; no. 53.
BT1390.L3813 1981   229'.93   80-28612
ISBN 0-89130-463-0 (pbk.)

Printed in the United States of America
1 2 3 4 5
Edwards Brothers, Inc.
Ann Arbor, Michigan 48106

To my grandmother, my mother, and my wife:

ⲚⲦⲰⲦⲚ ⲚⲈⲚⲦⲀ₂† ⲚⲀⲈⲒ ⲘⲠⲰⲚⲌ̄

TABLE OF CONTENTS

ABBREVIATIONS AND SIGLA

The abbreviations used follow the guidelines set forth in "Instructions for Contributors," *Journal of Biblical Literature* 95 (1976) 331-46. In addition to the abbreviations listed there, the following should also be noted.

Bethge	Hans-Gebhard Bethge. "Der sogenannte 'Brief des Petrus an Philippus': Die zweite 'Schrift' aus Nag-Hammadi-Codex VIII," *Theologische Literaturzeitung* 103 (1978) 161-70.
Crum	Walter E. Crum. *A Coptic Dictionary.* Oxford: Clarendon, 1939.
Foerster	Werner Foerster, ed. *Gnosis.* 2 vols. Oxford: Clarendon, 1972.
Hennecke-Schneemelcher	Edgar Hennecke. *New Testament Apocrypha.* 2 vols. Ed. Wilhelm Schneemelcher. Philadelphia: Westminster, 1963.
Ménard	Jacques-E. Ménard. *La Lettre de Pierre à Philippe.* Bibliothèque copte de Nag Hammadi 1. Quebec: Université Laval, 1977.
Wisse	Frederik Wisse. Transcription and translation of *The Letter of Peter to Philip.* Wisse's transcription has not yet been published; a final transcription will appear in *Nag Hammadi Codex VIII* of The Coptic Gnostic Library (Nag Hammadi Studies). For the sake of this study, I have used the most recent transcription available, and have also consulted earlier notes and transcriptions. Wisse's translation has been published in *The Nag Hammadi Library in English* (San Francisco: Harper & Row; Leiden: Brill, 1977) 394-98.

The sigla utilized for the texts and translations follow the format adopted for the volumes in The Coptic Gnostic Library; see Alexander Böhlig and Frederik Wisse, *Nag Hammadi Codices III,2 and IV,2: The Gospel of the Egyptians (The Holy Book of the Great Invisible Spirit)* (Nag Hammadi Studies 4; Leiden: Brill, 1975) xiii. The following are most significant.

A dot under a letter signifies that the letter is
visually uncertain. Occasionally a dot is used
without a letter to indicate an ink trace that is
so ambiguous that no letter may confidently be
suggested.

[ ]   Square brackets indicate a lacuna in the manuscript.
When the text cannot be reconstructed, dots occasionally may be used to indicate the approximate
number of letters suggested by the size of the
lacuna.

< >   Pointed brackets indicate a correction of a scribal
omission or error. The correction may insert
letters unintentionally omitted by the scribe, or
replace letters erroneously inserted with what the
scribe presumably intended to write.

{ }   Braces signify superfluous letters or words added
by the scribe.

( )   Parentheses indicate helpful material supplied by
the editor or translator. Although this material
may not directly reflect the text being examined,
it provides useful information for the reader.
Greek forms of the Greek loan words are included
in the translation in parentheses.

PREFACE TO THE PUBLISHED EDITION

In keeping with the principles of the SBLDS, this dissertation is here published in a form nearly identical with that
of the dissertation as original submitted to the faculty of
Claremont Graduate School. It has been shortened a bit, and
several typographical errors and stylistic infelicities have
been improved. In addition, bibliographical entries have been
updated when an article or book previously available only in
typescript has now appeared, and a few new references also
have been included.

My thanks to the staff of Scholars Press, and particularly
Joann Burnich, for help in the final preparation of the manuscript.

Claremont, CA

March, 1981

PREFACE

This dissertation grew out of my participation as research associate in the Coptic Gnostic Library Project of the Institute for Antiquity and Christianity, Claremont, California, from the spring of 1975 until the spring of 1978. My experience on the Project piqued my interest in Gnostic studies, and also provided me with a unique opportunity for access to photographs as well as published and unpublished materials pertaining to the Nag Hammadi library. Furthermore, during late January and early February of 1978, after the conclusion of the archaeological season at Nag Hammadi (Faw Qibli), I was able to spend valuable time at the Coptic Museum in Cairo, and work on the papyrus of Codex VIII. Such opportunities have all been very formative for the present investigation of the second tractate from Codex VIII, *The Letter of Peter to Philip*.

I would like to acknowledge the support and assistance I have received from several people. To my supervisory committee, James Brashler, Elaine H. Pagels, and the chairman, James M. Robinson, I extend a hearty word of thanks, for they have provided useful guidance and saved me from many a foolish blunder. James M. Robinson deserves a special expression of appreciation. He has functioned as my professor, supervisor, advisor, and friend, and I am indebted to him in many ways. Hans Dieter Betz and Kathleen O'Brien Wicker also offered helpful counsel during an earlier stage of the research.

I wish to single out three other people who have been most influential in the production of this study. From my early years my mother and father instilled within me a love of learning, and to them I owe a tremendous debt of gratitude. And to my wife Bonita I offer my most profound thanks. She not only endured but also typed this dissertation.

New York, NY
March, 1979

CHAPTER I

INTRODUCTION

The Letter of Peter to Philip (Ep. Pet. Phil.) is one
of the tractates located in the collection of codices known as
the Nag Hammadi library.[1] The Nag Hammadi library consists of
twelve codices along with eight additional leaves, now designated Codex XIII, which were removed from a codex in antiquity
and slipped inside the front cover of Codex VI. These thirteen
codices contain some fifty-two tractates, with additional
scribal notes and colophons; in addition, tractate 2 from Codex
XI includes five appended subtractates on sacramental matters.
Of these tractates, forty are texts which are neither duplicates nor texts previously known, and of those forty texts
about thirty have survived in rather complete condition. One
of the well-preserved texts is the *Ep. Pet. Phil.*

The Nag Hammadi library was discovered, according to reports, in December of 1945 by Muhammad Ali al-Samman Muhammad
Khalifah, the fertilizer-hunter and blood-avenger.[2] Subsequent
to the discovery, these codices were treated in a rather harsh
manner. They were transported about, passed from hand to hand,
put up for sale, apparently even partly burned in the oven of
the widowed mother of Muhammad Ali, and taken into protective
custody by the Egyptian Department of Antiquities. In the case
of Codex I, the "Jung Codex," most of it was sold abroad to the
Jung Institute, and has only recently been returned to the
Coptic Museum in Cairo, where all the codices now reside in
their conserved state. Although over thirty years have passed
since this discovery, the major portion of the Nag Hammadi
library was not made available for some time on account of
various political and monopolistic roadblocks.[3] However, since
the involvement of UNESCO in the 1960s, and the appointment of
the International Committee for the Nag Hammadi Codices at the
end of 1970, the materials have become increasingly available
to the scholarly world, and now at last the Coptic text and one
or more modern translations of each of the tractates are at the
disposal of the reading public.[4]

Nag Hammadi Codex (NHC) VIII was one of the very last
codices to be made available, and finally was published in the
Facsimile Edition in 1976. Among the more fragmentary of the
codices, Codex VIII has received comparatively little attention
while some of the more complete and seemingly spectacular
codices have attracted the interest of the scholarly world.
This fragmentary codex is best preserved at the beginning and
the end; the first and the last twenty or thirty pages are preserved fairly well. In fact, the loose central portion of the
codex was removed from the cover before the photographs by Jean
Doresse were taken in late 1948, and in 1949 Codex VIII was
packed in a suitcase by Doresse. In 1958 the codex was inven-
toried as consisting of twenty-seven folios (or fifty-four
pages) together with a collection of fragments in envelopes.
In 1961 the pages of Codex VIII which were still in the cover
(pages 1-26 and 113-40) were conserved, and labeled with numbers 1-54.[5] As Martin Krause and Pahor Labib report,

> Alle anderen Seiten waren, meist in mehrere Teile
> zerbrochen und nicht mehr in der richtigen Reihen-
> folge, von den Findern oder Händlern aus dem Leder-
> einband genommen und in Cellophantüten gelegt
> worden....Die Fragmente der übrigen Seiten 27-112,
> die ungeordnet in den Cellophantüten lagen, wurden
> in der vorgefundenen Reihenfolge verglast und er-
> hielten die Nummern 55-128.[6]

Since then the pagination of the central section has been
established, fragments have been placed, and the codex has
been presented in facsimile edition in 1976.[7]

The cover of Codex VIII is of particular interest. Like
the covers of most of the Nag Hammadi codices, the cover of
Codex VIII was made from a piece of sheepskin leather. Darkened on the outside, the hair side, the cover was tooled with
various lines, some of which form a St. Andrew's cross when the
cover is fully opened, and provided with thongs for closing and
tying the codex.[8] On the basis of such features as the dimen-
sions of the cover, the presence or absence of a flap, the use
of staining and tooling, the characteristics of the thongs and
the binding, and the rigidity of the cartonnage-backed leather,
James M. Robinson has suggested a classification of the leather
covers of the various codices.[9] On those bases Robinson

proposes that the covers of VIII and IV, and to some extent V, can be said to belong together. Such correlations between codices, like those between scribal hands, may provide valuable information on the production of the codices within the Nag Hammadi library. Furthermore, the cartonnage lining the cover of Codex VIII has yielded a Greek document which can be dated after 309 C.E. Such a date would suggest that Codex VIII was manufactured at a time well into the fourth century, a date which relates well to other datable clues for the manufacture of the codices in the Nag Hammadi collection.[10]

Codex VIII is dominated by the first long tractate, entitled *Zostrianos*.[11] Most of the tractates in the Nag Hammadi corpus are relatively short. *Zost.*, however, like *Marsanes*, is an exception to this tendency, and occupies most of Codex VIII: pages 1-132. *Zost.* actually occupies more pages than any other tractate in the Nag Hammadi library, although many of the pages have deteriorated so badly that a clear translation and comprehension of the text is often impossible. *Zost.* is provided with the subscribed title ⲍⲱⲥⲧⲣⲓⲁⲛⲟⲥ as well as an appended cryptogram which mentions both Zostrianos and Zoroaster. Zostrianos is also mentioned in the *incipit* (1,3), and although the reference is partially in a lacuna (ⲍⲱⲥ[   ]) the restoration seems certain. Zoroaster was the founder of the Persian Zoroastrian religious heritage, and an exceedingly significant figure in late antiquity, while Zostrianos was said to have been a close relative of Zoroaster.[12]

Zost. is a Gnostic tractate which provides a series of revelations about the heavenly realm. Zostrianos, it seems, is living a life of separation in this world of darkness, and raises some difficult questions concerning the meaning of existence and the nature of the heavenly realm. Deeply troubled about these questions he raises, Zostrianos finally is visited by the angel of the knowledge of the Light, and is given a guided tour of the glorious heavens. Consequently, Zostrianos ascends on high, is baptized in the names of powers at the various levels, and receives instruction about the beings and glories in the heavenly regions. Following those revelations,

Zostrianos concludes his ecstatic trip, returns back to earth,
and records his γνῶσις on three tablets. The tractate closes
with a stirring sermon in which Zostrianos awakens "an erring
crowd" (130,14) by proclaiming, "Know those who are living,
and the holy seed of Seth" (130,16-17). Continuing, Zostrianos
cautions against a wanton participation in corporeality: "Flee
from the madness and the bondage of femaleness, and choose for
yourselves the salvation of maleness" (131,5-8). For "the
gentle Father has sent you the savior, and has given you power"
(131,14-16).

      Zost. stands as representative of a non-Christian Gnosti-
cism, with notable Jewish and Neoplatonic affinities.[13] On
account of the several references to Seth as well as other
names and distinctive features, *Zost.* is claimed by some to
be a representative document of Sethian Gnosticism.[14]

      If such is the nature of *Zost.*, how does this tractate
relate to the second and concluding tractate in Codex VIII,
the *Ep. Pet. Phil.*? The *Ep. Pet. Phil.* is tucked away quite
unobtrusively into the final eight and one-half pages of the
codex; is there any particular reason for its inclusion with
Zost. in Codex VIII? We do suspect that scribes may have
selected documents for inclusion in certain codices on account
of characteristics shared by all the tractates. Thus Codex I
may be a collection of Valentinian tractates, and Codex V is,
in large part, an "apocalyptic" codex. When we look for cor-
responding comparisons between *Zost.* and the *Ep. Pet. Phil.*,
we note a few similarities in terminology, perspective, and
revelatory concern, including some general similarities between the Sophia material in *Zost.* and the non-Christian
"Sophia" myth embedded within the *Ep. Pet. Phil.* Yet it is
clear that, as they now stand, *Zost.* is a non-Christian Gnostic
tractate while the *Ep. Pet. Phil.* has a Christian Gnostic
character. Hence it may be the case that the *Ep. Pet. Phil.*
was included in Codex VIII not so much because of affinities
with *Zost.* as because of the amount of valuable space available
to the scribe after the conclusion of *Zost.* The scribe apparently had a number of tractates and codices to copy, and the

Ep. Pet. Phil. was of an appropriate length to function as
the concluding tractate to Codex VIII.[15]

For around two decades little was known or written about
the *Ep. Pet. Phil.* While the attention of the scholarly
world was riveted upon the few tractates which were coming
to light, such as the *Gos. Truth* and the *Gos. Thom.*, practically the only information on the *Ep. Pet. Phil.* available
to the reading public came from a couple of early inventories
by Jean Doresse. Doresse describes his experiences in Cairo
during the autumn of 1948 as exciting but traumatic. He was
asked to assist in the examination of the Nag Hammadi codices
while war raged all around.

> I was allowed to make no more than a rapid inspection
> of them--given just time enough to identify, to my
> personal satisfaction, the principal works they con-
> tained and to take notes of a few characteristic
> passages. Egypt was then at war with Israel, and on
> several occasions air-raid warnings (sounded on the
> slightest justification) cut short the few evenings
> upon which I was allowed access to the documents.[16]

During the following spring, Doresse was commissioned by the
Council of the Coptic Museum

> to draw up an expert description, more detailed than
> the first notes I had been able to make, and this
> second description remains, up to the present, *the
> only complete and direct inventory of the documents*
> that has been made: no other title of any work has
> yet been added to the list that I then prepared.[17]

Just when it seemed that the documents were about to be made
available, however, political and military chaos broke loose,
and much of the Nag Hammadi library was inaccessible for years.[18]

In an essay by Jean Doresse and Togo Mina which was composed shortly before the death of Togo Mina in 1949, a very
brief reference is made to our tractate. After mentioning the
three (*sic!*) tractates of the codex,[19] and providing a few
remarks on *Zost.* and its cryptogram, the authors finally
mention the *Ep. Pet. Phil.*: "Le volume se termine enfin par
une *Epître de Pierre à Philippe*, moins chrétienne toutefois
que son titre ne le ferait supposer."[20] This terse reference
passes on little information other than the title and the
marginally Christian character of at least part of the

tractate. Even in 1958 Doresse had little to say about the
Ep. Pet. Phil. Although he comments extensively on *Zost.*,
he breezes by the *Ep. Pet. Phil.* by noting that just as we
can leave aside the *Apoc. Pet.* from further discussion, so
too "we can also pass by the *Epistle of Peter to Philip* (No.
15)."[21] Apparently Doresse had not directed much attention,
during his early inventories, to our tractate. Thus later,
secondary descriptions also reflect this paucity of knowledge
about the *Ep. Pet. Phil.* In 1950 Henri-Charles Puech writes,
"L'ignorance où nous sommes du contenu de l'*Epître de Pierre
à Philippe* (36) interdit de hasarder à son propos la moindre
hypothèse,"[22] and in 1957 he must be content merely to refer
to "une épître de 'Pierre à Philippe, son frère aîné et son
compagnon.'"[23] In 1971 Martin Krause and Pahor Labib only
quote the title, provide the line numbers, and add in a foot-
note, "Zum Inhalt machen weder Doresse noch Puech Angaben."[24]

Meanwhile, exciting events were transpiring elsewhere.[25]
While in attendance at the Messina Colloquium in April of 1966,
James Robinson spoke with Martin Krause concerning the materials in the Nag Hammadi library which were still unassigned.
In particular they discussed the *Ep. Pet. Phil.* Krause indicated that he had made a German précis of the tractate for
Wilhelm Schneemelcher, who was making plans for the third
edition of *Neutestamentliche Apokryphen*. In addition, Krause
mentioned that he had a transcription of the tractate in his
notebook of transcriptions in Münster, transcriptions made
while he was working at the Coptic Museum in Cairo. Krause
invited Robinson to come to Münster and copy his transcription
of the *Ep. Pet. Phil.* While still in Messina, however, Krause
showed Robinson a photograph of the first page, page 132, of
the tractate. Robinson stayed up late into the night studying
the photograph; he prepared a preliminary transcription and
translation, and showed it to Krause the next morning. Subsequently, Robinson did in fact visit Münster, and was able
to obtain copies of Krause's transcription of the *Ep. Pet.
Phil.*

These copies of the tractate were carried by Robinson to
Claremont, and were the focus of attention for some time.
Already during the summer of 1966 Ernest Tune, Robinson, and
several graduate students began to study the *Ep. Pet. Phil.*
During this summer, too, the newspapers began to pick up the
story of this tractate. In July the Los Angeles *Times*, the
Pomona *Progress-Bulletin*, and other newspapers printed
articles on the Nag Hammadi library and the *Ep. Pet. Phil.*
On July 13, for example, the *Times* published a story which
was entitled as follows: "Letter Tells of Risen Christ's
Unrecorded Visit: Coptic Document Found in Egypt Rivals Dead
Sea Scrolls, Claremont Scholar Says." The *Progress-Bulletin*
carried stories on both July 13 and July 14; the July 14
account was accompanied by a photograph with a caption which
stated that Robinson was pictured holding a letter of Peter
in his hands, a letter which Robinson had found while in the
Near East. Not wishing to be taken for a thief or a smuggler,
Robinson quickly corrected this and other errors in a letter
to the editor of the *Progress-Bulletin*.

During the autumn semester of 1966-67 Ernest Tune offered
a course at Claremont Graduate School entitled "Religion 234:
Coptic Gnostic Literature." In this seminar various people
from Claremont were initiated into Coptic and Gnostic studies
through an exposure specifically to the *Ep. Pet. Phil.* During
the fall of 1966 the Institute for Antiquity and Christianity
was also being founded, and the Coptic Gnostic Library Project
was envisaged. The Project team was even able to travel to
Ann Arbor, Michigan, during the summer of 1967, in order to
study with H. J. Polotsky. Members of the team took on various tasks and tractates within the Nag Hammadi corpus, and the
Ep. Pet. Phil. was assigned to Frederik Wisse.

Currently more attention is being shown to the *Ep. Pet.
Phil.*[26] Part of the reason for this increased attention involves the greater willingness of scholars to share insights
and materials relating to the tractate. In 1972 Krause published a lengthy summation of the contents of the *Ep. Pet.
Phil.* as a part of a discussion which focused upon *Acts Pet.
12 Apost.*[27] In 1974 Pheme Perkins presented a paper at the

annual meeting of the Society of Biblical Literature on the
place of Peter in Gnostic revelatory documents, and included a
brief analysis of our tractate.[28]

Later, in December of 1976, several papers read at the
Colloquium on the Future of Coptic Studies in Cairo provided
hints of research taking place on the *Ep. Pet. Phil.*[29] On
December 10, Jacques-E. Ménard read a brief introductory paper
entitled "La Lettre de Pierre à Philippe: sa structure."
Later, in 1977, Ménard published one of his contributions in
the Bibliothèque copte de Nag Hammadi, *La Lettre de Pierre à
Philippe*,[30] a booklet in which he provides primarily a Coptic
text, a French translation, and notes on the transcription of
the tractate, although he does also add (pp. 40-47) a very
brief "Commentaire." On that same day in Cairo Gerard P.
Luttikhuizen also read a brief paper on "The Letter of Peter
to Philip and the New Testament." Luttikhuizen is cooperating
with Krause and Theofried Baumeister on a German edition of
the *Ep. Pet. Phil.*, to appear as a volume in the Nag Hammadi
Studies series.[31] On December 12, Hans-Martin Schenke presented his paper "On the Middle Egyptian Dialect of the Coptic
Language," a paper which relates importantly to our tractate.
Schenke is leader of the Berlin Arbeitskreis, which has published a study of the tractate under the particular leadership
of Hans-Gebhard Bethge.[32] This study by the members of the
Arbeitskreis presents, in the usual fashion, a brief introduction, German translation, and notes for the *Ep. Pet. Phil.*
Also in typical fashion, the Arbeitskreis offers some very
engaging suggestions, particularly the thesis that the tractate is actually the opening of a Gnostic version of the *Acts
of Philip*. Finally, on December 13 Frederik Wisse presented
his paper on "Gnosticism and Early Monasticism in Egypt," a
paper which relates to Wisse's interest in the relationship
between the Nag Hammadi corpus and the monastic communities.[33]
Wisse has contributed the brief introduction and translation
of the *Ep. Pet. Phil.* in *The Nag Hammadi Library*,[34] and currently he is working with me at finalizing our analysis of
the *Ep. Pet. Phil.* for the critical edition of Codex VIII, to

be published in a volume of Nag Hammadi Studies. Furthermore,
as his Cairo paper intimated, Wisse is preparing a volume on
Gnosticism and the Nag Hammadi codices, and an analysis of the
Ep. Pet. Phil. will function as one portion of this study.

Now that texts, translations, and studies of the *Ep. Pet.
Phil.* are becoming available, we expect to notice an increas-
ing number of references to the tractate in dissertations and
secondary literature. Such references can already be noted.
In his Th.D. dissertation, Klaus Koschorke has produced a
study of Gnostic polemics with particular attention to the
Apoc. Pet. and *Testim. Truth* of the Nag Hammadi library.[35]
As a part of his discussion he provides an analysis of the
Ep. Pet. Phil., since it is clear that this tractate contrib-
utes to our understanding of Christian Gnosticism in relation
to the Great Church. On the basis of this dissertation
Koschorke has also explored certain themes in the tractate,
for example, the Gnostic "Pentecost" sermon in the *Ep. Pet.
Phil.*,[36] and the similarities between the *Ep. Pet. Phil.*
136,16-137,4 and the prologue to the Gospel of John.[37] Again,
Jesse Jeremiah Sell has completed a Ph.D. dissertation at
Duke University (1976) on "A Study of the Self-Predication
Statements Attributed to 'Jesus Christ' in the Naga-Hammadi
Coptic 'Gnostic' Corpus," and has spent some time analyzing
the relevant self-predication statements in the *Ep. Pet. Phil.*

The present volume is intended to contribute to the discussion of this tractate by providing what is most needed at
this time: a commentary on the *Ep. Pet. Phil.* This study
reflects the accomplishments already made by colleagues who
previously have turned their attention to this fascinating
text. It is hoped that my work is inspired by their wise insights, and will advance our knowledge of Gnosticism and the
Nag Hammadi library. I begin by establishing a Coptic text and
offering an English translation. The text provided builds upon
the pioneering works of others, particularly Frederik Wisse,
who first turned his attention to this text over a decade ago.
The text suggested was also established by comparison with the
Coptic text provided by Ménard, who was able to do an ultraviolet

collation in preparing his edition. Another (ultraviolet)
collation was accomplished by Bentley Layton, John Sieber, and
Frederik Wisse; and during January and February of 1978 I was
also able to do my own ultraviolet collation at the Coptic
Museum in Old Cairo. Indices to proper names, Greek loan words,
and Coptic words in the text are also provided. These indices
are more complete and helpful than previous indices compiled by
Wisse and Ménard. The grammatical discussion which follows the
indices considers the sorts of questions which have been discussed among members of the Coptic Gnostic Library Project at
Claremont for some time, and portrays the philological side of
our tractate. The commentary, with the conclusion, seeks to
clarify the message of the *Ep. Pet. Phil.*, while pointing out
important parallels and significant allusions. Finally, a
selected bibliography is appended to the conclusion.

To cite the *Gos. Thom.*: may we find ⲑⲉⲣⲙⲏⲛⲉⲓⲁ ⲛ̄ⲛⲉⲉⲓϣⲁⲝⲉ![38]

CHAPTER I

NOTES

[1]For a general introduction to the Nag Hammadi library,
see James M. Robinson, "Introduction," *The Nag Hammadi Library
in English* (San Francisco: Harper & Row; Leiden: Brill, 1977)
1-25; idem, *The Nag Hammadi Codices* (Claremont: Institute for
Antiquity and Christianity, 1977); George MacRae, "Nag Hammadi," IDBSup, 613-19, with additional bibliography; also
the popular book by John Dart, *The Laughing Savior* (New York:
Harper & Row, 1976); or the somewhat outdated volume by Jean
Doresse, *The Secret Books of the Egyptian Gnostics* (New York:
Viking, 1960). A comprehensive bibliography is provided by
David M. Scholer, *Nag Hammadi Bibliography 1948-1969* (NHS 1;
Leiden: Brill, 1971), supplemented annually in the autumn issue
of *NovT*.

[2]On the story of the discovery of the library, see James
M. Robinson, "The Discovery of the Nag Hammadi Codices," *BA* 42
(1979) 206-24, as well as his prefaces to the volumes in *The
Facsimile Edition of the Nag Hammadi Codices* (Leiden: Brill,
1972-77); the introductory volume, currently in preparation,
will give a full account of the discovery. More briefly, see
his "Introduction" and his booklet published by the Institute
for Antiquity and Christianity, as cited above, n. 1.

[3]See James M. Robinson's review article, "The Jung Codex:
The Rise and Fall of a Monopoly," *RelSRev* 3 (1977) 17-30.

[4]The *Facsimile Edition* is now reaching completion. The
photographs of the Coptic pages have all been available since
the end of 1977, when the last of these volumes appeared; the
cartonnage was published in 1979, and the introductory volume
should be available in the near future. In conjunction with
the publication of the last volume of codex pages, the one-
volume edition of *The Nag Hammadi Library* appeared, with English translations of all the tractates (except the duplicates)
in the Nag Hammadi codices plus the Berlin Gnostic (BG) Codex
8502. Furthermore, two of the eleven volumes in The Coptic
Gnostic Library have been completed: *The Gospel of the Egyptians
(The Holy Book of the Great Invisible Spirit)* (ed. Alexander
Böhlig and Frederik Wisse; NHS 4; Leiden: Brill, 1975); and *Nag
Hammadi Codices V, 2-5 and VI with Papyrus Berolinensis 8502,
1 and 4* (ed. Douglas M. Parrott; NHS 11; Leiden: Brill, 1979).
The other volumes are all nearing completion. In addition,
German and French translations have also been appearing during
the past few years.

[5]See James M. Robinson, "Preface," *Facsimile Edition:
Codex VIII*, xi-xiii.

[6]Martin Krause and Pahor Labib (eds.), *Gnostische und
hermetische Schriften aus Codex II und Codex VI* (Abhandlungen

11

des Deutschen Archäologischen Instituts Kairo, Koptische Reihe, Band 2; Glückstadt: J. J. Augustin, 1971) 4-5.

[7]For an acknowledgement of those who effected the pagination and fragment placement, see the "Preface," *Facsimile Edition: Codex VIII*, especially xxi.

[8]For a more complete description of the cover, see Robinson, "Preface," *Facsimile Edition: Codex VIII*, ix-xi.

[9]J. M. Robinson, "The Construction of the Nag Hammadi Codices," *Essays on the Nag Hammadi Texts in Honour of Pahor Labib* (ed. Martin Krause; NHS 6; Leiden: Brill, 1975) 170-90, esp. 184-86. More briefly, see his "Preface," *Facsimile Edition: Codex VIII*, ix.

[10]See Robinson, "Introduction," *The Nag Hammadi Library*, 15-16; idem, "The Construction of the Nag Hammadi Codices," 189.

[11]An introduction to *Zost.* is provided by John H. Sieber, "An Introduction to the Tractate Zostrianos from Nag Hammadi," *NovT* 15 (1973) 233-40; also see *The Nag Hammadi Library*, 368-93.

[12]See Sieber, "An Introduction to the Tractate Zostrianos from Nag Hammadi," 235-37; Doresse, *Secret Books*, "Index," s.v. "Zoroaster" and "Zostrian."

[13]See Robinson, "The Three Steles of Seth and the Gnostics of Plotinus," *Proceedings of the International Colloquium on Gnosticism* (ed. Geo Widengren; Stockholm: Almquist & Wiksell, 1977) 132-42, esp. 136-42.

[14]The question of Sethian Gnosticism is currently being debated, and the issues are by no means resolved. Note especially A. F. J. Klijn, *Seth in Jewish, Christian and Gnostic Literature* (Leiden: Brill, 1977), with bibliography.

[15]Cp. the scribal note at NHC VI 65,8-14, where the scribe states that he copied only certain tractates from a larger collection.

[16]Doresse, *Secret Books*, 120.

[17]Ibid., 122.

[18]See Robinson, "The Coptic Gnostic Library Today," *NTS* 12 (1968) 357.

[19]Doresse and Mina refer to our codex as Codex VII, though later in his *Secret Books* Doresse calls it Codex IV; Puech numbers it Codex IX; and Krause and Robinson opt for Codex VIII.

[20]Jean Doresse and Togo Mina, "Nouveaux textes gnostiques coptes découverts en Haute-Egypte: La bibliothèque de Chenoboskion," *VC* 3 (1949) 136. See also Doresse, "Une bibliothèque gnostique copte," *La Nouvelle Clio* 1 (1949) 64.

[21]Doresse, *Secret Books*, 236; his inventory is on p. 142.

[22]H.-Ch. Puech, "Les nouveaux écrits gnostiques découverts en Haute-Egypte (premier inventaire et essai d'identification)," *Coptic Studies in Honor of Walter Ewing Crum* (Boston: Byzantine Institute, 1950) 117. Note also p. 108, where Puech lists the title of the document, stating that it is "de huit pages seulement," and quotes Doresse's brief description from *VC*.

[23]H.-Ch. Puech, "Découverte d'une bibliothèque gnostique en Haute-Egypte," *Encyclopédie Française* 19: *Philosophie, Religion* (Paris: Société Nouvelle de l'Encyclopédie Française, 1957) 10. It is apparent from his use of quotation marks that Puech must intend to provide a quotation or close paraphrase of the *incipit* of the *Ep. Pet. Phil.* It is equally apparent that he is somewhat mistaken in his citation of this *incipit*.

[24]Krause and Labib, *Gnostische und hermetische Schriften*, 6-7. See also the notation by Krause, in his publication of 1962, of the title of the tractate and the page and line numbers ("Der koptische Handschriftenfund bei Nag Hammadi: Umfang und Inhalt," *Mitteilungen des Deutschen Archäologischen Instituts, Abteilung Kairo* [Wiesbaden: Otto Harrassowitz, 1962] 18.128). As Krause notes, both Doresse and Puech had previously assumed that Codex VIII contained three tractates rather than two.

[25]The following paragraphs are based on materials in the Nag Hammadi Archive at the Institute for Antiquity and Christianity, and conversations with James Robinson.

[26]The following paragraphs will cite relevant contributions on the *Ep. Pet. Phil.* In the body of the work we shall discuss many of these contributions in greater detail.

[27]M. Krause, "Die Petrusakten in Codex VI von Nag Hammadi," *Essays on the Nag Hammadi Texts in Honor of Alexander Böhlig* (ed. M. Krause; NHS 3; Leiden: Brill, 1972) 42-45.

[28]P. Perkins, "Peter in Gnostic Revelation," *SBL 1974 Seminar Papers* (ed. George MacRae; Cambridge, MA: Society of Biblical Literature, 1974) 2.1-13, esp. 4.

[29]Several of the papers, including those by Jacques-E. Ménard and Gerard P. Luttikhuizen, have recently been published in *Nag Hammadi and Gnosis* (ed. R. McL. Wilson; NHS 14; Leiden: Brill, 1978); Hans-Martin Schenke's paper has appeared in *Enchoria* 8 (1978, Sonderband) 43*(89)-58*(104).

[30]J.-E. Ménard, *La Lettre de Pierre à Philippe* (Bibliothèque copte de Nag Hammadi 1; Quebec: Université Laval, 1977).

[31]Baumeister has recently published an article which I have not yet seen: "Montanismus und Gnostizismus. Die Frage der

Identität und Akkommodation des Christentums im 2. Jahrhundert,"
Trierer Theologische Zeitschrift 87 (1978) 44-60. From reports
I understand that this article considers certain passages in
the *Ep. Pet. Phil.*

[32]H.-G. Bethge, "Der sogenannte 'Brief des Petrus an
Philippus': Die zweite 'Schrift' aus Nag-Hammadi-Codex VIII,"
TLZ 103 (1978) cols. 161-70.

[33]See F. Wisse, "Die Sextus-Sprüche und das Problem der
gnostischen Ethik," *Zum Hellenismus in den Schriften von Nag
Hammadi* (Göttinger Orientforschungen, 6. Reihe: Hellenistica,
Band 2; Wiesbaden: Otto Harrassowitz, 1975) 55-86.

[34]*The Nag Hammadi Library*, 394-98.

[35]K. Koschorke, *Die Polemik der Gnostiker gegen das kirch-
liche Christentum, unter besonderer Berücksichtigung der Nag-
Hammadi-Traktate 'Apokalypse des Petrus' (NHC VII,3) und
'Testimonium Veritatis' (NHC IX,3)* (NHS 12; Leiden: Brill,
1978) 192-95 [previously Th.D. dissertation, Ruprecht-Karl-
Universität zu Heidelberg, 1976, cp. 187-90].

[36]K. Koschorke, "Eine gnostische Pfingstpredigt: Zur Aus-
einandersetzung zwischen gnostischem und kirchlichem Christentum am Beispiel der 'Epistula Petri ad Philippum' (NHC VIII,2),"
ZTK 74 (1977) 323-43.

[37]K. Koschorke, "Eine gnostische Paraphrase des johanneischen Prologs: Zur Interpretation von 'Epistula Petri ad
Philippum' (NHC VIII,2) 136,16-137,4," *VC* 33 (1979) 383-92.

[38]The Coptic and Greek texts used in this study are taken
from a variety of sources. In most instances the references to
texts from the Nag Hammadi library are based upon transcriptions prepared by members of the Coptic Gnostic Library Project
of the Institute for Antiquity and Christianity. Exceptions to
this are the following: for Codex I, the several volumes of the
editio princeps edited by Kasser, Malinine, Puech, Quispel, et
al., and published by Rascher Verlag and Franke Verlag, 1968-
1975; for the *Ap. John, Die drei Versionen des Apokryphon des
Johannes im Koptischen Museum zu Alt-Kairo* (ed. Martin Krause
and Pahor Labib; Abhandlungen des Deutschen Archäologischen
Instituts Kairo, Koptische Reihe, Band 1; Wiesbaden: Otto
Harrassowitz, 1962), with corrections by members of the Coptic
Gnostic Library Project; for the *Gos. Thom., The Gospel According to Thomas* (ed. A. Guillaumont, H.-Ch. Puech, et al.; Leiden:
Brill, 1959), with corrections; for the *Gos. Phil.*, J.-E. Ménard, *L'Evangile selon Philippe* (Paris: Letouzey & Ané, 1967);
for the *Hyp. Arch.*, Bentley Layton, "The Hypostasis of the
Archons, or *The Reality of the Rulers*," *HTR* 67 (1974) 351-425;
for *Orig. World*, Hans-Gebhard Bethge, "'Vom Ursprung der Welt':
Die fünfte Schrift aus Nag-Hammadi-Codex II neu herausgegeben
und unter bevorzugter Auswertung anderer Nag-Hammadi-Texte
erklärt" (Th.D. dissertation, Humboldt-Universität zu Berlin,
1975). For BG 8502, the edition of W. C. Till is used; for

Pistis Sophia, that of C. Schmidt; for Irenaeus, the text of
W. W. Harvey; for Hippolytus, that of P. Wendland; for the
Excerpta ex Theodoto, that of R. P. Casey; for the apocryphal
Acts of the Apostles, that of R. A. Lipsius and M. Bonnet.
Unless otherwise indicated, all translations are my own.

CHAPTER II

TEXT, TRANSLATION, NOTES, AND INDICES

132,10   ⲧⲉⲡⲓⲥⲧⲟⲗⲏ ⲛ̄ⲡⲉⲧⲣⲟⲥ ⲉⲧⲁϥ

11   ϫⲟⲟⲩⲥ ⲛ̄ⲫⲓⲗⲓⲡⲡⲟⲥ: >——

12   ⲡⲉⲧⲣⲟⲥ ⲡⲁⲡⲟⲥⲧⲟⲗⲟⲥ ⲛ̄ⲧⲉ ⲓ̄ⲥ̄]

13   ⲡⲉⲭ̄ⲥ̄ ⲛ̄ⲫⲓⲗⲓⲡⲡⲟⲥ ⲡⲉⲛⲥⲟⲛ ⲙ̄

14   ⲙⲉⲣⲓⲧ ⲙⲛ̄ ⲡⲉⲛϣⲃⲏⲣⲁⲡⲟⲥⲧ[ⲟ]

15   ⲗⲟⲥ ⲙⲛ̄ ⲛ̄ⲥⲛⲏⲩ ⲉⲧⲛ̄ⲙⲙⲁⲕ ϫⲉ

16   ϯⲟⲩⲱϣ ⲇⲉ ⲛ̄ⲕⲓⲙⲉ ⲡⲉⲛⲥⲟⲛ [ϫⲉ]

17   ⲁⲛⲭⲓ ⲛ̄ϩⲉⲛⲉⲛⲧⲟⲗⲏ ⲛ̄[ⲧ]ⲟⲟⲧ[ϥ̄ ⲙ̄]

18   ⲡⲉⲛϫⲟⲉⲓⲥ ⲙⲛ̄ ⲡⲥⲱ[ⲧ]ⲏⲣ ⲛ̄[ⲧⲉ]

19   ⲡⲕⲟⲥⲙⲟⲥ ⲧⲏⲣϥ̄ ϫⲉ [ⲉⲛ]ⲁⲉ̄ⲓ ⲉ[ⲩ]

20   [ⲙ]ⲁ ϫⲉ ⲉⲛⲁϯ ⲥⲃⲱ ⲁⲩ[ⲱ] ⲛ̄ⲧⲛ̄ⲧⲁ

21   ϣⲉ ⲟⲉⲓϣ ϩⲣⲁⲓ̈ ϩ̄ⲙ ⲡⲓ[ⲟ]ⲩϫⲁⲓ̈ ⲉ

22   ⲧⲁⲩⲉⲣⲏⲧ ⲙ̄ⲙⲟϥ ⲛⲁⲛ ⲉⲃⲟⲗ ϩⲓ̄

133,1   [ⲧ̄]ⲛ̄ ⲡⲉⲛϫⲟⲉⲓⲥ ⲓ̄ⲥ̄ ⲡⲉⲭ̄ⲥ̄·] ⲛ̄ⲧⲟⲕ ⲇⲉ

2   [ⲛ]ⲉϣⲁⲕⲡⲱⲣ̄ϫ̄ ⲉⲃⲟⲗ ⲙ̄ⲙⲟⲛ· ⲁⲩⲱ

3   ⲛ̄ⲡⲉⲕⲙⲉⲣⲉ ⲡⲓⲧⲣⲉⲛⲉ̄ⲓ ⲉⲩⲙⲁ

4   ⲁⲩⲱ ⲛ̄ⲧⲛ̄ⲉⲓⲙⲉ ϫⲉ ⲉⲛⲁⲧⲟϣⲛ̄ ⲛ̄

5   ⲁϣ ⲛ̄ϩⲉ ϫⲉ ⲉⲛⲁϩ̄ⲓ ϣ̄ⲙⲛⲟⲩϥⲉ·

6   ⲉϣϫⲉ ⲟⲩⲛ ⲁⲥⲣ̄ ⲁⲛⲁⲕ ⲡⲉⲛⲥⲟⲛ ϫⲉ

7   ⲉⲕⲉⲉ̄ⲓ ⲕⲁⲧⲁ ⲛⲉⲛⲧⲟⲗⲏ ⲛ̄ⲧⲉ ⲡⲉⲛ

8   ⲛⲟⲩⲧⲉ ⲓ̄ⲥ̄· ⲛⲁⲓ̈ ⲛ̄ⲧⲉⲣⲉϥϫⲓⲧⲟⲩ

9   ⲛ̄ϭⲓ ⲫ[ⲓⲗⲓ]ⲡⲡⲟⲥ ⲁⲩⲱ ⲛ̄ⲧⲉⲣⲉϥⲟ

10   ϣⲟⲩ ⲁϥⲃⲱⲕ ⲉⲣⲁⲧϥ̄ ⲙ̄ⲡⲉⲧⲣⲟⲥ

11   ϩ̄ⲛ̄ ⲟⲩⲣⲁϣⲉ ⲉϥⲧⲉⲗⲏⲗ ⲙ̄ⲙⲟϥ·

12   ⲧⲟⲧⲉ ⲁⲡⲉⲧⲣⲟⲥ ⲁϥⲥⲱⲟⲩϩ

13   ⲙ̄ⲡⲕⲉⲥⲉⲉⲡⲉ ⲁⲩⲃⲱⲕ ⲉϫⲙ̄

14   ⲡⲧⲟⲟⲩ ⲉⲧⲉ ϣⲁⲩⲙⲟⲩⲧⲉ ⲉⲣⲟϥ

15   ϫⲉ ⲡⲁⲛⲓϫⲟⲉⲓⲧ ⲡⲙⲁ ⲉⲧⲉ ϣⲁⲩ

16   ⲥⲱⲟⲩϩ ⲉⲙⲁⲩ ⲙⲛ̄ ⲡⲙⲁⲕⲁⲣⲓⲟⲥ

17   ⲛ̄ⲭ̄ⲥ̄ ϩⲟⲧⲁⲛ ⲉϥϩ̄ⲛ̄ ⲥⲱⲙⲁ· ⲧⲟ

18   ⲧⲉ ⲛ̄ⲧⲉⲣⲟⲩⲉ̄ⲓ ⲉⲩⲙⲁ ⲛ̄ϭⲓ ⲛⲁⲡⲟⲥ

19   ⲧⲟⲗⲟⲥ ⲁⲩⲱ ⲁⲩⲛⲟⲭⲟⲩ ⲉϫⲛ̄

20   ⲛⲉⲩⲡⲁⲧ ⲁⲩϣⲗⲏⲗ ⲛ̄ϯϩⲉ ⲉⲩ

132,10   The letter (ἐπιστολή) of Peter which he
   11   sent to Philip:

   12   "Peter the apostle (ἀπόστολος) of Jesus
   13   Christ, to Philip our beloved
   14   brother and our fellow apostle (-ἀπόστολος),
   15   and the brothers who are with you: greetings (χαίρειν)!
   16   "Now (δέ) I want you to understand, our brother,
              [that]
   17   we received orders (ἐντολή) from
   18   our Lord and the savior (σωτήρ) [of]
   19   the whole world (κόσμος), that [we] should come
   20   together to teach and
   21   preach in the salvation
   22   that was promised to us by
133,1   our Lord Jesus Christ. But (δέ) as for you,
    2   you were separated from us; and
    3   you did not desire that we come together
    4   and learn how to orient ourselves
    5   that we might tell the good news.
    6   So (οὖν) would it be agreeable to you, our brother, to
    7   come according to (κατά) the orders (ἐντολή) of our
    8   God Jesus?"
                 When Philip had received these (words)
    9   and had read
   10   them, he went to Peter,
   11   rejoicing with gladness.
   12   Then (τότε) Peter gathered
   13   the rest. They went upon
   14   the mountain which is called
   15   "Olivet," the place where they used to
   16   gather with the blessed (μακάριος)
   17   Christ when (ὅταν) he was in (the) body (σῶμα).
                 Then (τότε)
   18   when the apostles (ἀπόστολος) had come together,
   19   and had thrown themselves upon
   20   their knees, they prayed in this way,

133,21	[x]ⲱ ⲙ̄[ⲙⲟ]ⲥ ⲭⲉ ⲡⲓⲱⲧ ⲡⲓⲱⲧ
22	ⲡ̣ⲓⲱⲧ ⲛ̄ⲧⲉ ⲡⲟⲩⲟⲉⲓⲛ ⲡⲁⲓ̈ ⲉ
23	ⲧⲉⲩⲛ̄ⲧⲁ̣ϥ ⲛ̄ⲛⲓⲁⲫⲑⲁⲣⲥⲓⲁ
24	ⲥⲱⲧ[ⲙ̄] ⲉⲣⲟⲛ ⲕⲁⲧⲁ ⲑⲉ ⲉⲧⲁ[ⲕ]
25	ⲙ̄ⲧⲱ[ⲟ]ⲩ ⲋⲙ̄ ⲡⲉⲕⲁⲗⲟⲩ ⲉⲧ
26	ⲟⲩⲁⲁ̣ⲃ̣ [ⲧ]ⲓⲥ ⲡⲉⲭ̄ⲥ̄· ⲛ̄ⲧⲟϥ ⲅⲁⲣ
27	ⲁϥϣⲱⲡⲉ ⲛⲁⲛ ⲛ̄ⲟⲩⲫⲱⲥⲧⲏⲣ
134,1	ⲋ̄ⲙ̄ ⲡⲕⲁ̣[ⲕ]ⲉ̣ ⲁⲉ̄ⲓ̄ⲟ ⲥⲱⲧⲙ̄ ⲉⲣⲟ̣[ⲛ]
2	ⲁⲩⲱ ⲁⲩⲕⲟⲧⲟⲩ ⲛ̄ⲕⲉⲥⲟⲡ ⲁⲩ
3	ϣⲁⲏⲗ ⲉⲩϫⲱ ⲙ̄ⲙⲟⲥ ϫⲉ ⲡϣⲏ
4	ⲣⲉ ⲛ̄ⲧⲉ ⲡⲱⲛ̄ⲋ̄ ⲡϣⲏⲣⲉ ⲛ̄ⲧⲉ †
5	ⲙⲛ̄ⲧⲁⲧⲙⲟⲩ· ⲡⲁⲓ̈ ⲉⲧϣⲟⲟⲡ ⲋⲙ̄
6	ⲡⲟⲩⲟⲉⲓⲛ· ⲡϣⲏⲣⲉ ⲡⲉⲭ̄ⲥ̄ ⲛ̄ⲧⲉ
7	†ⲙⲛ̄ⲧⲁⲧⲙⲟⲩ· ⲡⲉⲛⲣ̄ϥ̄ⲥⲱⲧⲉ
8	ⲙⲁ† ⲛⲁⲛ ⲛ̄ⲛⲟⲩϭⲁⲙ· ⲉⲡⲓⲁ̣ⲏ ⲥⲉ
9	ⲕⲱⲧⲉ ⲛ̄ⲥⲱⲛ ⲉⲋⲟⲧⲃ̄ⲛ [ⲧ]ⲟ̣ⲧⲉ ⲁϥ
10	ⲟⲩⲱⲛ̄ⲋ̄ ⲉⲃⲟⲗ ⲛ̄ϭⲓ ⲟⲩⲛⲟϭ ⲛ̄ⲟⲩⲟⲉⲓ[ⲛ]
11	ⲋⲱⲥⲧⲉ ⲛ̄ⲧⲉⲡⲓⲧⲟⲟⲩ ⲣ̄ ⲟⲩⲟⲉⲓⲛ
12	ⲉⲃⲟⲗ ⲋⲙ̄ ⲡⲓⲱⲣ̄ⲋ̄ ⲛ̄ⲧⲉ ⲡⲏ ⲉⲧⲁϥⲟⲩ
13	ⲱⲛ̄ⲋ̄ ⲉⲃⲟⲗ· ⲁⲩⲱ ⲁⲩⲥⲙⲏ ⲁⲥⲱϣ
14	ⲉⲃⲟⲗ ϣⲁⲣⲟⲟⲩ ⲉⲥϫⲱ ⲙ̄ⲙⲟⲥ ϫⲉ
15	ⲭⲓ ⲥⲙⲏ ⲉⲛⲁϣⲁϫⲉ ϫⲉ ⲉⲉ̄ⲓⲉⲭ[ⲟⲥ]
16	ⲛⲏⲧⲛ̄· ⲉⲧⲃⲉ ⲟⲩ ⲧⲉⲧⲛ̄ϣⲓⲛⲉ ⲙ̄
17	ⲙⲟⲉⲓ ⲁⲛⲟⲕ ⲡⲉ ⲓ̄ⲥ̄ ⲡⲉⲭ̄ⲥ̄ ⲉⲧϣ[ⲟ]
18	ⲟⲡ ⲙⲛ̄ ⲧⲏⲩⲧⲛ̄ ϣⲁ ⲉⲛⲉⲋ̄· ⲧⲟⲧ[ⲉ]
19	ⲁⲛⲁⲡⲟⲥⲧⲟⲗⲟⲥ ⲁⲩⲟⲩⲱϣ[ⲃ̄]
20	ⲁⲩⲱ ⲛⲁⲩϫⲱ ⲙ̄ⲙⲟⲥ ϫⲉ ⲡⲭ̄[ⲟ]
21	ⲉⲓⲥ †ⲛⲟⲩⲱϣ ⲉⲉⲓⲙⲉ ⲉⲡⲁϣ
22	ⲱⲧ ⲛ̄ⲧⲉ ⲛⲉⲱⲛ ⲙⲛ̄ ⲡⲉⲩⲡⲗⲏ
23	ⲣⲱⲙⲁ· ⲁⲩⲱ ϫⲉ ⲡϣ[ⲥ] ⲥⲉⲁⲙⲁ[ⲋ]
24	ⲧⲉ ⲙ̄ⲙⲟⲛ ⲋ̄ⲙ̄ ⲡⲓⲙⲁ ⲛ̄ϣ̄ϣⲱⲡⲉ·
25	ⲏ̄ ⲡⲱⲥ ⲁⲛⲉ̄ⲓ̄ ⲉⲡⲓⲙⲁ ⲏ̄ ⲉⲛⲁⲃⲱⲕ
26	ⲛ̄ⲁϣ ⲛ̄ⲣⲏⲧⲉ· ⲏ̄ ⲡⲱⲥ ⲟⲩⲛ̄ⲧⲁⲛ
135,1	[ⲛ̄†ⲉ̄ⲋⲟ]ⲩⲥⲓⲁ ⲛ̄ⲧⲉ †ⲡⲁ̣ⲣ̄ⲋⲏⲥⲓⲁ·
2	[ⲏ̄] ⲉ[ⲧ]ⲃⲉ ⲟⲩ ⲛⲓϭⲟⲙ ⲥⲉ† ⲛ̄ⲙ̄ⲙⲁⲛ·

133,21 saying, "Father, Father,

22   Father of the light, who

23   possesses the incorruptions (ἀφθαρσία),

24   hear us just as (κατά) [you] have

25   taken pleasure in your holy child

26   Jesus Christ. For (γάρ) he

27   became for us an illuminator (φωστήρ)

134,1   in the darkness. Yea, hear us!"

2   And they resumed again and

3   prayed, saying, "Son

4   of life, Son of

5   immortality, who is in

6   the light, Son, Christ of

7   immortality, our redeemer,

8   give us power, because (ἐπειδή) they

9   are searching for us in order to kill us."
            Then (τότε)

10   a great light appeared

11   so that (ὥστε) the mountain shone

12   from the sight of him who

13   appeared. And a voice cried

14   out to them, saying,

15   "Listen to my words that I may speak

16   to you. Why are you seeking

17   me? I am Jesus Christ who is

18   with you for ever."
            Then (τότε)

19   the apostles (ἀπόστολος) answered

20   and said, "Lord,

21   we would like to understand the deficiency

22   of the aeons (αἰών) and their

23   fullness (πλήρωμα)." And, "How (πῶς) are we detained

24   in this dwelling place?

25   Or (ἤ), how (πῶς) have we come to this place?
        Also (ἤ), in what way

26   shall we leave? Also (ἤ), how (πῶς) do we possess

135,1   [the] authority (ἐξουσία) of boldness (παρρησία)?

2   [Also (ἤ)], why do the powers fight against us?"

135,3 ⲧⲟⲧⲉ ⲁⲩⲥⲙⲏ ϣⲱⲡⲉ ⲛⲁⲩ ⲉⲃⲟⲗ

  4 ϩⲙ̄ ⲡ[ⲟ]ⲩⲟⲉⲓⲛ ⲉⲥϫⲱ ⲙ̄ⲙⲟⲥ ϫⲉ ⲛ̄

  5 ⲧⲱⲧⲛ̄ ⲟⲩⲁⲧⲧⲏⲩⲧⲛ̄ ⲉⲧⲡ̄ ⲙ̄ⲛ

  6 ⲧⲣⲉ ϫⲉ ⲁⲉⲓϫⲉ ⲛⲁⲓ̈ ⲧⲏⲣⲟⲩ ⲛⲏⲧⲛ̄

  7 ⲁ[ⲗⲗ]ⲁ [ⲉ]ⲧⲃⲉ ⲧⲉⲧⲛ̄ⲙⲛ̄ⲧⲁⲧⲛⲁϩⲧⲉ

  8 ϯ[ⲛ]ⲁϣⲁϫⲉ ⲛ̄ⲕⲉⲥⲟⲡ· ⲉⲧⲃⲉ

  9 [ⲡⲓϣⲱ]ⲧ ⲙⲉⲛ ⲛ̄ⲧⲉ ⲛⲉⲱⲛ ⲡⲁⲓ̈

  10 [ⲡⲉ] ⲡ̣ⲓ̣ϣⲱⲧ ⲉⲧ<ⲁ>ϯⲙⲛ̄ⲧⲁⲧ

  11 ϭⲱⲧⲙ̄ ⲇⲉ ⲙⲛ̄ ϯⲙⲛ̄ⲧⲁⲧϣⲟⲭⲛⲉ

  12 ⲛ̄ⲧⲉ ⲧⲙⲁⲁⲩ ⲉⲧⲁⲥⲟⲩⲱⲛϩ̄ ⲉⲃⲟⲗ

  13 ⲉϫⲙ̄ ⲡⲟⲩⲁϩ ⲥⲁϩⲛⲉ ⲛ̄ⲧⲉ ϯⲙⲛ̄ⲧ

  14 ⲛⲟϭ ⲛ̄ⲧⲉ ⲡⲓⲱⲧ· ⲁⲥⲟⲩⲱϣ ⲉ

  15 ⲧⲟⲩⲛⲟⲥ ⲛ̄ϩⲉⲛⲉⲱⲛ· ⲁⲩⲱ ⲉⲧⲁⲥ

  16 ϣⲁϫⲉ ⲁϥⲟⲩⲱϩ ⲉⲃⲟⲗ ⲛ̄ϭⲓ ⲡⲓⲁⲩ

  17 ⲑⲁⲗⲏⲥ· ⲉⲧⲁⲥϣⲱϫⲛ̄ ⲇⲉ ⲛ̄ⲟⲩ

  18 ⲙⲉⲣⲟⲥ ⲁϥⲁⲙⲁϩⲧⲉ ⲙ̄ⲙⲟϥ ⲛ̄ϭⲓ ⲡⲓ

  19 ⲁⲩⲑⲁⲗⲏⲥ· ⲁⲩⲱ ⲁϥϣⲱⲡⲉ ⲛ̄

  20 ⲟⲩϣⲱⲧ ⲡⲁⲓ̈ ⲡⲉ ⲡϣⲱⲧ

  21 [ⲛ̄]ⲧⲉ ⲛⲓⲉⲱⲛ· ⲉⲧⲁⲡⲓⲁⲩⲑⲁⲗⲏⲥ

  22 ϭⲉ ⲉⲧⲁϥϫⲓ ⲛ̄ⲟⲩⲙⲉⲣⲟⲥ ⲁϥϫⲟϥ

  23 ⲁⲩⲱ ⲁϥⲕⲱ ⲛ̄ϩⲉⲛϭⲟⲙ ⲉϩⲣⲁⲓ̈

  24 ⲉϫⲱϥ ⲙⲛ̄ ϩⲉⲛⲉϩⲟⲩⲥⲓⲁ

  25 ⲁⲩⲱ [ⲁ]ϥⲟⲗϥ̄ ⲉϩⲟⲩⲛ ⲉⲛⲓⲉⲱⲛ

  26 ⲉⲧⲙⲟ[ⲟ]ⲩⲧ· ⲁⲩⲱ ⲁⲩⲣⲁϣⲉ

  27 ⲛ̄ϭⲓ ⲛⲓϭⲟⲙ ⲧⲏⲣⲟⲩ ⲛ̄ⲧⲉ ⲡⲕⲟⲥ

  28 ⲙⲟⲥ ϫⲉ ⲁⲩϫⲡⲟⲟⲩ· ⲛ̄ⲧⲟⲟⲩ

136,1 ⲇⲉ ⲛ̄ⲥⲉⲥ̣[ⲟ]ⲟⲩⲛ ⲁⲛ ⲙ̄ⲡⲓ̣[ϣⲟⲧ ⲉⲧⲡ̄]

  2 ϣ̄ⲣⲡ̄ ⲛ̄ϣⲟⲟⲡ· ⲉⲡⲓⲇⲏ ϩⲉⲛϣⲙ̄

  3 ⲙⲟ ⲙ̄ⲙⲟϥ ⲛⲉ· ⲁⲗⲗⲁ ⲡⲁⲓ̈ ⲡ[ⲉ]ⲧⲉⲁ[ⲩ]

  4 ϯ ϭⲟⲙ ⲛⲁϥ ⲁⲩⲱ ⲁⲩϣ̄ⲙ̄ϣⲉ ⲙ̄ⲙⲟϥ

  5 ⲉⲁⲩⲥⲙⲟⲩ ⲉⲣⲟϥ· ⲛ̄ⲧⲟϥ ⲇⲉ ⲡⲓⲁⲩ

  6 ⲑⲁⲗⲏⲥ ⲁϥϫⲓⲥⲉ ⲛ̄ϩⲏⲧ ⲉϩⲣⲁⲓ̈ ⲉϫⲙ̄

  7 ⲡⲓⲥⲙⲟⲩ ⲛ̄ⲧⲉ ⲛⲓϭⲟⲙ· ⲁϥ[ϣ]ⲱⲡ[ⲉ] ⲛ̄

  8 ⲟⲩⲣⲉϥⲕⲱϩ· ⲁⲩⲱ ⲁϥⲟ[ⲩ]ⲱϣ [ⲉ]ⲧⲁ

  9 ⲙⲓⲟ ⲛ̄ⲛⲟⲩϩ̄ⲓⲕⲱⲛ ⲉⲡⲙ[ⲁ ⲛ̄ⲛⲟⲩϩ̄ⲓⲕⲱⲛ]

135,3   Then (τότε) a voice came to them from
4   the light, saying,
5   "It is you yourselves who bear
6   witness that I said all these things to you.
7   But (ἀλλά) because of your unbelief
8   I shall speak again.
        "To begin with (μέν), concerning
9   [the deficiency] of the aeons (αἰών), this
10   [is] the deficiency. Now (δέ) <when> the
11   disobedience and the foolishness
12   of the mother appeared,
13   without the command of the majesty
14   of the Father, she wanted to
15   set up aeons (αἰών). And when she
16   spoke, the Arrogant One (αὐθάδης) followed.
17   So (δέ) when she left behind a
18   portion (μέρος), the Arrogant One (αὐθάδης) grabbed it,
19   and it became
20   a deficiency. This is the deficiency
21   of the aeons (αἰών).
        "So then, when the Arrogant One (αὐθάδης)
22   had taken a portion (μέρος), he sowed it.
23   And he placed powers
24   and authorities (ἐξουσία) over it.
25   And he confined it within the mortal aeons (αἰών).
26   And all the powers
27   of the world (κόσμος) rejoiced
28   that they had been brought forth. But (δέ) they
136,1   do not know the preexistent [Father],
2   since (ἐπειδή) they are strangers
3   to him. But (ἀλλά) this one is he to whom
4   power was given; and they served him
5   after having praised him.
        "So (δέ) he, the
6   Arrogant One (αὐθάδης), became haughty because of
7   the praise of the powers. He became
8   a rival, and he wanted [to]
9   make an image (εἰκών) in place [of an image (εἰκών)],

136,10   ⲙ̄ⲛ ⲟⲩⲙⲟⲣⲫⲏ ⲉⲡⲙⲁ ⲛ̄ⲛⲟⲩⲙ̄[ⲟⲣ]

11   ⲫⲏ· ⲁϥⲧⲱϣ ⲇⲉ ⲛ̄ⲛⲓϭⲟⲙ ϩⲣⲁⲓ̈ ϩⲛ̄

12   ⲧⲉϥⲉϧⲟⲩⲥⲓⲁ ϫⲉ ⲉⲩⲉⲡⲗⲁⲥⲥⲁ ⲛ̄ϩⲉ[ⲛ]

13   ⲥⲱⲙⲁ ⲉⲩⲙⲟⲟⲩⲧ· ⲁⲩⲱ ⲁⲩϣ̄

14   ⲡⲉ ⲉⲃⲟⲗ ϩⲛ̄ ⲟⲩⲙ̄ⲛ̄ⲧⲁⲧⲉⲓⲛⲉ ⲉⲃⲟⲗ

15   ϩⲛ̄ †ⲉⲓⲇⲉⲁ ⲉⲧⲉⲁⲥϣⲱⲡⲉ:

16   ⲉⲧⲃⲉ ⲡⲓⲡⲗⲏⲣⲱⲙⲁ ⲇⲉ ⲁⲛⲟⲕ ⲡⲉ ⲁ[ⲩⲱ]

17   ⲁⲩⲧ̄ⲛ̄ⲛⲟⲟⲩⲧ ⲉϩⲣⲁⲓ̈ ϩⲙ̄ ⲡⲥⲱⲙⲁ ⲉ̣

18   ⲧⲃⲉ ⲡⲓⲥⲡⲉⲣⲙⲁ ⲉⲧⲉⲁϥϩⲉ ⲉⲃⲟⲗ

19   ⲁⲩⲱ ⲁⲓ̈ⲉ̄ⲓ ⲉϩⲣⲁⲓ̈ ⲉⲡⲉⲩⲡⲗⲁⲥⲙⲁ ⲉ[ⲧ]

20   ⲙⲟⲟⲩⲧ· ⲛ̄ⲧⲟⲟⲩ ⲇⲉ ⲙ̄ⲡⲟⲩϭ[ⲟⲩ]

21   ⲱⲛ̄ⲧ ⲛⲉⲩⲙⲉⲉⲩⲉ ⲉⲣⲟⲉⲓ ϫⲉ ⲁⲛ[ⲟⲕ]

22   ⲟⲩⲣⲱⲙⲉ ⲉϥⲙⲟⲟⲩⲧ· ⲁⲩⲱ ⲁⲓ̈ϣ[ⲁ]

23   ϫⲉ ⲙ̄ⲛ ⲡⲉⲧⲉ ⲡⲱⲓ̈ ⲛ̄ⲧⲟϥ ⲇⲉ ⲁϥⲥⲱ

24   ⲧ̄ⲙ ⲛⲁⲓ̈ ⲕⲁⲧⲁ ⲧⲉⲧ̄ⲛ̄ϩ[ⲉ] ϩⲱⲧ

25   ⲧⲏⲩⲧ̄ⲛ ⲛⲁⲓ̈ ⲉⲧⲁⲩⲥⲱ[ⲧ̄]ⲙ̄ ⲙ̄ⲡⲟⲟⲩ

26   ⲁⲩⲱ ⲁⲓ̈† ⲛⲁϥ ⲛ̄ⲛⲟⲩⲉϧⲟⲩⲥⲓⲁ ϫⲉ

27   ⲉϥⲉⲃ̄ⲓ ⲉϩⲟⲩⲛ ⲉ†ⲕⲗⲏⲣⲟⲛⲟⲙⲓⲁ

28   ⲛ̄ⲧⲉ ⲧⲉϥⲙ̄ⲛ̄ⲧⲉⲓⲱⲧ· ⲁⲩⲱ ⲁⲓ̈ϥⲓ

137,1   [ⲁ]ⲩⲙⲟⲩϩ ⲉⲃⲟⲗ

2   [   ].. ϩⲣⲁⲓ̈ ϩⲙ̄ ⲡⲉϥⲟⲩϫⲁⲓ̈· ⲉⲡⲓⲇⲏ

3   [ⲇⲉ] ϫⲉ ⲛ̄[ⲉ]ⲟⲩϣ̄ϣⲱⲧ ⲡⲉ ⲉⲧⲃⲉ ⲡⲁⲓ̈ ⲁϥ

4   ϣⲱⲡⲉ [ⲛ̄]ⲟⲩⲡⲗⲏⲣⲱⲙⲁ· ⲉⲧⲃⲉ ⲡⲏ

5   [ⲁ]ⲉ ϫⲉ ⲥⲉⲁⲙⲁ̣ϩⲧⲉ ⲙ̄ⲙⲱⲧ̄ⲛ ϫⲉ ⲛ̄ⲧⲱⲧ̄ⲛ

6   ⲛⲉⲧⲉ ⲛⲟⲩⲉ̄ⲓ· ⲉϣⲱⲡⲉ ⲉⲧⲉⲧⲛⲁⲕⲁⲕ

7   ⲧⲏⲛⲉ ⲕⲁϩⲏⲩ ⲙ̄ⲡⲁⲓ̈ ⲉⲧⲧⲁⲕⲏⲟⲩⲧ· ⲧⲟ

8   ⲧⲉ ⲉⲧⲉⲧⲛⲁϣⲱⲡⲉ ⲛ̄ϩⲉⲛⲫⲱⲥⲧⲏⲣ

9   ϩⲛ̄ ⲧⲙⲏⲧⲉ ⲛ̄ϩⲉⲛⲣⲱⲙⲉ ⲉⲩⲙⲟⲟⲩⲧ

10   ⲡⲏ ⲁ[ⲉ] ϫⲉ [ⲛ̄]ⲧⲱⲧ̄ⲛ ⲉⲧⲛⲁ† ⲙ̄ⲛ ⲛⲓϭⲟⲙ

11   ϫⲉ ⲛ̄[ⲧ]ⲟⲟⲩ ⲙ̄ⲙ̄ⲛ̄ⲧⲁⲩ ⲛ̄ⲟⲩⲙ̄ⲧⲟⲛ ⲕⲁ

12   [ⲧⲁ] ⲧⲉⲧ̄ⲛ̄ϩⲉ· ⲉⲡⲓⲇⲏ ⲛ̄ⲥⲉⲟⲩⲱϣ ⲁⲛ

13   [ϩⲓ]ⲛⲁ ⲛ̄ⲧⲉⲧ̄ⲛ̄ⲛⲟⲩϩ̄ⲙ· ⲧⲟⲧⲉ ⲁⲛⲁⲡⲟⲥ

136,10   and a form (μορφή) in place of a form (μορφή).
11   So (δέ) he assigned the powers within
12   his authority (ἐξουσία) to mold (πλάσσειν)
13   mortal bodies (σῶμα); and they came
14   into being from a misrepresentation of
15   the semblance (ἰδέα) that had come forth.
16   "Now (δέ) concerning the fullness (πλήρωμα),
     it is I. [And]
17   I was sent down in the body (σῶμα)
18   for the sake of the seed (σπέρμα) that had fallen away.
19   And I came down to their mortal model (πλάσμα).
20   But (δέ) as for them, they did not recognize
21   me; they were thinking of me that I
22   was a mortal person. And I spoke
23   with him who is mine, and (δέ) he hearkened
24   to me just (κατά) as you
25   also who hearkened today.
26   And I gave him authority (ἐξουσία) that
27   he might enter into the inheritance (κληρονομία)
28   of his fatherhood. And I took
137,1   [was] filled
2   [   ] in his salvation. [So (δέ)]
     since (ἐπειδή)
3   he was deficiency, for this reason he
4   became fullness (πλήρωμα).
     "Now (δέ) concerning this,
5   that you are being detained; (this is) because you
6   are mine. When you strip
7   yourselves of that which is corruptible, then (τότε)
8   you will become illuminators (φωστήρ)
9   in the midst of mortal people.
10   "Now (δέ) (concerning) this, that it is you who
     will fight against the powers;
11   (this is) because they do not have rest like (κατά)
12   you, since (ἐπειδή) they do not want
13   (ἵνα) you to be saved."

137,14   [т]олос оүϣⲟ̄т ⲛ̄ⲕⲉⲥⲟⲡ ⲉⲩⲭⲱ ⲙ̄
     15   ⲙⲟⲥ ϫⲉ ⲡⲭⲟⲉⲓⲥ ⲙⲁⲧⲁⲙⲟⲛ ϫⲉ ⲁϣ
     16   [т]ⲉ ⲑⲉ ⲉⲧⲛ̄ⲛⲁ† ⲙ̄ⲛ ⲛⲓⲁⲣⲭⲱⲛ·   ⲉⲡⲓⲁⲏ
     17   [ⲛⲓⲁ]ⲣⲭⲱⲛ ⲥⲉⲛ̄ⲧⲡⲉ ⲙ̄ⲙⲟⲛ·   ⲧⲟⲧⲉ
     18   [ⲁⲩⲥ]ⲙⲏ ⲁⲥⲱϣ ⲉⲃⲟⲗ ϣⲁⲣⲟⲟⲩ ⲉⲃⲟⲗ-
     19   [ϩ̄ⲙ] ⲡⲏ ⲉⲧⲉ ⲛⲉϥⲟⲩⲟⲛϩ̄ ⲉⲃⲟⲗ ⲉⲥϫⲱ
     20   [ⲙ̄]ⲙⲟⲥ ϫⲉ ⲛ̄ⲧⲱⲧ̄ⲛ ⲇⲉ ⲉⲧⲉⲧⲛⲁ†
     21   [ⲛ̄ⲧ̄]ⲙ̄ⲙⲁⲩ ⲛ̄†ϩⲉ·   ⲛⲓⲁⲣⲭⲱⲛ ⲅⲁⲣ ⲉⲩ†
     22   ⲙ̄ⲛ ⲡⲓⲣⲱⲙⲉ ⲉⲧⲥⲁϩⲟⲩⲛ·   ⲛ̄ⲧⲱⲧ̄ⲛ
     23   [ⲁ]ⲉ ⲉⲧⲉⲧⲛⲉ† ⲛ̄ⲙⲙⲁⲩ ⲛ̄†ϩⲉ·   ⲁⲙⲏ
     24   ⲉⲓⲧⲛ ⲉⲩⲙⲁ ⲁⲩⲱ † ⲥⲃⲱ ϩ̄ⲙ ⲡⲕⲟⲥ
     25   ⲙⲟⲥ ⲙ̄ⲡⲓⲟⲩϫⲁ̈ⲓ ϩ̄ⲛ ⲟⲩϩⲣⲏⲧ·   ⲁⲩⲱ
     26   ⲛ̄ⲧⲱⲧ̄ⲛ ϩⲱⲕⲧⲏⲩⲧ̄ⲛ ⲛ̄ϩⲣⲁ̈ⲓ ϩ̄ⲛ †ϭⲟⲙ
     27   ⲛ̄ⲧⲉ ⲡⲁϩⲓⲱⲧ·   ⲁⲩⲱ ⲟⲩⲱⲛϩ̄ ⲙ̄
     28   ⲡⲉⲧⲛ̄ⲧⲱⲃϩ̄ ⲉⲃⲟⲗ·   ⲁⲩⲱ ⲛ̄ⲧⲟϥ ⲡⲓ
     29   ⲱⲧ ϥⲛⲁⲣ̄ⲃⲟⲏⲑⲓ ⲉⲣⲱⲧ̄ⲛ·   ϩⲱⲥ ⲉⲁϥ
     30   ⲣ̄ⲃⲟⲏⲑⲓ ⲉⲣⲱⲧ̄ⲛ ⲉⲁϥⲧⲁⲩⲟϥ̄ⲓ·
138,1   ⲙ̄ⲡⲣ̄[.]ⲁⲃ[   ]
      2   ⲕⲁⲧⲁ ⲑⲉ ⲉⲧⲁⲓⲣ̄ ϣⲣ̄ⲡ ⲛ̄ⲭⲟ̣[ⲟ]ⲥ̣ [ⲛⲏ]
      3   ⲧ̄ⲛ ϩⲟⲧⲁⲛ ⲉⲉⲓϩ̄ⲙ ⲡ[ⲥ]ⲱⲙⲁ·   [ⲧ]ⲟⲧⲉ̣
      4   ⲁⲥϣⲱⲡⲉ ⲛ̄ϭⲓ ⲟⲩⲉⲃⲣⲏϭⲉⲥ ⲙ̄ⲛ ⲟⲩ
      5   ϩⲣⲟⲩⲙ̄ⲡⲉ ⲉⲃⲟⲗ ϩ̄ⲛ ⲧⲡⲉ·   ⲁⲩⲱ ⲁⲩ
      6   ⲧⲱⲣ̄ⲡ ⲙ̄ⲡⲉⲧⲁϥⲟⲩⲱⲛϩ̄ ⲛⲁⲩ ⲉⲃⲟⲗ
      7   ⲙ̄ⲡⲓⲙⲁ ⲉⲧⲙ̄ⲙⲁⲩ ⲉϩⲣⲁ̈ⲓ ⲉⲧⲡⲉ·   ⲧⲟⲧⲉ
      8   ⲁⲛⲁⲡⲟⲥⲧⲟⲗⲟⲥ ⲁⲩϣ̄ⲡ ϩⲙⲟⲧ ⲛ̄ⲧⲙ̄
      9   ⲡⲭⲟⲉⲓⲥ ϩⲣⲁ̈ⲓ ϩ̄ⲛ ⲥⲙⲟⲩ ⲛⲓⲙ ⲁⲩⲱ
     10   ⲁⲩⲕⲟⲧⲟⲩ ⲉϩⲣⲁ̈ⲓ ⲉⲑⲓⲗⲏ̄ⲙ ⲉ[ⲩ]ⲛ̄
     11   ⲛⲏⲩ ⲇⲉ ⲉϩⲣⲁ̈ⲓ ⲛⲁⲩϣⲁϫⲉ ⲙ̄ⲛ ⲛⲉ[ⲩ]
     12   ⲉⲣⲏⲩ ϩ̄ⲓⲧⲉϩ̄ⲓⲏ·   ⲉⲧⲃⲉ ⲡⲓⲟⲩⲟⲉⲓⲛ [ⲉ]
     13   ⲧⲉⲁϥϣⲱⲡⲉ·   ⲁⲩⲱ ⲁϥϣⲱⲡⲉ ⲛ̄
     14   ϭⲓ ⲟⲩϣⲁϫⲉ ⲉⲧⲃⲉ ⲡⲭⲟⲉⲓⲥ ⲉⲩϫⲱ̣

Then (τότε) the
137,14 apostles (ἀπόστολος) worshiped again, saying,
15 "Lord, tell us, how
16 shall we fight against the archons (ἄρχων), since
(ἐπειδή)
17 [the] archons (ἄρχων) are over us?"
Then (τότε)
18 [a] voice cried out unto them from
19 what was appearing, saying,
20 "Well (δέ), you will fight
21 against them in this way, for (γάρ) the archons
(ἄρχων) fight
22 against the inner person. So (δέ) you
23 shall fight against them in this way:
24 come together and teach in the world (κόσμος)
25 the salvation with a promise. And
26 gird yourselves with the power
27 of my Father, and express
28 your prayer. And surely the
29 Father will help (βοηθεῖν) you, as (ὡς) he
30 helped (βοηθεῖν) you by sending me.
138,1 Do not [   ]
2 just as (κατά) I previously said [to]
3 you when (ὅταν) I was in the body (σῶμα)."
Then (τότε)
4 came lightning and
5 thunder from heaven, and
6 what appeared to them there was carried
7 up to heaven.
Then (τότε)
8 the apostles (ἀπόστολος) gave thanks to
9 the Lord with every praise. And
10 they returned to Jerusalem.
11   Now (δέ) as they were going up, they spoke with each
12 other on the way about the light
13 which had come forth. And a statement was made
14 about the Lord, for it was said,

138,15   ⲙⲙⲟⲥ ϫⲉ ⲉϣϫⲉ ⲛⲧⲟϥ ⲡⲉⲛϫⲟ[ⲉⲓⲥ]

16   ⲁϥϫⲓ ⲙⲕⲁϩ ⲉⲓⲉ ⲁⲟⲩⲏⲣ ϭⲉ ⲁⲛⲟⲛ[:]

17   ⲁϥⲟⲩⲱϣⲃ ⲛϭⲓ ⲡⲉⲧⲣⲟⲥ ⲉϥϫⲱ

18   ⲙⲙⲟⲥ ϫⲉ ⲁϥϫⲓ ⲙⲕⲁϩ ⲉⲧⲃⲏⲏⲧ[ⲛ]

19   ⲁⲩⲱ ϩⲁⲡⲥ ⲉⲣⲟⲛ ϩⲱⲱⲛ ⲉⲧⲣⲉ[ⲛ]

20   ϫⲓ ⲙⲕⲁϩ ⲉⲧⲃⲉ ⲧⲉⲛⲙⲛⲧⲕⲟⲩ[ⲓ]

21   ⲧⲟⲧⲉ ⲁⲩⲥⲙⲏ ϣⲱⲡⲉ ϣⲁⲣⲟⲟⲩ

22   ⲉⲥϫⲱ ⲙⲙⲟⲥ ϫⲉ ⲁⲓ̈ϫⲟⲥ ⲛⲏⲧⲛ

23   ⲛϩⲁϩ ⲛⲥⲟⲡ ϫⲉ ϩⲁⲡⲥ ⲉⲣⲱⲧⲛ

24   ⲉⲧⲣⲉⲧⲉⲛϫⲓ ⲙⲕⲁϩ· ϩⲁ

25   ⲡⲥ ⲉⲧⲣⲉⲩⲛⲧⲏⲩⲧⲛ ⲉϩⲉⲛⲥⲩ

26   ⲛⲁⲅⲱⲅⲏ ⲙⲛ ϩⲉⲛϩⲏⲅⲉⲙⲱⲛ

27   ϩⲱⲥⲧⲉ ⲛⲧⲉⲧⲛϫⲓ ⲙⲕⲁϩ· ⲡⲏ ⲇⲉ

28   ⲉⲧⲉ ⲛϥⲛⲁϫⲓ ⲙⲕⲁϩ ⲁⲛ ⲟⲩⲇⲉ

139,1   [   ]

2   [   ] ⲡ[ⲉⲛ]ⲓⲱⲧ

3   [   ]. ϫⲉⲕⲁⲁⲥ ⲉϥ

4   [ⲉ.].ⲣ.[ⲁ]ⲛⲁⲡⲟⲥⲧⲟⲗⲟⲥ ⲇⲉ

5   [ⲁⲩ]ⲣⲁϣ[ⲉ ⲉⲙⲁ]ⲧⲉ ⲁⲩⲱ ⲁⲩⲉⲓ ⲉϩⲣⲁⲓ̈

6   [ⲉⲑⲓ]ⲏⲙ ⲁⲩⲱ ⲁⲩⲉⲓ ⲉϩⲣⲁⲓ̈ ⲉⲡⲣⲡⲉ ⲁⲩϯ

7   [ⲥⲃ]ⲱ ϩⲛ ⲟⲩⲟⲩϫⲁⲓ̈ ϩⲣⲁⲓ̈ ϩⲙ ⲡⲣⲁⲛ ⲛⲧⲉ

8   [ⲡⲭ]ⲟⲉⲓⲥ ⲓⲥ ⲡⲉⲭⲥ· ⲁⲩⲱ ⲁⲩⲣ ⲡⲁϩⲣⲉ

9   [ⲉⲩ]ⲙⲏⲏϣⲉ· ⲁϥⲟⲩⲱⲛ ⲇⲉ ⲉⲣⲱϥ ⲛϭⲓ

10   [ⲡⲉⲧ]ⲣⲟⲥ ⲡ[ⲉ]ϫⲁϥ ⲛⲛⲉϥⲙⲁⲑⲏⲧⲏⲥ ϫⲉ

11   [ⲉϩ]ⲉ ⲡⲉⲛϫⲟⲉⲓⲥ ⲓⲥ ϩⲟⲧⲁⲛ ⲉϥϩⲛ ⲥⲱⲙⲁ

12   [ⲁϥ]ϯ ⲙⲁⲉⲓⲛ ⲛⲁⲛ ⲉϩⲱⲃ ⲛⲓⲙ ⲛⲧⲟϥ ⲅⲁⲣ

13   [ⲁϥ]ⲉⲓ ⲉϩⲣⲁⲓ̈· ⲛⲁⲥⲛⲏⲩ ϫⲓ ⲥⲙⲏ ⲉⲧⲁⲥⲙⲏ

14   [ⲁⲩ]ⲱ ⲁϥⲙⲟⲩϩ ⲉⲃⲟⲗ ϩⲛ ⲟⲩⲡⲛⲁ ⲉϥⲟⲩⲁⲁⲃ

15   [ⲡⲉ]ϫⲁϥ ⲛϯϩⲉ ϫⲉ ⲡⲉⲛⲫⲱⲥⲧⲏⲣ ⲓⲥ

16   [ⲁϥⲉⲓ] ⲉϩⲣⲁⲓ̈ ⲁⲩⲱ ⲁⲩⲁϣⲧϥ· ⲁⲩⲱ ⲁϥⲣⲫⲟ

17   [ⲣⲉⲓ ⲛⲟ]ⲩⲕⲗⲟⲙ ⲛϣⲟ<ⲛ>ⲧⲉ· ⲁⲩⲱ ⲁϥϯ ϩⲓ

18   [ⲱⲱϥ] ⲛⲛⲟⲩⲥⲧⲟⲗⲏ ⲛⲭⲏϭⲉ ⲁⲩⲱ ⲁⲩ

19   [ⲁϣ]ⲧϥ ⲉϫⲛ ⲟⲩϣⲉ ⲁⲩⲱ ⲁⲩⲧⲟⲙⲥϥ ϩⲛ

20   ⲟ[ⲩ]ⲙϩⲁⲟⲩ ⲁⲩⲱ ⲁϥⲧⲱⲛϥ ⲉⲃⲟⲗ ϩⲛ ⲛⲉⲧ

21   ⲙ[ⲟⲟ]ⲩⲧ: ⲛⲁⲥⲛⲏⲩ ⲟⲩϣⲙⲙⲟ ⲙ

138,15   "If he, our [Lord],
16   suffered, then how much (more are) we (to suffer)?"
17   Peter answered, saying,
18   "He suffered on account of [us],
19   and it is necessary for us also to
20   suffer on account of our smallness."
21   Then (τότε) a voice came unto them,
22   saying, "I have said to you
23   often: it is necessary for you
24   to suffer. It is necessary
25   for you to be brought to
26   synagogues (συναγωγή) and governors (ἡγεμών),
27   so that (ὥστε) you will suffer. But (δέ) the one
28   who will not suffer nor (οὐδέ)
139,1   [   ]
2   [our] Father
3   [   ] so that he
4   [may   ]."
             And (δέ) the apostles (ἀπόστολος)
5   rejoiced [greatly], and they went up
6   [to] Jerusalem. And they went up to the temple and
7   taught concerning salvation in the name of
8   [the] Lord Jesus Christ. And they healed
9   [a] crowd.
             Now (δέ) Peter opened his mouth
10   and said to his disciples (μαθητής),
11   "[Indeed], our Lord Jesus, when (ὅταν) he was in
         (the) body (σῶμα),
12   indicated everything to us. For (γάρ)
13   he came down. My brothers, listen to my voice."
14   [And] he was filled with holy spirit (πνεῦμα)
15   and spoke in this way: "Our illuminator (φωστήρ) Jesus
16   [came] down and was crucified. And he
17   [wore (φορεῖν)] a crown of thorns. And he put
18   [on] a purple robe (στολή); and he was
19   [crucified] upon a cross; and he was buried in
20   a tomb; and he rose from the
21   dead.

139,22   пеïхι ⲙ̄ⲕⲁ₂ пе ⲓ̄ⲥ· ⲁⲗⲗⲁ ⲁⲛⲟⲛ пете

23   ⲁ[ⲛ]ⲭⲓ ⲙ̄ⲕⲁ₂ ⲍ̄ⲛ ⲧⲡⲁⲣⲁⲃⲁⲥⲓⲥ ⲛ̄ⲧⲙⲁⲁⲩ

24   ⲁⲩⲱ ⲉⲧⲃⲉ ⲡⲁï ⲁ⳿ⲉⲓⲣⲉ ⲛ̄₂ⲱⲃ ⲛⲓⲙ

25   ⲕⲁⲧⲁ ⲟⲩⲉⲓⲛⲉ ₂ⲣⲁï ⲛ̄₂ⲏ̄ⲧ̄ⲛ̄· ⲡⲭⲟⲉⲓⲥ

26   ⲅⲁⲣ ⲓ̄ⲥ ⲡϣⲏⲣⲉ ⲛ̄ⲧⲉ ⲡⲉⲟⲟⲩ ⲙ̄ⲡⲓⲱⲧ

27   ⲛ̄ⲁⲧ† ϣⲓ ⲉⲣⲟ⳿ ⲡⲁï ⲡⲉ ⲡⲓⲁⲣⲭⲏⲅⲟⲥ

28   ⲛ̄ⲧⲉ ⲡⲉⲛⲱⲛ̄₂·   ⲛⲁⲥⲛⲏⲩ ⲙ̄ⲡⲣ̄

29   ⲧⲣⲉⲛⲥⲱⲧ̄ⲙ ⲟⲩⲛ ⲛ̄ⲥⲁ ⲛⲉ†ⲁⲛⲟ

30   ⲙⲟⲥ ⲁⲩⲱ ⲛ̄ⲧ̄ⲛ̄ⲙⲟⲟϣⲉ ₂ⲣⲁï ⲍ̄ⲛ

140,1   [ⲁⲡⲉ]

2   ⲧⲣⲟⲥ ⲁ⳿[ⲥ]ⲱⲟ̣[ⲩ₂   ]

3   [.]ⲡⲉ ⲉ⳿ⲭⲱ [ⲙ̄ⲙⲟⲥ ⲭⲉ ⲡⲉⲛⲭⲟⲉ]ⲓ̣ⲥ̣ ⳾ⲓ̄ⲥ̄]

4   ⲡⲉⲭ̄ⲥ̄ ⲡⲁⲣⲭⲏⲅⲟⲥ ⲛ̄[ⲧⲉ ⲡⲉ]ⲛ̣ⲙ̄ⲧⲟ[ⲛ]

5   ⲙⲁ† ⲛⲁⲛ ⲛ̄ⲟⲩⲡⲛ̄ⲁ̄ ⲛ̄ⲧⲉ ⲟⲩⲉⲡⲓ[ⲥ]

6   ⲧⲏⲙⲏ ₂̄ⲓ̄ⲛⲁ ⲁⲛⲟⲛ ₂ⲱⲱⲛ ⲭⲉ ⲉⲛⲉ

7   ⲉⲓⲣⲉ ⲛ̄₂ⲉⲛϭⲟⲙ· ⲧⲟⲧⲉ ⲁⲡⲉⲧ[ⲣⲟⲥ]

8   ⲙ̄ⲛ ⲛⲓⲕⲉⲁⲡⲟⲥⲧⲟⲗⲟⲥ ⲁⲩⲛⲁⲩ ⲉ[ⲣⲟ⳿]

9   ⲁⲩⲱ ⲁⲩⲙⲟⲩ₂ ⲉⲃⲟⲗ [ⲍ̄ⲛ] ⲟ̣ⲩⲡⲛ̄ⲛ̄[ⲁ̄]

10   ⲉ⳿ⲟⲩⲁⲁⲃ· ⲁⲩⲱ ⲁⲡⲟⲩⲁ ⲡⲟⲩⲁ

11   ⲉⲓⲣⲉ ⲛ̄₂ⲉⲛⲧⲁⲗϭⲟ· ⲁⲩⲱ ⲁⲩⲡⲱⲣ̄ⲭ̄

12   ⲉⲃⲟⲗ ⲭⲉ ⲉⲩⲉⲧⲁϣⲉ ⲟⲉⲓϣ ⲙ̄ⲡⲭⲟ

13   ⲉⲓⲥ ⲓ̄ⲥ̄ ⲁⲩⲱ ⲁⲩⲥⲱⲟⲩ₂ ϣⲁ ⲛⲉ[ⲩ]

14   ⲉⲣⲏⲩ ⲁⲩⲣ̄ⲁⲥⲡⲁⲍⲉ ⲙ̄ⲙⲟⲟⲩ [ⲉⲩ]

15   ⲭⲱ ⲙ̄ⲙⲟⲥ ⲭⲉ ₂ⲁⲙⲏⲛ: ⲧⲟ[ⲧⲉ]

16   ⲁ⳿ⲟⲩⲱⲛ̄₂ ⲉⲃⲟⲗ ⲛ̄ϭⲓ ⲓ̄ⲥ̄ ⲉ⳿ⲭⲱ [ⲙ̄]

17   ⲙⲟⲥ ⲛⲁⲩ ⲭⲉ †ⲣⲏⲛⲏ ⲛⲏⲧ̄ⲛ [ⲧⲏⲣ]

18   ⲧ̄ⲛ ⲙ̄ⲛ ⲟⲩⲟⲛ ⲛⲓⲙ ⲉⲧⲛⲁ₂ⲧⲉ ⲉ̣

19   ⲡⲁⲣⲁⲛ· ⲉⲧⲉⲧⲛⲁⲃⲱⲕ ⲇⲉ ⲉ⳿ⲉ̣

20   ϣⲱⲡⲉ ⲛⲏⲧ̄ⲛ ⲛ̄ϭⲓ ⲟⲩⲣⲁϣⲉ ⲙ̄ⲛ

21   ⲟⲩ₂ⲙⲟⲧ ⲙ̄ⲛ ⲟⲩϭⲁⲙ· ⲙ̄ⲡⲣ̄ⲣ̄

"My brothers, Jesus is a stranger to
139,22   this suffering. But (ἀλλά) we are the ones who
23   have suffered through the transgression (παράβασις)
of the mother.
24   And for this reason he did everything
25   in (κατά) a likeness to us. For (γάρ) the Lord
26   Jesus, the Son of the immeasurable glory of the
Father,
27   is the author (ἀρχηγός)
28   of our life.
"So (οὖν), my brothers, let us not
29   hearken to these lawless
30   ones (ἄνομος) and walk in
140,1   [   ]."
2   Peter [gathered   ]
3   [   ], saying, "[Our Lord Jesus]
4   Christ, author (ἀρχηγός) [of our] rest,
5   give us a spirit (πνεῦμα) of understanding (ἐπιστήμη),
6   so that (ἵνα) we also may
7   perform mighty deeds."
Then (τότε) Peter
8   and the other apostles (ἀπόστολος) saw [him],
9   and they were filled with holy spirit (πνεῦμα).
10   And each one
11   performed healings. And they parted
12   so that they might preach the
13   Lord Jesus.
And they gathered with their
14   companions and greeted (ἀσπάζεσθαι) them,
15   saying, "Amen (ἀμήν)!"
Then (τότε)
16   Jesus appeared, saying
17   to them, "Peace (εἰρήνη) to [all] of you
18   and everyone who believes in
19   my name! Now (δέ) as you go,
20   there shall be for you joy and
21   grace and power. So (δέ) do not be

140,22   ϭⲁⲃϩⲏⲧ ⲇⲉ ⲉⲓⲥ ϩⲏⲧⲉ ϯⲛⲉⲙⲏⲧⲛ̄

23   ϣⲁ ⲉⲛⲉϩ· ⲧⲟⲧⲉ ⲁⲛ<ⲁ>ⲡ[ⲟ]ⲥⲧⲟ

24   ⲗⲟⲥ ⲁⲩⲡⲱⲣϫ̄ ⲙ̄ⲙⲟⲟⲩ ⲉⲃⲟⲗ

25   ⲉϩⲣⲁⲓ̈ ⲉⲡⲓϥⲧⲟⲟⲩ ⲛ̄ϣⲁⲭⲉ ϫⲉ ⲉⲩ

26   ⲉⲧⲁϣⲉ ⲟⲉⲓϣ ⲁⲩⲱ ⲁⲩⲃⲱⲕ

27   ϩⲛ̄ ⲟⲩϭⲟⲙ ⲛ̄ⲧⲉ ⲓ̄ⲥ̄ ϩⲛ̄ ⲟⲩⲉⲓⲣⲏⲛ[ⲏ]:>———

140,22   afraid; behold, I am with you

    23   for ever."

              Then (τότε) the apostles (ἀπόστολος)

    24   parted from each other

    25   with four messages, so that they

    26   might preach. And they went

    27   in the power of Jesus, in peace (εἰρήνη).

Notes to the Text and Translation

132,10 Two sets of decorative lines added by the scribe
        above the superscribed title of the *Ep. Pet. Phil.*
        separate this tractate from the previous trac-
        tate, *Zost.*, with its subscribed title and
        cryptogram.

13   The reading ⲛ̇ is based on an apparent minute trace
        of ink, and provides the anticipated ⲛ̄ for ⲛ̄ⲙⲉⲣⲓⲧ.

15   ⲭⲉ seems likely, on account of the usual length of
        a line. The ⲉ appears certain under ultraviolet
        light, though part of the ⲉ is in a lacuna.
        ⲭⲉ[ⲓⲣⲉ] would necessitate an unusually long line,
        although the scribe does not hesitate to employ a
        longer line occasionally to avoid clumsy word
        divisions, particularly with Greek loan words (see
        133,16.18.27; 135,25; 137,16). On ⲭⲉ as an abbrevi-
        ation, among others, for the greeting in Greek
        letters, see below, p. 93. It also remains a
        distinct possibility that some sort of punctuation,
        perhaps a supralinear dot, was placed after the ⲭⲉ,
        although the position of the ✝ in line 16 may have
        provided such an indication of the opening of a new
        "paragraph" or section.

16   ✝ is written noticeably to the left of the left
        margin, perhaps to emphasize the beginning of the
        body of the letter.

19   A less likely translation of lines 19-21 would be
        as follows: "that [we] should come together, teach,
        and preach." The syntax of the sentence, however,
        with the two ⲭⲉ clauses and second future verbs,
        and the third clause containing a conjunctive form,
        substantiates the translation given above. The
        reading ⲉ̄ⲓ ⲉ[ⲩⲙ]ⲁ ⲭⲉ, "come together," represents a
        common verbal construction in the tractate, and thus
        is preferable to a variant restoration, ⲉ̄ⲓ
        ⲉ[ⲛⲁⲱ]ⲁⲭⲉ, "come to speak." See Bethge, col. 168
        n. 1, as well as 133,3.18; 137,24.

21   The reading [ⲟ]ⲩ remains visually ambiguous. Under
        ultraviolet light ink traces or shadows are some-
        what clearer for ⲩ.

133,1   The restoration of the supralinear punctuation mark
        is supported by the size of the lacuna.

4   Here it is most appropriate to translate ⲧⲱϣ with a
        verb like "orient." Hence Wisse suggests "locate,"
        Ménard "répartir," and Bethge "verteilen." ⲧⲱϣ can
        also be translated as "limit," "determine,"
        "appoint," and even "prepare."

133,6   ϵϣⲭⲉ is here translated as an interrogative; see
Walter C. Till, *Koptische Grammatik (Saïdischer
Dialekt)* (Leipzig: VEB, 1966) §434. ϵϣⲭⲉ could also
be understood in an intensive or exclamatory sense,
and be translated "surely." Again, the clause could
possibly be translated as follows, with ⲭⲉ plus the
third future verb functioning to express a wish (see
ibid., §361): "So if it would be agreeable to you,
our brother, may you come."

10   In ⲟϣⲟⲩ ⲁϥⲃⲱⲕ, the ⲩ and the ϥ are visually certain,
especially under ultraviolet light. Both the ink
traces (the tip of the left stroke and the base of
the ⲩ, and the right vertical stroke of the ϥ) and
the spacing contribute to this certainty.

15   The Berlin Arbeitskreis suggests the possibility
of emending the text as follows: ϵⲧⲉ<ⲛⲉ>ϣⲁⲩ; see
Bethge, col. 168 n. 6. This emendation to the
preterite does not seem necessary; see the discussion of the temporal value of the habitude (*praesens
consuetudinis*) in Till, *Koptische Grammatik*, §304;
and C. C. Walters, *An Elementary Coptic Grammar*
(Oxford: Blackwell, 1972) §61.

16   ⲙⲁⲕⲁⲣⲓⲟⲥ intrudes somewhat into the right margin;
see above, the note to 132,15.

17   Here ϵϥⲍ̄ⲛ ⲥⲱⲙⲁ is used without the article; the
clause could be translated "he was embodied." See
especially 139,11, and also 136,17; 138,3.

18   ⲁⲡⲟⲥ- intrudes somewhat into the right margin; see
above, the note to 132,15.

19   The first perfect appended to the past temporal is
awkward. An alternate translation would be as
follows: "when the apostles had come together, they
threw themselves upon their knees and prayed." In
such a translation, however, the ⲁⲩⲱ in line 19
becomes problematic. On the possibility of using a
series of first perfect verbs without the conjunction, see the *Gos. Thom.* II 34,3 and following, and
the comments of Orval Wintermute ("Coptic Grammar
to the Gospel of Thomas" [unpublished typescript
available at the Institute for Antiquity and
Christianity] 53). In the *Ep. Pet. Phil.*, note
similar constructions elsewhere, for example at
134,2; 139,9-10; 140,13-14.

22   Syntactically ϵⲧⲉⲩⲛ̄ⲧⲁϥ can modify either ⲡⲓⲱⲧ or
ⲡⲟⲩⲟⲉⲓⲛ; the use of ⲡⲁ̈ⲓ would seem to tip the
balance in favor of ⲡⲓⲱⲧ. See also 134,5, where the
structure parallels that of the first prayer, but
where the gender of ⲡⲁ̈ⲓ makes it highly unlikely
that it refers to ⲙ̄ⲛ̄ⲧⲁⲧⲙⲟⲩ.

133,24   On the restoration of the lacunae at the end of
          line 24 and the beginning of line 25, see below, pp.
          80-81. Both of the lacunae are of such a size as
          to suggest that one Coptic letter may be restored
          in each case; were two letters to be restored in
          either case, these letters would have to be exceed-
          ingly small. Furthermore, the scribe's system of
          dividing words at the end of lines suggests the
          plausibility of a pronominal prefix at the end of
          line 24. Our English translation of the clause in
          lines 24-25 could also make use of the sense of the
          present tense: "just as [you] take pleasure in";
          see below, pp. 103-04.

27   ϕⲱⲥⲧⲏⲣ intrudes considerably into the right margin;
          see above, the note to 132,15.

134,2   ⲁⲩⲕⲟⲧⲟⲩ is literally "they turned themselves,
          returned, repeated" (Crum, 125a). A freer transla-
          tion might be as follows: "they returned again to
          prayer" or "they prayed again another time" (so
          Wisse).

5   See 133,22, and the relevant note.

7   The ⲉ is based upon minute ink traces or shadows
          visible under ultraviolet light.

15   On ⲭⲉ with ⲉⲉ̄ⲓⲉⲝ[ⲟⲥ], see below, p. 75; the
          usual form for the prefix is ⲉⲓ̈ⲉ-. The sentence
          remains difficult, and has prompted additional sug-
          gestions for emendation. Ménard (pp. 16-17) suggests
          ⲉ<ⲓ̈>ⲉ̄ⲓ ⲉⲭⲱ ⲛⲏⲧⲛ̄, "<je> viens pour vous parler."
          Such an emendation is not unreasonable, and the
          suggested omission by the scribe of the ⲓ in this
          context would be understandable enough. (At the
          end of line 15, I was unable to ascertain, even
          under ultraviolet light, whether or not ink traces
          are indeed visible; the rough papyrus surface,
          faded and with lacuna, is now difficult to read
          and interpret.) Bethge (cols. 166, 168 n. 12) opts
          for a reading of Wisse, ⲭ[ⲉ]ⲛⲏⲧⲛ̄, and translates
          this as a form of ⲭⲛⲁ, "send" (Crum, 774a). We
          have opted for ⲭⲟ⸗ as being most reasonable (see
          also 138,22: ⲁⲓ̈ⲭⲟⲥ). A form of ⲭⲱ fits the context
          well; ⲭⲱ is rarely used as an intransitive verb
          (see Crum, 754a), and the space at the end of the
          line could easily accommodate [ⲟⲥ].

18   Note the misprint in Ménard: ⲛ̄ⲛ̄ⲧⲩⲏⲧⲛ̄.

22   ⲩ is written in conjunction with a ⲕ on the papyrus,
          the result being ⳤ. From the regular shape of the
          ⲕ and the heavy character of its vertical stroke, it
          is apparent that the scribe first copied ⲕ; later a
          scribe or reader modestly added ⲩ over the ⲕ. Hence

134,22   the reading was changed from "your fullness" to
"their fullness." See also 136,16, and the discussion below, p. 113.

23   Although most of the ⲱ in ⲡⲗⲏⲣⲱⲙⲁ is missing, the
size of the space, the shape of the ink remnants,
and the lack of the tail of a ⳅ make ⲱ visually
certain. The rather unusual translation and punctuation of this section are derived from the Coptic.
ⲁⲩⲱ ⲭⲉ ⲡⲱ[ⲥ] accounts for the translation "And,
'How....'" Bethge (col. 166) suggests, parentheti-
cally after "und," that "sie fuhren fort" be understood as providing the sense of this passage. On
the peculiar syntax of this section, see the discussion below, p. 113. The clause which opens in
line 23 is translated as a passive; the active voice
could also be used, although the pronominal subject
then would have an uncertain antecedent: "How do
they detain us in this dwelling place?" For another
such pronominal subject with an uncertain antecedent, see 134,8. Also note the beginning of the
answer to this question at 137,4-5.

135,1   ⲧ is provided for the article in the lacuna in part
on the basis of the parallel in the same line; also
see the discussion below, p. 70. ⲛ is certain on
the basis of ink traces and space.

9   [ⲡⲓⳅⲱⲱ]ⲧ is certain on the basis of 134,21-22 and
135,10. ⲛⲓ- rather than ⲛ- is suggested by 135,10.
Between lines 9 and 10 the scribe left extra space
on account of a bad horizontal papyrus fiber.

10   <ⲁ> follows the suggestion of Wisse, also adopted by
both Bethge and Ménard. The manuscript has ⲉ.

16   It is very tempting to follow Wisse, Bethge, and
Ménard in emending ⲁⳅⲟⲩⲱ̇ ⲉⲃⲟⲗ to ⲁⳅⲟⲩⲱ<ⲛ>̇ ⲉⲃⲟⲗ,
"appeared." ⲟⲩⲱ̇ ⲉⲃⲟⲗ frequently means "set down,
bring down, pause"; see Bethge, col. 168 n. 17,
where he maintains that the meaning of ⲟⲩⲱ̇ with
ⲉⲃⲟⲗ "hier nicht passt," and the discussion of this
passage below, pp. 124-25.

17   Under ultraviolet light, ink traces of ⲉ̣ and the
certainty of the following ⲗ are established.

19   The first ⲁ of ⲁⲩⲑⲁⲗⲏⲥ is verified under ultraviolet
light: the loop and tail are visible.

25   The ink remnants and space for the vertical stroke
make certain the first ⳅ in [ⲁ]ⳅⲟⲛ̄ⳅ.

26   The first ⲟ in ⲉⲧⲙⲟ[ⲟ]ⲩⲧ is verified by the pattern
and thickness of the ink traces, which conform to
the scribe's usual method of writing ⲟ.

136,1   Wisse suggests N̄n[ετρ̄], but this suggestion is
         unlikely. Not only does the probable space used
         after the n (about 2.5-2.8 cm.) appear sufficient
         to have contained five or six letters; but also a
         vertical stroke, most likely a ι, seems to appear
         to the right of the n. Hence we select, with
         Ménard, a different emendation better suited to the
         data.

3   Within this context the passive, "he to whom power
         was given," seems the most appropriate translation.
         An active construction, however, is possible, though
         vague: "they gave power." Bethge (col. 168 n. 18)
         also suggests the following as a possible text and
         translation: n[ε]τελ[c]† бoм, "he to whom [she]
         (viz. the mother) gave power."

8   From line 8 through line 14, a bad vertical fiber
         caused the scribe to leave extra space between ϥ and
         o in line 8, ε and o in line 11, and τ and ε in line
         14. Evidence of this fiber can also be seen within
         the first n of N̄noyм[op]φн (line 10).

9   The conjecture that N̄noyζ̄ικωn concludes line 9 is
         based on the weighty evidence of the parallel in
         line 10. On similarly long lines, see the note to
         132,15.

10   Minute ink traces of м are visible under ultraviolet
         light.

14   Wisse translates the difficult phrase in lines 14-15
         as follows: "from an untrue copy, from the semblance
         which had emerged." The division of the phrase into
         two parallel phrases, à la Wisse, seems to make
         matters unnecessarily complicated; see the discus-
         sion on this passage below, p. 128.

16   The λ of λ[γω] is quite certain under ultraviolet
         light; the ink traces even hint at the curved loop
         of the λ.

17   On λγτ̄nnooyτ εζρλï, "I was sent down," see Crum,
         420a and 700ab. From the context, the translation
         "down" seems much preferable to "up." On ζ̄м ncωмλ,
         see the slightly different construction at 133,17,
         as well as the note there.

20   Instead of the ç, an o̧ would also be theoretically
         possible. The consistently thin character of the
         top of the stroke, however, makes a ç almost cer-
         tain, as an examination of the scribal hand would
         seem to indicate.

21   The n of λn[oκ] is certain under careful examination
         in both natural and ultraviolet light.

136,25   The ⲅ of ⲙ̄ⲡⲟⲟⲩ is verified by the height, thickness,
and angle of the opening (left) stroke.

26   A dot of ink (confirmed by ultraviolet light)
appears after the ⲭⲉ at the end of the line; this
could indicate a drop of ink that splashed onto the
papyrus, or a punctuation mark of unknown purpose.
See also Ménard (pp. 20 and 34), who makes a highly
unlikely suggestion, considering the length of the
line: "est-ce le début d'une autre lettre?"

137,1   Lines 1 and 2 cannot be restored with any degree of
confidence. Bethge (col. 168 n. 21) suggests that
line 2 be restored with [ⲙⲡⲉϥⲭ]ⲱⲕ, so that the
clause could be translated as follows: "es [wurde]
vollkommen gemacht [seine Vollendu]ng in seiner
Erlösung." The ink traces, however, of the two
letters to the right of the lacuna at the beginning
of line 2 may not suggest ⲱⲕ as the most likely
restoration. (The ink traces could indicate ⲟ, ⲉ,
or ⲥ for the first letter, and perhaps ⲛ for the
second letter.) Ménard (p. 22) is more ambitious
in his restoration: ⲁⲓ̈ϥⲓ[ϥ̄ ⲉⲃⲟⲗ ⲍ̄ⲙ ⲡϣⲱⲱⲧ ⲁ]ⲩⲙⲟⲩ₂
ⲉⲃⲟⲗ [ⲉⲓ̈ⲟⲩⲁⲍ̄ϥ] ⲉ̄ⲛ₂ⲣⲁⲓ̈ ⲍ̄ⲙ ⲡⲉϥⲟⲩⲭⲁⲓ̈, "je la fis passer
[de Déficience à Plénitude, l'établissant] dans
son salut." While this restoration is provocative,
one might question both the inconsistency in the
definite article before ϣⲱⲱⲧ and the indefinite
article before ⲙⲟⲩ₂ (the transcription of the
former, however, could be modified easily enough),
and the likelihood of using ⲙⲟⲩ₂ ⲉⲃⲟⲗ practically
as a Coptic equivalent of ⲡⲗⲏⲣⲱⲙⲁ in the tractate.
Many restorations are possible, of course. Even if
we retain the ϣⲱⲱⲧ, a reasonable conjecture, and
emphasize the concept of being filled, we can still
restore the passage as follows: ⲁⲓ̈ϥⲓ[ϥ̄ ⲉⲃⲟⲗ ⲍ̄ⲙ
ⲡϣⲱⲱⲧ ⲁ]ⲩⲙⲟⲩ₂ ⲉⲃⲟⲗ [(ⲁⲉ) ⲙ̄ⲙⲟϥ] ⲉ̄ⲛ₂ⲣⲁⲓ̈ ⲍ̄ⲙ ⲡⲉϥⲟⲩⲭⲁⲓ̈,
"I took [him out of deficiency, and he] was filled
with his salvation." The ⲉ̄ⲛ₂ⲣⲁⲓ̈ ⲍ̄ⲙ with ⲉ is quite awkward, however, and does not fit the apparent syntax
and style of this tractate (cp. 137,26: ⲛ̄₂ⲣⲁⲓ̈ ⲍ̄ⲙ-).
The juxtaposition of first perfect verbs without
ⲁⲩⲱ presents no problem; see above, the note to
133,19. More serious may be the placement of the
ⲁⲉ, which is desirable for reasons of spacing in
the construction suggested above; this postpositive
particle is not placed precisely where one would
expect it, though it seems that the scribe could
easily compromise the position in the interest of
maintaining the unity of a phrase (see 136,16;
137,4-5). We may also consider the following for
137,2: [ⲙ̄ⲙⲟϥ ⲍ̄ⲛ (ⲟⲩ)ⲙ̄ⲧ]ⲟⲛ ₂ⲣⲁⲓ̈ ⲍ̄ⲙ ⲡⲉϥⲟⲩⲭⲁⲓ̈, "[he]
(was filled) [with peace] in his salvation." Yet
another possibility for the very end of the lacuna:
ⲥⲟⲛ, "brother."

137,3   The ϫ could conceivably be ϧ, though the beginning
          of the bottom horizontal stroke of the ϫ seems to
          be visible.

   15   A rough and imperfect vertical fiber near the left
          margin extends downward from approximately line 15.
          Hence the scribe was compelled to leave extra space
          between certain letters in order to avoid writing
          upon the rough papyrus. Space is clearly notice-
          able between ο and ϲ of line 15, ι and τ of line
          24, ϵ and τ of line 28, τ and ϥ of line 29, and ε
          and ο of line 30.

   27   The ⲁ of ⲡⲁϵⲓⲱⲧ is verified by ultraviolet light.
          ϵⲓⲱⲧ is used here, after ⲡⲁ-, instead of the more
          usual ⲓⲱⲧ; a trace of ink from the ϵ seems visible.

   30   Blotting from p. 136 is apparent near the right
          margin of several lines on p. 137, and creates
          difficulties in determining the text at the end of
          line 30. The ο of ϵⲁϥⲧⲁⲅⲟϥ̄ⲓ is quite clear, espe-
          cially under ultraviolet light. The ϵ is very
          likely, and the ι and the supralinear stroke are
          likewise quite certain. Images of the following
          letters from 136,28 can be discerned in the blotted
          ink on p. 137: ⲛ, τ, apparently ϵ, τ, ϵ, ϥ, ⲙ, ⲛ,
          and so on, plus the tail of the ϥ from 136,27.
          Though the blotting is certain, for some reason
          Ménard suggests a curious sort of phenomenon involv-
          ing "une surimpression visible par transparence de
          la p. 139 sur la p. 138" (p. 35). The end of
          137,30 has created problems for some time. Wisse
          and Ménard suggest that the last two letters are ⲍ̄ⲓ,
          and even maintain that the ⲍ is certain. Such a
          suggestion, however, creates problems in the transi-
          tion from 137,30 to 138,1, where the first few
          letters are visible. Bethge once suggested (p. 14
          n. 30 of his earlier typescript) that "vielleicht
          liegt hier der Versuch einer Verbesserung und Rasur
          eines versehentlich geschriebenen hitn und dem
          Anfang eines weitergehenden Wortes zu ei vor";
          Bethge did not have access to the manuscript itself,
          and apparently was not aware of the blotting problem.
          Yet, as Stephen Emmel has suggested to me privately,
          Bethge's conjecture was essentially correct, apart
          from the misinterpretation of the blotted ink.
          Following correspondence with Emmel, Bethge modi-
          fied his comment somewhat (col. 168 n. 30). When
          the blotted ink traces are mentally removed, the
          remaining ink traces on 137,30 include an upper and
          lower arc (appropriate for a ⲍ but also for an ϵ)
          and probably a supralinear dot. On the supralinear
          stroke over the suffix -ϵⲓ, compare 137,6: ⲛⲟⲩϥ̄ⲓ.

138,1   In the first line м is clear; п is quite certain,
          since a т does not fit the remaining ink traces;
          ρ is clear, and a minute trace of ink above the ρ
          (verified under ultraviolet light) must be a portion
          of a supralinear stroke; the lacuna contained one
          or two letters; the λ is very likely on the basis
          of the part of the tail that has been preserved;
          and the в is obvious. Unfortunately line 1 cannot
          be restored with confidence. It seems likely, how-
          ever, that 138,1 begins with a negative imperative.
          Ménard (pp. 24-25, 36) conjectures that the passage
          may possibly be restored with [π̄] (*sic*! He must have
          meant to place only the supralinear stroke in square
          brackets.) π̄ρ[ρ̄6]λв[2нт], "Ne craignez pas," and
          also refers to 140,21-22 for a parallel construction.
          Also note Bethge, col. 168 n. 31.

2   The ρ in ετλϊρ̄ is very probable, since there does
          not seem to be sufficient room for the left portion
          of a ϥ, the other possible interpretation of the
          ink traces. Likewise, the х of n̄хρ[ο]ϲ is quite
          likely from the pattern of ink traces remaining.

3   On the phrase "in the body," see the note to 133,17.

4   The в and ρ of ογεвρнϬεϲ are verified by the spacing
          and ink traces observed under ultraviolet light.

9   The λ in λγω nearly attains visual certainty; λ is
          much less likely, for the pattern of ink traces is
          not quite appropriate. The γ is not certain, since
          only a trace of the ink from the tip of the right
          tail is visible.

10   The н of εοτ̄нм̄ is certain enough; part of the
          horizontal stroke can be observed. In other manu-
          scripts, "Jerusalem" (ειερογϲλλнм) can also be
          abbreviated ετ̄λнм̄; see Till, *Koptische Grammatik*,
          §26.

14   Apparently the γ of εγхω has been corrected over a ϥ.
          This correction is apparent from the increased di-
          mensions of the γ, and the traces of the left curved
          arm and the right vertical stroke of the ϥ. Slight
          papyrus damage may indicate an attempt to erase part
          of the ϥ.

16   It seems reasonable to follow Wisse's suggestion of
          [:], particularly on account of the *paragraphus* in
          the left margin. Line 16 also seems to be slightly
          shorter than many other lines, and thus easily could
          accommodate such a *dicolon*. See also 136,15; 140,15.
          An alternate English translation of the apodosis in
          line 16 is as follows: "then how much (are) we
          (to suffer)?"

138,20   A supralinear dot possibly may be restored after
          the ι.

21   The two letters o in ϣⲁⲣⲟⲟⲩ were written with some
          extra space between them, on account of an imperfect
          vertical papyrus fiber running down toward the
          bottom of the page.

23   From about line 23 down to the last lines on the
          page some blotting is visible near the left margin.
          In this case the blotting does not interfere with
          the reading of the text of p. 138.

25   The English active voice could also be used here:
          "that they bring you."

139,1   The additional line at the top of the page seems
          likely for several reasons. Toward the end of the
          tractate (and thus also the codex) the pages tend
          to have an increasing number of lines per page.
          Thus pp. 132 and following have, successively, 22,
          27, 26, 28, 30, and 28 lines; hence it is by no
          means unlikely that p. 139 could have as many as
          30 lines. Again, it seems, on the basis of profile,
          that 138,1 begins one-half to one full line higher
          on the page than most of the other pages in the
          tractate, and even 137,1 begins slightly higher than
          most pages. Yet 138,1 is nearly a line higher than
          the line here termed 139,2, thus suggesting that a
          line once existed above 139,2. Again, as both Wisse
          and Ménard (after Wisse) rightly note, an extra
          line at the top of p. 139 would be very helpful in
          making the transition from p. 138 to p. 139 as
          smooth as possible. It may also be mentioned that
          Ménard suggests in his transcription and notes that
          he observed just a trace of ink which derived,
          perhaps, from a ⲣ, ⲋ, ⲯ, or ⲫ in 139,1; see his
          pp. 26-27, 37.

2   Instead of ⲡ[ⲉⲛ]ⲓⲱⲧ we may possibly read ⲡ[ⲗⲉ]ⲓⲱⲧ,
          as at 137,27.

3   The trace of ink before ⲭⲉⲕⲗⲗⲥ seems to be from a
          rather thick stroke at an angle, and could suggest
          ⲙ, ⲗ, ⲱ, ⲯ, or perhaps even ⲛ. Ménard suggests ⲙ,
          perhaps as good a judgment as can be made.

4   The [ⲉ] is suggested by the use of the third future
          with ⲭⲉⲕⲗⲗⲥ. One additional letter seems probable
          in the lacuna. An apparent trace of a tail visible
          under ultraviolet light would suggest an ⲗ before
          the ⲣ, though the trace is ambiguous enough so that
          Ménard can suggest ⲉ. Following the certain ⲣ,
          the ink traces may indicate an o or ⲉ or even ⲍ
          (so Ménard).

139,9   Ménard suggests [ⲛ̄ⲟⲩ]ⲙⲏⲛⲱ̄ϣⲉ. Not only does the
          reconstruction suggested here fit the size of the
          lacuna better than the reconstruction of Ménard, but
          ⲣ̄ ⲡⲗ̲ⲣⲉ ⲉ- is also clearly attested (see Crum, 282b).

11   The approximate distance from the left margin (which
          can no longer be located precisely) to the extant ⲛ
          is 1.5 cm., enough space for two or more probably
          three letters.   Hence ⲉ₂ⲉ is a reasonable sugges-
          tion for the restoration. A photograph taken some
          time ago by Jean Doresse shows a clear ⲉ (before
          ⲡⲉⲛⲭⲟⲉⲓⲥ) on a fragment of papyrus which since then
          has broken off and been lost. This Doresse photo-
          graph is located at the Institute for Antiquity and
          Christianity, where I examined it; it shows the
          papyrus pages when still located within their cover.
          Furthermore, it was used for Plate 6 of the *Facsimile
          Edition: Codex VIII*, and is entitled "Codex VIII
          Open to Pages [138]-[139]." The examination of old
          photographs may provide valuable evidence for papyrus
          fragments which have been lost over the years be-
          cause of the handling and examination of the manu-
          scripts. The pages of the Nag Hammadi codices in
          particular have been extensively photographed, and
          hence provide a fine opportunity for such examina-
          tion. Note, for example, the work already done
          by Stephen Emmel,("Unique Photographic Evidence for
          Nag Hammadi Texts: CG II *2-7*, III *5* and XIII *2**,"
          BASP 14 [1977] 109-21 [continued]). Earlier tran-
          scriptions of line 11, before the evidence of the
          Doresse photographs had come to light, suggested
          [ⲙⲏ] instead of [ⲉ₂]ⲉ, and presented the sentence
          as a question introduced by the Greek loan word μή.
          Thus note Bethge's translation, as well as his
          comment (col. 169 n. 41): "Die erwartete Antwort auf
          diese Frage kann nur 'nein' lauten, und d.h.: er hat
          nicht alles gezeigt." On the phrase "in (the) body,"
          see above, the note to 133,17.

12   The ϯ seems certain; the spacing is inappropriate
          for a ϥ, and no ink traces are present for the
          loop of a ⲣ.

15   The ⲝ of [ⲡⲉ]ⲭⲗϥ is certain under ultraviolet light;
          the slight loop on the right diagonal, consistent
          with the scribal hand, verifies the ⲝ. On account
          of an apparent imperfection in the papyrus, a
          slightly larger space was left between ⲛ̄ and ϯ.

16   Literally ⲗⲩⲗⲱⲧϥ̄ is "he was hanged"; also see line
          19. Instead of ⲫⲟ[ⲣⲉⲓ] we may prefer ⲫⲟ[ⲣⲓ]; cp.
          ⲃⲟⲏⲉⲓ (137,29-30), and the discussion below, p. 69.
          If ⲫⲟ[ⲣⲓ] is used, then there may be enough space
          for a doubled ⲛ before ⲟⲩ, as in line 18.

139,17   The м of the manuscript has been corrected (with
         Wisse and Ménard) to н. м and н may easily be
         confused because of their similarity in sound and
         appearance; thus whether the scribe was copying
         from dictation or from another manuscript, the
         error was simple enough. On ϣомтє as "three" (fem.),
         see Crum (566b). Bethge (cols. 168, 169 n. 43)
         prefers to emend ᴀϥ† to ᴀ<ʏ>†. This emendation,
         however, does not seem necessary; see John 19:5,
         and the discussion below, pp. 152 and 185 n. 208.

19   Instead of the ᴀʏ[ᴀϣ]ϥ̄ϥ suggested by Wisse, Ménard
         prefers ᴀʏ[оϥт̄]ϥ, "they [nailed] him." Ménard's
         reading remains a possibility, and the occurrence
         of ω̄ϥт with єх̄н is attested. Yet єιϣє with єх̄н
         is also well attested (Crum, 88b; it is found else-
         where with "cross" also), and fits the context
         better. Here it may also be noted that ϣє, like
         ξύλον, literally means "wood." From about line 19
         down an imperfect vertical fiber near the right
         margin caused the scribe occasionally to leave extra
         space between letters, so that he would not be
         forced to write upon a poor papyrus surface; note
         the space between ᴀ and ʏ (of ᴀʏтомс̄ϥ) in line 19,
         ϥ and є in line 20, н and о in line 22, ω and в in
         line 24, п and х in line 25, м and п in line 26,
         ρ and х as well as х and н in line 27, м and п in
         line 28, and н and о in line 29. In addition, the
         н of н̄тмᴀᴀʏ in line 23 is written somewhat defec-
         tively because of this imperfect papyrus; the right
         vertical stroke is disconnected from the body of
         the н.

20   The phrase "he rose" can be understood more literally
         in two ways: "he (viz. God) raised him (viz. Jesus)
         from the dead," or "he (viz. Jesus) raised himself
         from the dead."

21   Extra space was left between м[оо]ʏт: and нᴀснну.
         In conjunction with the *dicolon*, this space seems
         to provide an indication of something comparable to
         our paragraph. The two clauses in lines 21-23 are
         nicely constructed as a chiasm: ...пє т̄с̄· ᴀᴧᴧᴀ
         ᴀнон пє....

23   From approximately line 23 down, some blotting from
         p. 138 occurs near the right margin of p. 139.

26   Instead of "the immeasurable glory of the Father,"
         we may also translate this passage as "the glory of
         the immeasurable Father."

27   To avoid writing upon a rough spot on an imperfect
         part of the papyrus, the scribe left a bit of extra
         space between т and †.

139,28   As in line 21, extra space was left after the
          supralinear dot and before naᴄnhy.

140,1   A line, of which no ink traces remain, is posited
          as line 1 of the page; see the note to 139,1. Here
          the line seems necessary for the transition from
          139,30 to 140,1. It is quite possible that ⲧⲟⲧⲉ
          may have existed in the lacuna of line 1, so that
          the new paragraph may begin as follows: [ⲧⲟⲧⲉ
          ⲁⲛⲉ]ⲧⲣⲟⲥ ⲁϥ[ⲥ]ⲱⲟ̣[ⲩ₂], "[Then] Peter [gathered]."

    2   For lines 2 and 3, Bethge (cols. 168, 169 n. 51)
          suggests ⲁϥ[ⲥ]ⲱⲟ[ⲩ₂ ⲉ₂ⲟⲩⲛ ⲛ̄ⲡⲕⲉⲥⲉⲉ]ⲡⲉ, "he [gathered
          together the rest]." Based on 133,12-13, this
          reading is appropriate to the context, and accounts
          for the ink traces as well as the space available
          in the lacunae. Ink traces, apparently of the left
          leg of the ⲛ in line 3, are clearly visible under
          ultraviolet light. It is also conceivable, though
          probably less likely, that ⲧ should be read instead
          of ⲛ̣, and that the ink traces derive from a letter
          just to the left of ⲧ.

    4   The ⲥ and the ⲛ before the lacuna are clear enough
          from the ink traces. The ⲛ̣ is based upon ink
          traces of the right vertical stroke. The ⲙ and the
          ⲧ are obvious; and the ⲟ seems quite certain under
          ultraviolet light, which shows that the visible ink
          marks from the sides of the ⲟ appear closed at the
          top and the bottom. Ménard and Bethge agree with
          this analysis of the ink traces, and suggest, very
          plausibly, the restoration of the lacunae adopted
          here.

   10   The final ⲁ of the line is verified, under ultra-
          violet light, by the ink traces of the tail of the ⲁ.

   11   The ⲣ and ⲝ of ⲁⲩⲡⲱⲣ̄ⲝ are certain on the basis of
          the ink traces which clearly outline the letters
          and the supralinear stroke under ultraviolet light.

   15   The scribe left some extra space after the *dicolon*
          and before the ⲧⲟ[ⲧⲉ]; see also 139,21.28. At the
          left margin, between lines 15 and 16, the scribe
          has used a *paragraphus*; see 136,15; 138,16.

   21   From line 21 to the bottom of the page an imperfect
          vertical papyrus fiber near the left margin prompted
          the scribe to leave extra space occasionally between
          letters, thereby to avoid writing upon a rough
          surface; thus note the space between ⲩ and ₂ in
          line 21, ⲃ and ₂ in line 22, ⲉ and ₂ in line 25,
          and ⲉ and ⲧ in line 26. In addition, the first ⲟ of
          line 27 is poorly written on account of the rough
          papyrus.

140,23   The <ⲁ> corrects the ⲟ of the manuscript.

25   Bethge (cols. 168, 169-170 n. 58) suggests the
          possibility of dittography in order to explain the
          difficult words ⲉⲡⲓϥⲧⲟⲟⲩ ⲛ̄ⲱ̄ⲁ̄ⲝ̄ⲉ ⲝⲉ. Bethge posits
          that perhaps the original text was ⲉⲡⲓϥⲧⲟⲟⲩ ⲛ̄ⲥⲁ ⲝⲉ,
          "in the four directions, so that," which through
          dittography became ⲉⲡⲓϥⲧⲟⲟⲩ ⲛ̄ⲥⲁ ⲝⲉ {ⲝⲉ}; this text
          could have been modified to ⲉⲡⲓϥⲧⲟⲟⲩ ⲛ̄ⲱ̄ⲁ̄ⲝ̄ⲉ ⲝⲉ, "eine
          Verschlimmbesserung zum normalen Sahidisch." See
          additional discussion below, pp. 160-61.

27   As is the case with many of the Nag Hammadi codices,
          blotted ink is visible at the beginning and here at
          the end of Codex VIII. The blotted ink visible on
          the verso of the front flyleaf has proved very
          helpful in reconstructing part of the text of VIII
          1,1-2. Blotted ink from p. 140 likewise is visible
          on the recto of the back flyleaf, particularly near
          the bottom of the page, but this ink does not
          influence any of the readings on p. 140.

Indices to the Text

The following indices include indices of proper names, Greek loan words, and Coptic words. The Greek loan words are listed as they appear in the Coptic script, although allowances have been made for those unaccustomed to the peculiarities of the Coptic alphabet. At the left margin of the index of Coptic words are listed the appropriate page and column references in Crum's *Coptic Dictionary*. The abbreviations used for nouns (masc., fem., sing., pl.) are obvious.

Proper Names

ⲁⲅⲑⲁⲗⲏⲥ cp. Greek loan word

ⲑⲓⲏⲙ (Ἱερουσαλήμ) Jerusalem 138,10; 139,6

ⲓ̅ⲥ̅ (Ἰησοῦς) Jesus 139,22; 140,16.27

    ⲓ̅ⲥ̅ ⲡⲉⲭ̅ⲥ̅ Jesus Christ 132,12-13; 133,26; 134,17

    ⲡⲉⲛⲛⲟⲩⲧⲉ ⲓ̅ⲥ̅ our God Jesus 133,7-8

    ⲡⲉⲛⲫⲱⲥⲧⲏⲣ ⲓ̅ⲥ̅ our illuminator Jesus 139,15

    ⲡⲉⲛⲭⲟⲉⲓⲥ ⲓ̅ⲥ̅ our Lord Jesus 139,11

    ⲡⲭⲟⲉⲓⲥ ⲓ̅ⲥ̅ the Lord Jesus 139,25-26; 140,12-13

    ⲡⲉⲛⲭⲟⲉⲓⲥ ⲓ̅ⲥ̅ ⲡⲉⲭ̅ⲥ̅ our Lord Jesus Christ 133,1; 140,[3-4]

    ⲡⲭⲟⲉⲓⲥ ⲓ̅ⲥ̅ ⲡⲉⲭ̅ⲥ̅ the Lord Jesus Christ 139,8

ⲡⲁⲛⲓⲭⲟⲉⲓⲧ cp. ⲭⲟⲉⲓⲧ (Coptic word)

ⲡⲉⲧⲣⲟⲥ (Πέτρος) Peter 132,10.12; 133,10.12; 138,17; 139,10; 140,1-2.7

ⲫⲓⲗⲓⲡⲡⲟⲥ (Φίλιππος) Philip 132,11.13; 133,9

ⲭ̅ⲥ̅ (Χριστός) Christ 133,1.17; 134,6; 139,8; 140,4

    ⲓ̅ⲥ̅ ⲡⲉⲭ̅ⲥ̅ Jesus Christ 132,12-13; 133,26; 134,17

Greek Loan Words

ⲁⲓⲱⲛ cp. ⲉⲱⲛ

ⲁⲗⲗⲁ (ἀλλά) but 135,7; 136,3; 139,22

ⲁⲙⲏⲛ cp. ϩⲁⲙⲏⲛ

ⲁⲛⲟⲙⲟⲥ (ἄνομος) lawless 139,29-30

ⲁⲡⲟⲥⲧⲟⲗⲟⲥ (ἀπόστολος) masc. apostle 132,12.14-15; 133,18-19; 134,19; 137,13-14; 138,8; 139,4; 140,8.23-24

    cp. also ϣⲃⲏⲣ

ⲁⲣⲭⲏⲅⲟⲥ (ἀρχηγός) masc. author 139,27; 140,4

ⲁⲣⲭⲱⲛ (ἄρχων) masc. archon 137,16.17.21

ⲁⲥⲡⲁⲍⲉ (ἀσπάζεσθαι) greet

    140,14 ⲁⲩⲅⲁⲥⲡⲁⲍⲉ

ⲁⲩⲑⲁⲗⲏⲥ (αὐθάδης) masc. arrogant one 135,16-17.19.21;
136,5-6

ⲁⲫⲑⲁⲣⲥⲓⲁ (ἀφθαρσία) fem. incorruption 133,23

ⲃⲟⲏⲑⲓ (βοήθειν) help

    137,29 ϥⲛⲁⲣ̄ⲃⲟⲏⲑⲓ

    137,29-30 ⲉⲁϥⲣ̄ⲃⲟⲏⲑⲓ

ⲅⲁⲣ (γάρ) for 133,26; 137,21; 139,12.26

ⲇⲉ (δέ) and, but, well, so 132,16; 133,1; 135,11.17;
136,1.5.11.16.20.23; 137,[3].5.10.20.23; 138,11.27;
139,4.9; 140,19.22

εἰκών cp. ⲉ̅ⲓⲕⲱⲛ

εἰρήνη cp. ⲉⲓⲣⲏⲛⲏ

ⲉⲛⲧⲟⲗⲏ (ἐντολή) fem. order 132,17; 133,7

ⲉⲝⲟⲩⲥⲓⲁ (ἐξουσία) fem. authority 135,1.24; 136,12.26

ⲉⲡⲓⲇⲏ (ἐπειδή) since 134,8; 136,2; 137,2.12.16

ⲉⲡⲓⲥⲧⲏⲙⲏ (ἐπιστήμη) fem. understanding 140,5-6

ⲉⲡⲓⲥⲧⲟⲗⲏ (ἐπιστολή) fem. letter 132,10

ⲉⲱⲛ (αἰών) masc. aeon 134,22; 135,9.15.21.25

ⲏ̅ (ἤ) or, also 134,25(bis).26; 135,[2]

ἡγεμών cp. ⲍ̄ⲏⲅⲉⲙⲱⲛ

ⲉⲓⲗⲉⲁ (ἰδέα) fem. semblance 136,15

ἵνα cp. ⲉ̅ⲓⲛⲁ

ⲉⲓⲣⲏⲛⲏ (εἰρήνη) fem. peace 140,27

    †ⲣⲏⲛⲏ 140,17

ⲕⲁⲧⲁ (κατά) according to, like, as, in 133,7.24; 136,24;
137,11-12; 138,2; 139,25

    cp. also ⲍⲉ

ⲕⲗⲏⲣⲟⲛⲟⲙⲓⲁ (κληρονομία) fem. inheritance 136,27

ⲕⲟⲥⲙⲟⲥ (κόσμος) masc. world 132,19; 135,27-28; 137,24-25

ⲙⲁⲑⲏⲧⲏⲥ (μαθητής) masc. disciple 139,10

ⲙⲁⲕⲁⲣⲓⲟⲥ (μακάριος) blessed 133,16

ⲙⲉⲛ (μέν) to begin with, now 135,9

ⲙⲉⲣⲟⲥ (μέρος) masc. portion 135,18.22

ⲙⲟⲣⲫⲏ (μορφή) fem. form 136,10.[10-11]

ὅταν cp. ⲍⲟⲧⲁⲛ

οὐδέ cp. ⲟⲩⲇⲉ

οὖν cp. ⲟⲩⲛ

ⲡⲁⲣⲁⲃⲁⲥⲓⲥ (παράβασις) fem. transgression 139,23

ⲡⲁⲣⲍⲏⲥⲓⲁ (παρρησία) fem. boldness 135,1

ⲡⲗⲁⲥⲙⲁ (πλάσμα) masc. model 136,19

ⲡⲗⲁⲥⲥⲁ (πλάσσειν) mold
      136,12 ⲉⲩⲉⲡⲗⲁⲥⲥⲁ

ⲡⲗⲏⲣⲱⲙⲁ (πλήρωμα) masc. fullness 134,22-23; 136,16; 137,4

ⲡⲛ̅ⲁ̅ (πνεῦμα) masc. spirit 139,14; 140,5.9

ⲡⲱⲥ (πῶς) how? 134,23.25.26

ⲥⲡⲉⲣⲙⲁ (σπέρμα) masc. seed 136,18

ⲥⲧⲟⲗⲏ (στολή) fem. robe 139,18

ⲥⲩⲛⲁⲅⲱⲅⲏ (συναγωγή) fem. synagogue 138,25-26

ⲥⲱⲙⲁ (σῶμα) masc. body 133,17; 136,13.17; 138,3; 139,11

ⲥⲱⲧⲏⲣ (σωτήρ) masc. savior 132,18

ⲧⲟⲧⲉ (τότε) then 133,12.17-18; 134,9.18; 135,3;
    137,7-8.13.17; 138,3.7.21; 140,7.15.23

ⲟⲩⲗⲉ (οὐδέ) nor 138,28

ⲟⲩⲛ (οὖν) so 133,6; 139,29

ⲫⲟⲣⲉⲓ (φορεῖν) bear, wear
      139,[16-17] ⲁϥ̅ⲫⲟⲣⲉⲓ

ⲫⲱⲥⲧⲏⲣ (φωστήρ) masc. illuminator 133,27; 137,8; 139,15

ⲭⲉ(ⲓⲣⲉ) (χαίρειν) greet
      132,15 ⲭⲉ

ὡς cp. ⲍⲱⲥ

ὥστε cp. ⲍⲱⲥⲧⲉ

ⲍⲁⲙⲏⲛ (ἀμήν) amen 140,15

ⲍⲏⲅⲉⲙⲱⲛ (ἡγεμών) masc. governor 138,26

ⲍⲓ̄ⲕⲱⲛ (εἰκών) fem. image 136,9.[9]

ⲍⲓ̄ⲛⲁ (ἵνα) that, so that 137,[13]; 140,6

ⲍⲟⲧⲁⲛ (ὅταν) when 133,17; 138,3; 139,11

ⲍⲱⲥ (ὡς) as 137,29

ⲍⲱⲥⲧⲉ (ὥστε) so that 134,11; 138,27

                    Coptic Words

(2a)   ⲁⲉ̄ⲓⲟ cp. ⲍⲁⲉ̄ⲓⲟ
(5a)   ⲁⲗⲟⲩ masc. child 133,25
(7b)   ⲁⲙⲟⲩ, ⲁⲙⲏⲉⲓⲧⲛ (pl.) come (used as imperative of
              ⲉ̄ⲓ)

              ⲁⲙⲏⲉⲓⲧⲛ ⲉⲩⲙⲁ come together 137,23-24
              cp. ⲉ̄ⲓ

(9a)   ⲁⲙⲁϩⲧⲉ hold, detain, grab
                      134,23-24 ⲥⲉⲁⲙⲁϩⲧⲉ
                      135,18 ⲁϥⲁⲙⲁϩⲧⲉ
                      137,5 ⲥⲉⲁⲙⲁϩⲧⲉ

(10b)   ⲁⲛ not (negative particle used with ⲛ̄: ⲛ̄- ⲁⲛ)
                 136,1; 137,12; 138,28

(11a)   ⲁⲛⲁⲓ be pleasing
                 ⲡ̄ ⲁⲛ⸗ be agreeable to
                      133,6 ⲁⲥⲡ̄ ⲁⲛⲁⲕ

(11b)   ⲁⲛⲟⲕ personal pronoun
                 ⲁⲛⲟⲕ I 134,17; 136,16.21
                 ⲛ̄ⲧⲟⲕ you (masc. sing.) 133,1
                 ⲛ̄ⲧⲟϥ he 133,26; 136,5.23; 137,28; 138,15;
                      139,12
                 ⲁⲛⲟⲛ we 138,16; 139,22; 140,6
                 ⲛ̄ⲧⲱⲧⲛ̄ you (pl.) 135,4-5; 137,5.10.20.22.26
                 ⲛ̄ⲧⲟⲟⲩ they 135,28; 136,20; 137,11
                 ⲁⲛⲟⲛ personal pronoun cp. ⲁⲛⲟⲕ

(19b)   ⲁⲩⲱ and 132,20; 133,2.4.9.19; 134,2.13.20.23;
                 135,15.19.23.25.26; 136,4.8.13.[16].19.22.
                 26.28; 137,24.25.27.28; 138,5.9.13.19;
                 139,5.6.8.[14].16(bis).17.18.19.20.24.30;
                 140,9.10.11.13.26

(21b)   ⲗⲟⲩⲏⲣ cp. ⲟⲩⲏⲣ

(22a)   ⲁϣ what? 137,15
                 ⲛ̄ⲁϣ ⲛ̄ⲣⲏⲧⲉ in what way? 134,26
                 ⲛ̄ⲁϣ ⲛ̄ϩⲉ how? 133,4-5
              ⲁϣⲧ⸗ cp. ⲉⲓϣⲉ

(25b)   ⲁⲭⲛ̄-, ⲉⲭⲛ̄- without
                 ⲉⲭⲛ̄- 135,13

(29a)   ⲃⲱⲕ leave, depart
                      134,25 ⲉⲛⲁⲃⲱⲕ
                      140,19 ⲉⲧⲉⲧⲛⲁⲃⲱⲕ
                      140,26 ⲁⲩⲃⲱⲕ
                 ⲃⲱⲕ ⲉⲣⲁⲧ⸗ go to
                      133,10 ⲁϥⲃⲱⲕ ⲉⲣⲁⲧϥ̄
                 ⲃⲱⲕ ⲉⲭⲛ̄- go up upon
                      133,13 ⲁⲩⲃⲱⲕ ⲉⲭⲛ̄-

(32a)   ⲃⲱⲗ loosen, ⲃⲟⲗ masc. outside
                 ⲉⲃⲟⲗ out, forth, away cp. ⲙⲟⲩϩ, ⲡⲱⲣⲝ, ⲟⲩⲱⲛϩ̄,
                      ⲟⲩⲱϩ, ⲱϣ, ϩⲉ

ⲉⲃⲟⲗ ⳅⲛ̄- ⲥⲡ. ⳅⲛ̄-

ⲉⲃⲟⲗ ⳅⲓ ⲧ̄ⲛ̄- ⲥⲡ. ⲧⲱⲣⲉ

(50a) ⲉ-, ⲉⲣⲟ⸗, ⲉⲣⲱ⸗ (with 2nd pl. suffix; once, 139,9, with 3rd masc. sing.)

to, for 132,19; 133,3.10.14.16.18.24; 134,1.9.15.21.25; 135,14.25(bis); 136,5.[8].9.10.21.27(bis); 137,24.29.30; 138,19.23.24.25(bis); 139,[9].9.12.13.27; 140,18

direct object indicator 134,21; 140,[8]

ⲉ₂ⲣⲁⲓ̈ ⲉ- ⲥⲡ. ₂ⲣⲁⲓ̈

(53b) ⲉⲃⲣⲏⲅⲉⲥ fem. lightning 138,4

(56a) ⲉⲙⲁⲧⲉ ⲥⲡ. ⲙⲁⲧⲉ

ⲉⲙⲁⲩ ⲥⲡ. ⲙⲁⲩ

(57a) ⲉⲛⲉⳅ masc. eternity

ⲱⲁ ⲉⲛⲉⳅ for ever 134,18; 140,23

ⲉⲣⲁⲧ⸗ ⲥⲡ. ⲣⲁⲧ

(58a) ⲉⲣⲏⲧ promise

132,21-22 ⲉⲧⲁⲩⲉⲣⲏⲧ

masc. promise 137,25

(59a) ⲉⲣⲏⲩ masc. companion, each other 138,12; 140,14

(61a) ⲉⲧ-, ⲉⲧⲉ- who, which, that 132,10.15.21-22; 133,14.15.22-23.24.25; 134,5.12.17; 135,5.26; 136,[1].3.15.18.19.23.25; 137,6.7.10.16.19. 22; 138,2.6.7.12-13.28; 139,20.22; 140,18

(61a) ⲉⲧⲃⲉ-, ⲉⲧⲃⲏⲏⲧ⸗ because of, on account of, for the sake of, concerning, about 135,7.8; 136,16.17-18; 137,4; 138,12.14.18.20

ⲉⲧⲃⲉ ⲡⲁⲓ̈ for this reason 137,3; 139,24

ⲉⲧⲃⲉ ⲟⲩ why? 134,16; 135,2

(62a) ⲉⲟⲟⲩ masc. glory 139,26

(63b) ⲉⲱⲱⲡⲉ ⲥⲡ. ⲱⲱⲡⲉ

(63b) ⲉⲱⲝⲉ interrogative, if 133,6; 138,15

(64b) ⲉ₂ⲉ indeed 139,[11]

(65b) ⲉⲝⲛ̄-, ⲉⲝⲱ⸗ upon, on, over ⲥⲡ. ⲝⲱ

(65b) ⲉⲝⲛ̄- without ⲥⲡ. ⲁⲝⲛ̄-

(70a) ⲉⲓ, ⲛ̄ⲛⲏⲩ† (used as qualitative), ⲁⲙⲟⲩ (used as imperative) come, go

133,7 ⲉⲕⲉⲉⲓ

134,25 ⲁⲛⲉⲓ

ⲉ̄ⲓ ⲉⲩⲙⲁ   come together
    132,19   ⲉⲛⲁⲉ̄ⲓ ⲉⲩⲙⲁ
    133,3   ⲡⲓⲧⲣⲉⲛⲉ̄ⲓ ⲉⲩⲙⲁ
    133,18   ⲛ̄ⲧⲉⲣⲟⲩⲉ̄ⲓ ⲉⲩⲙⲁ
    137,23-24   ⲁⲙⲏⲉⲓⲧⲛ ⲉⲩⲙⲁ

ⲉ̄ⲓ ⲉ₂ⲟⲩⲛ ⲉ-   enter into
    136,27   ⲉⲅⲉⲉ̄ⲓ ⲉ₂ⲟⲩⲛ ⲉ-

ⲉ̄ⲓ ⲉ₂ⲣⲁ̈ⲓ (ⲉ-)   come, go down (to), up (to)
    136,19   ⲁ̈ⲓⲉ̄ⲓ ⲉ₂ⲣⲁ̈ⲓ ⲉ-
    138,10-11   ⲉⲩⲛ̄ⲛⲏⲩ ⲉ₂ⲣⲁ̈ⲓ
    139,5-6   ⲁⲅⲉ̄ⲓ ⲉ₂ⲣⲁ̈ⲓ ⲉ-
    139,6   ⲁⲅⲉ̄ⲓ ⲉ₂ⲣⲁ̈ⲓ ⲉ-
    139,13   ⲁⲅⲉ̄ⲓ ⲉ₂ⲣⲁ̈ⲓ
    139,[16]   ⲁⲅⲉ̄ⲓ ⲉ₂ⲣⲁ̈ⲓ

(74a)   ⲉⲓⲉ, ₂ⲓⲉ   then
    ₂ⲓⲉ 138,16
(77b)   ⲉⲓⲙⲉ, ⲓⲙⲉ   know, understand
    132,16   ⲛ̄ⲕⲓⲙⲉ
    133,4   ⲛ̄ⲧⲛ̄ⲉⲓⲙⲉ
    134,21   ⲉⲉⲓⲙⲉ
(78b)   ⲉⲓⲛⲉ, ⲛ̄ⲧ⸱   bring
    ⲉⲓⲛⲉ ⲉ-   bring to
    138,25   ⲉⲧⲣⲉⲩⲛ̄ⲧⲏⲩⲧⲛ̄ ⲉ-
(80b)   ⲉⲓⲛⲉ   masc. likeness   139,25
    ⲙ̄ⲛ̄ⲧⲁⲧⲉⲓⲛⲉ   fem. misrepresentation   136,14
(83a)   ⲉⲓⲣⲉ   do, perform
    139,24   ⲁⲅⲉⲓⲣⲉ
    140,6-7   ⲉⲛⲉⲉⲓⲣⲉ
    140,10-11   ⲁ- ⲉⲓⲣⲉ
    ⲣ̄-   be (used with verbs)
    Greek verbs
      137,29   ⲅⲛⲁⲣ̄ⲃⲟⲏⲑⲓ
      137,29-30   ⲉⲁⲅⲣ̄ⲃⲟⲏⲑⲓ
      139,16-17   ⲁⲅⲣ̄ⲫⲟⲣⲉⲓ
      140,14   ⲁⲩⲣ̄ⲁⲥⲡⲁⲍⲉ
    ср. ⲁⲛⲁⲓ, ⲙ̄ⲛ̄ⲧⲣⲉ, ⲡⲁ₂ⲣⲉ, ⲟⲩⲟⲉⲓⲛ, ϣⲱⲣⲛ̄, ϭⲃⲃⲉ
(84b)   ⲉⲓⲱⲣ₂, ⲓⲱⲣ₂   masc. sight
    ⲓⲱⲣ₂ 134,12

(85a)   ειc   behold

               ειc ₂нтε   140,22

(86b)   ειωτ, ιωτ   masc. father   133,21(bis).22; 135,14; 136,[1]; 137,28-29; 139,2.26

               ειωτ   137,27

               м̄н̄тειωτ   fem. fatherhood   136,28

(88b)   ειωε, λωτ⁴   hang, crucify

                     139,16   λγλωт̄⁴

                     139,[18-19]   λγλωт̄⁴

(90b)   κε   other, rest   133,13; 140,8

               н̄κεcοπ   another time, again   134,2; 135,8; 137,14

(92b)   κογι   small

               м̄н̄тκογι   fem. smallness   138,20

(94b)   κω   place

               κω ε₂ρλϊ εχω⁴   place over

                   135,23-24   λ⁴κω ε₂ρλϊ εχω⁴

(100b)   κωκ, κλκ⁴   strip off

               κωκ κλ₂нγ   strip

                   137,6-7   ετετнλκλκ тннε κλ₂нγ

(101b)   κλκε   masc. darkness   134,1

(104b)   κλομ   masc. crown   139,17

(124a)   κωτε, κοτ⁴   turn, go round

               κοτ⁴   (reflexive) resume, return, repeat

                   134,2   λγκοτογ

                   138,10   λγκοτογ

               κωτε н̄cω⁴   seek

                   134,8-9   cεκωτε н̄cωн

(132b)   κω₂   be envious, imitate

               ρε⁴κω₂   masc. rival   136,8

        κλ₂нγ   ср. κωκ

(153a)   мλ   masc. place   133,15; 134,25

               мλ н̄ωωπε   dwelling place   134,24

               επмλ н̄-   in place of   136,9.10

               εγмλ   together   132,[19-20]; 133,3.18; 137,24

               м̄πιмλ εт̄м̄мλγ   there   138,7

(156a)   мε, мερε-   desire

                   133,3   н̄πεκмερε-

               мεριτ   beloved   132,14

(159a)   ⲙⲟⲩ die, ⲙⲟⲟⲩⲧ† be mortal
                    135,26 ⲉⲧⲙⲟⲟⲩⲧ
                    136,13 ⲉⲩⲙⲟⲟⲩⲧ
                    136,19-20 ⲉⲧⲙⲟⲟⲩⲧ
                    136,22 ⲉϥⲙⲟⲟⲩⲧ
                    137,9 ⲉⲩⲙⲟⲟⲩⲧ
                    139,20-21 ⲛⲉⲧⲙⲟⲟⲩⲧ
                ⲙⲛ̄ⲧⲁⲧⲙⲟⲩ fem. immortality 134,5.7

(163a)   ⲛ̄ⲕⲁϩ be painful
                    ϫⲓ ⲛ̄ⲕⲁϩ suffer
                    138,16 ⲁϥϫⲓ ⲛ̄ⲕⲁϩ
                    138,18 ⲁϥϫⲓ ⲛ̄ⲕⲁϩ
                    138,19-20 ⲉⲧⲣⲉⲛϫⲓ ⲛ̄ⲕⲁϩ
                    138,24 ⲉⲧⲣⲉⲧⲉⲧⲛ̄ϫⲓ ⲛ̄ⲕⲁϩ
                    138,27 ⲛ̄ⲧⲉⲧⲛ̄ϫⲓ ⲛ̄ⲕⲁϩ
                    138,28 ϥⲛⲁϫⲓ ⲛ̄ⲕⲁϩ
                    139,22-23 ⲡⲉⲧⲉⲁⲛϫⲓ ⲛ̄ⲕⲁϩ
                    ϫⲓ ⲛ̄ⲕⲁϩ masc. suffering 139,22

(166b)   ⲙⲙⲛ̄- there is not, ⲙⲙⲛ̄ⲧⲁⲥ not have
                    137,11 ⲙⲙⲛ̄ⲧⲁⲩ
                cp. also ⲟⲩⲟⲛ

(169b)   ⲙⲛ̄-, ⲛ̄ⲙⲙⲁⲥ, ⲛⲉⲙⲏⲥ (with 2nd pl. suffix)
                and, with 132,14.15(bis).18; 133,16;
                134,18.22; 135,2.11.24; 136,10.23; 137,10.
                16.21.22.23; 138,4.11.26; 140,8.18.20.21.22

(170b)   ⲙⲁⲉⲓⲛ masc. sign
                    † ⲙⲁⲉⲓⲛ ⲉ- indicate
                    139,12 ⲁϥ† ⲙⲁⲉⲓⲛ ⲉ-

(177a)   ⲙⲛ̄ⲧⲣⲉ masc. witness
                    ⲣ̄ ⲙⲛ̄ⲧⲣⲉ bear witness
                    135,5-6 ⲉⲧⲣ̄ ⲙⲛ̄ⲧⲣⲉ
                ⲙⲉⲣⲉ-, ⲙⲉⲣⲓⲧ cp. ⲙⲉ

(189a)   ⲙⲁⲧⲉ, ⲛ̄ⲧⲱⲟⲩ enjoy, take pleasure
                    ⲛ̄ⲧⲱⲟⲩ ϩⲛ̄ have, take pleasure in
                    133,24-25 ⲉⲧⲁⲕⲛ̄ⲧⲱⲟⲩ ϩⲙ̄-

(190a)   ⲙⲁⲧⲉ, ⲉⲙⲁⲧⲉ greatly
                    ⲉⲙⲁⲧⲉ 139,[5]

(190b)   ⲙⲏⲧⲉ fem. midst 137,9

(191b)   ⲙⲟⲩⲧⲉ call
                    133,14 ϣⲁⲩⲙⲟⲩⲧⲉ

(193b)   ⲛ̄ⲧⲟⲛ masc. rest 137,11; 140,4

              ⲛ̄ⲧⲱⲟⲩ cp. ⲙⲁⲧⲉ

(196b)   ⲙⲁⲩ the place there (noun), ⲙ̄ⲙⲁⲩ there

                   ⲉⲙⲁⲩ there

                        133,16 (ⲡⲙⲁ) ⲉⲧⲉ ⲉⲙⲁⲩ where

                   ⲉⲧⲙ̄ⲙⲁⲩ that, there 138,7

(197a)   ⲙⲁⲁⲩ fem. mother 135,12; 139,23

(199a)   ⲙⲉⲉⲩⲉ think

                        136,21 ⲛⲉⲩⲙⲉⲉⲩⲉ

(202a)   ⲙⲏⲛⲱϣⲉ masc. crowd 139,9

(203b)   ⲙⲟⲟⲱϣⲉ walk

                   ⲙⲟⲟϣⲉ ⲉ̣ⲣⲁⲓ̈ ⲍ̄ⲛ- walk in

                        139,30 ⲛ̄ⲧ̄ⲛⲙⲟⲟϣⲉ ⲉ̣ⲣⲁⲓ̈ ⲍ̄ⲛ-

(208a)   ⲙⲟⲩ₂ fill

                   ⲙⲟⲩ₂ ⲉⲃⲟⲗ be filled

                        137,1 ⲁⲩⲙⲟⲩ₂ ⲉⲃⲟⲗ

                        139,14 ⲁ̄ϥⲙⲟⲩ₂ ⲉⲃⲟⲗ

                        140,9 ⲁⲩⲙⲟⲩ₂ ⲉⲃⲟⲗ

(212b)   ⲙⲍⲁⲟⲩ masc. tomb 139,20

              ⲛ-, ⲛⲓ- definite article cp. ⲡ-

(215a)   ⲛ̄-, ⲙ̄ⲙⲟ⸗, ⲙ̄ⲙⲱ⸗¹

                   of (genitive particle) 132,10.13.[17];
                   133,5.10.11.17; 134,10.24.26; 136,2.[9].
                   10; 137,9; 138,5.23; 139,17.18.23.26.27;
                   140,25

                   cp. also ⲛ̄ⲧⲉ

                   direct object indicator 132,17.22; 133,13.
                   21.23.27; 134,3.8.14.16-17.20.24; 135,[1].
                   4.15.17.18.19.22.23; 136,1.4.6.7.9.11.12.
                   26; 137,[4].5.8.11.14-15.20.25.27; 138,6.
                   15.18.22; 139,17.18.24; 140,[3].5.7.11.
                   12.14.15.16-17

(215b)   ⲛ̄-, ⲙ̄ⲙⲟ⸗ in, on, from 133,2.4.20; 134,2.26;
                   135,8; 136,3.25; 137,7.14.17(bis).21.23.26;
                   138,2.7(bis).23; 139,15.21; 140,24

(216a)   ⲛ̄-, ⲛⲁ⸗, ⲛⲏ⸗ to, for 132,11.13.22; 133,27;
                   134,8.16; 135,3.6; 136,4.24.26; 138,[2].6.
                   22; 139,10.12; 140,5.17(bis).20

---

¹The entries for the varieties of ⲛ̄- are listed according
to the distinctions made in Crum 215a and following. In some
cases, however, a precise categorization is difficult.

(218b)   ΝΑ-, ΝΕϥ-, ΝΕΥ- possessive adjective   cp. ΠΑ-
                ΝΑΪ, ΝΕΪ- demonstrative pronoun   cp. ΠΑΪ
                ΝΟΥⁱ possessive pronoun   cp. ΠΩⁱ

(219a)   ΝΟΥ, Ν̄ΝΗΥ† (used as qualitative of ⲈⲒ) come, go
                    Ν̄ΝΗΥ Ε₂ΡΑΪ go up
                    138,10-11   ⲈΥΝ̄ΝΗΥ Ε₂ΡΑΪ

(225b)   ΝΙΜ every 138,9; 139,12.24; 140,18

                Ν̄Τⁱ cp. ⲈΙΝⲈ

(230a)   Ν̄ΤⲈ of (genitive particle)   132,12.[18];
                133,7.22; 134,4(bis).6.12.22; 135,1.9.12.
                13.14.21.27; 136,7.28; 137,27; 139,7.26.28;
                140,[4].5.27
                    cp. also Ν̄-

(230b)   ΝΟΥΤⲈ masc. God 133,8

(231b-232b)   Ν̄ΤΟΚ, Ν̄ΤΩΤΝ̄, Ν̄ΤΟΟΥ, Ν̄ΤΟϥ personal pronoun
                    cp. ΑΝΟΚ

(232a)   Ν̄ΤΝ̄-, Ν̄ΤΟΟΤⁱ cp. ΤΩΡⲈ

(233b)   ΝΑΥ see
                    140,8   ΑΥΝΑΥ

(235b)   ΝΗΥ, Ν̄ΝΗΥ cp. ΝΟΥ

(239b)   ΝΟΥϥΡ be good, ΝΟΥϥⲈ good
                    ϢⲘΝΟΥϥⲈ cp. ϢΙΝⲈ

(243b)   ΝΟΥ₂Μ̄ be saved
                    137,13   Ν̄ΤⲈΤΝ̄ΝΟΥ₂Μ̄

(246a)   ΝΑ₂ΤⲈ believe
                    ΝΑ₂ΤⲈ Ⲉ- believe in
                    140,18   ⲈΤΝΑ₂ΤⲈ Ⲉ-
                    Μ̄Ν̄ΤΑΤΝΑ₂ΤⲈ fem. unbelief 135,7

(247a)   ΝΟΥΧⲈ, ΝΟΧⁱ throw
                    ΝΟΧⁱ ⲈΧΝ̄- throw upon
                    133,19   ΑΥΝΟΧΟΥ ⲈΧΝ̄-

(250a)   ΝΟϬ great 134,10
                    Μ̄Ν̄ΤΝΟϬ fem. majesty 135,13-14

(252a)   Ν̄ϬΙ subject indicator 133,9.18; 134,10;
                135,16.18.27; 138,4.13-14.17; 139,9;
                140,16.20

(254b)   ΟΛⁱ cp. ΩΛ
                ΟϢⁱ cp. ΩϢ

(257b)   ΟⲈΙϢ cry, crying (noun)

ⲧⲁϣⲉ ⲟⲉⲓϣ   preach

    132,20-21   ⲛ̅ⲧ̅ⲛ̅ⲧⲁϣⲉ ⲟⲉⲓϣ

    140,12   ⲉⲩⲉⲧⲁϣⲉ ⲟⲉⲓϣ

    140,25-26   ⲉⲩⲉⲧⲁϣⲉ ⲟⲉⲓϣ

(258b)   ⲡ-, ⲡⲉ-, ⲡⲓ- (masc.), ⲧ-, ⲧⲉ-, ϯ- (fem.),
ⲛ-, ⲛⲓ- (pl.) definite article 132,10.12.
13.15.18.19.21; 133,1.3.7.13.14.15(bis).16.
18.21(bis).22(bis).23.24.26; 134,1.3.
4(tris).6(tris).7.11.12.17(bis).19.20.21.22;
135,[1].1.2.4.[9].9.[10].10(bis).11.12.
13(bis).14.16.18.20(bis).21(bis).25.27(bis);
136,1.3(bis).5.7(bis).9.10.11.15.16(bis).
17.18.23.25.27; 137,3.6.9.10.13.15.16(tris).
[17].17.21.22.24.25.26.28; 138,2.3.5.6.7.8.
9.12(bis).14; 139,4.6.7.[8].8.20.22(bis).
23(bis).25.26(tris).27(bis); 140,4(bis).8.
10(bis).12.17.23.25

(258b)   ⲡⲁ-   possessive adjective

    ⲡⲁ-, ⲧⲁ-, ⲛⲁ-   my 134,15; 137,27;
       139,13(bis).21.28; 140,19

    ⲡⲉⲕ-   your (masc. sing.) 133,25

    ⲡⲉϥ-, ⲧⲉϥ-, ⲛⲉϥ-   his 136,12.28; 137,2;
       139,10

    ⲡⲉⲛ-, ⲧⲉⲛ-   our 132,13.14.16.18; 133,1.6.7;
       134,7; 138,15.20; 139,[2].11.15.28;
       140,[3].[4]

    ⲡⲉⲧ̅ⲛ̅-, ⲧⲉⲧ̅ⲛ̅-   your (pl.) 136,24; 137,12.28

    ⲡⲉⲩ-, ⲛⲉⲩ-   their 133,20; 134,22; 136,19;
       138,11; 140,13

(259a)   ⲡⲁ-   possessive article

    133,15   ⲡⲁⲛⲓϫⲟⲉⲓⲧ the (Mount) of (the)
    Olives, Olivet

(259a)   ⲡⲁⲓ̈, ⲡⲉⲓ̈-, ⲡⲓ- (masc.), ϯ- (fem.), ⲛⲁⲓ̈, ⲛⲉⲓ̈-
(pl.) this, these (demonstrative pronoun)
133,8.20.22; 134,5.24.25; 135,6.9.20;
136,3.25; 137,3.7.21.23; 138,7; 139,15.
22.24.27.29

(259a)   ⲡⲉ   fem. heaven 138,5(bis).7

    ⲛ̅ⲧⲡⲉ ⲛ̅-   over, above 137,17

(260b)   ⲡⲏ   (masc.) that (demonstrative pronoun)
134,12; 137,4.10.19; 138,27

(260b)   ⲡⲱ⸗   (masc.), ⲛⲟⲩ⸗ (pl.) possessive pronoun

    ⲡⲱⲓ̈, ⲛⲟⲩⲉ̄ⲓ   mine 136,23; 137,6

(271b) ⲡⲱⲣ̄ϫ̄ separate

ⲡⲱⲣ̄ϫ̄ ⲉⲃⲟⲗ (ⲛ̄-) part, separate (from)

133,2 ⲛⲉϣⲁⲕⲡⲱⲣ̄ϫ̄ ⲉⲃⲟⲗ ⲙ̄ⲙⲟⲛ

140,11-12 ⲁⲩⲡⲱⲣ̄ϫ̄ ⲉⲃⲟⲗ

140,24 ⲁⲩⲡⲱⲣ̄ϫ̄ ⲙ̄ⲙⲟⲟⲩ ⲉⲃⲟⲗ

(273b) ⲡⲁⲧ fem. knee 133,20

(277a) ⲡⲟⲟⲩ ⲥⲡ. ⲅⲟⲟⲩ

(282b) ⲡⲁϩⲣⲉ masc. drug, medication

ⲣ̄ ⲡⲁϩⲣⲉ ⲉ- heal

139,8-9 ⲁⲩⲣ̄ ⲡⲁϩⲣⲉ ⲉ-

(285a) ⲡⲉϫⲉ-, ⲡⲉϫⲁ⸗ said

139,10 ⲡⲉϫⲁϥ

139,15 ⲡⲉϫⲁϥ

(288a) ⲣⲟ, ⲣⲱ⸗ masc. mouth

ⲣⲱ⸗ 139,9

(294b) ⲣⲱⲙⲉ masc. person, man 136,22; 137,9.22

(297b) ⲣⲁⲛ masc. name 139,7; 140,19

(298b) ⲣ̄ⲡⲉ masc. temple 139,6

(302b) ⲣⲁⲧ masc. foot

ⲉⲣⲁⲧ⸗ to the foot of, to ⲥⲡ. ⲃⲱⲕ

(304b) ⲣⲏⲧⲉ masc. manner, way

ⲛ̄ⲁϣ ⲛ̄ⲣⲏⲧⲉ ⲥⲡ. ⲁϣ

(308b) ⲣⲁϣⲉ rejoice

135,26 ⲁⲩⲣⲁϣⲉ

139,5 ⲁⲩⲣⲁϣⲉ

masc. gladness, joy 133,11; 140,20

(313a) ⲥⲁ masc. side

ⲛ̄ⲥⲁ-, ⲛ̄ⲥⲱ⸗ behind, after ⲥⲡ. ⲕⲱⲧⲉ, ⲥⲱⲧⲙ̄

ⲥⲁϩⲟⲩⲛ within, inner ⲥⲡ. ϩⲟⲩⲛ

(319a) ⲥⲁⲃⲉ masc. wise person, ⲥⲃⲱ fem. teaching

† ⲥⲃⲱ teach

132,20 ⲉⲛⲁ† ⲥⲃⲱ

137,24 † ⲥⲃⲱ

139,6-7 ⲁⲩ† ⲥⲃⲱ

(334b) ⲥⲙⲏ fem. voice 134,13; 135,3; 137,18; 138,21; 139,13

ϫⲓ ⲥⲙⲏ ⲉ- listen to

134,15 ϫⲓ ⲥⲙⲏ ⲉ-

139,13 ϫⲓ ⲥⲙⲏ ⲉ-

(335a)   ᴄᴍᴏʏ praise
             136,5 ᴇᴀʏᴄᴍᴏʏ
        masc. praise 136,7; 138,9

(342b)   ᴄᴏɴ, ᴄɴнʏ (pl.) masc. brother 132,13.15.16;
         133,6; 139,13.21.28

(349b)   ᴄᴏп masc. time
             ฬᴋᴇᴄᴏп another time, again 134,2; 135,8;
             137,14
             ฬ₂ᴀ₂ ฬᴄᴏп many times, often 138,23

(351a)   ᴄᴇᴇпᴇ masc. remainder, others 133,13

(362a)   ᴄωᴛᴇ redeem
             ᴩᴇɋᴄωᴛᴇ masc. redeemer 134,7

(363b)   ᴄωᴛฬ hear, hearken
             133,24 ᴄωᴛฬ
             134,1 ᴄωᴛฬ
             136,23-24 ᴀɋᴄωᴛฬ
             136,25 ᴇᴛᴀʏᴄωᴛฬ
        ᴄωᴛฬ ฬᴄᴀ- hearken to, obey
             139,28-29 ฬпᴩᴛᴩᴇɴᴄωᴛฬ ฬᴄᴀ-
        ฬฬᴛᴀᴛᴄωᴛฬ fem. disobedience 135,10-11

(369b)   ᴄᴏᴏʏɴ, ᴄᴏʏωɴˀ know, recognize
             136,1 ᴄᴇᴄᴏᴏʏɴ
             136,20-21 ฬпᴏʏᴄᴏʏωฬᴛ

(372b)   ᴄωᴏʏ₂ gather
             133,12 ᴀɋᴄωᴏʏ₂
             133,15-16 ϣᴀʏᴄωᴏʏ₂
             140,[2] ᴀɋᴄωᴏʏ₂
             140,13 ᴀʏᴄωᴏʏ₂

(385b)   ᴄᴀ₂ɴᴇ masc. provision, agreement
             ᴏʏᴀ₂ ᴄᴀ₂ɴᴇ masc. command 135,13
        ᴄᴀ₂ᴏʏɴ ᴄp. ₂ᴏʏɴ

(390a)   ᴛ-, ᴛᴇ-, ϯ- definite article cp. п-
(390a)   ᴛᴀ-, ᴛᴇɋ-, ᴛᴇɴ-, ᴛᴇᴛฬ- possessive adjective
         cp. пᴀ-
(390b)   ϯ- demonstrative pronoun cp. пᴀϊ
(392a)   ϯ give
             134,8 ᴍᴀϯ
             136,26 ᴀϊϯ
             140,5 ᴍᴀϯ

       † Ⲙ̄Ⲛ-   fight against
          135,2 Ⲥⲉ† Ⲛ̄ⲘⲘⲀⲚ
          137,10 ⲈⲦⲚⲀ† Ⲙ̄Ⲛ-
          137,16 ⲈⲦⲚ̄ⲚⲀ† Ⲙ̄Ⲛ-
          137,20-21 ⲈⲦⲈⲦⲚⲀ† Ⲛ̄ⲘⲘⲀⲨ
          137,21-22 ⲈⲨ† Ⲙ̄Ⲛ-
          137,23 ⲈⲦⲈⲦⲚⲈ† Ⲛ̄ⲘⲘⲀⲨ
       † Ⲍ̄ⲒⲰⲰ⸗ put on
          139,17-18 Ⲁϥ† Ⲍ̄ⲒⲰⲰϥ
       † ⲘⲀⲈⲒⲚ cp. ⲘⲀⲈⲒⲚ
       † ⲤⲂⲰ cp. ⲤⲀⲂⲈ
       † 6ⲟⲘ cp. 6ⲟⲘ
       ⲀⲦ† ϢⲒ cp. ϢⲒ

(402a)   ⲦⲰⲂ̄Ⲍ masc. prayer 137,28

(405a)   ⲦⲀⲔⲟ, ⲦⲀⲔⲎⲟⲨⲦ† be corruptible
          137,7 ⲈⲦⲦⲀⲔⲎⲟⲨⲦ

(410a)   ⲦⲈⲖⲎⲖ rejoice
          133,11 ⲈϥⲦⲈⲖⲎⲖ

(411b)   ⲦⲀⲖ6ⲟ masc. healing 140,11

(413a)   ⲦⲀⲘⲒⲟ make
          136,8-9 ⲈⲦⲀⲘⲒⲟ

(413b)   ⲦⲀⲘⲟ, ⲦⲀⲘⲟ⸗ tell
          137,15 ⲘⲀⲦⲀⲘⲟⲚ

(416a)   ⲦⲰⲘⲤ, ⲦⲟⲘⲤ⸗ bury
          139,19 ⲀⲨⲦⲟⲘⲤ̄ϥ

(419b)   Ⲧ̄ⲚⲚⲟⲟⲨ, Ⲧ̄ⲚⲚⲟⲟⲨ⸗ send
        Ⲧ̄ⲚⲚⲟⲟⲨ⸗ ⲈⲌ̄ⲣⲀⲒ̈ Ⲍ̄Ⲛ- send down in
          136,17 ⲀⲨⲦ̄ⲚⲚⲟⲟⲨⲦ ⲈⲌ̄ⲣⲀⲒ̈ Ⲍ̄Ⲙ-

(424a)   ⲦⲎⲣ⸗ whole, all 132,19; 135,6.27; 140,[17]

(425a)   ⲦⲰⲣⲈ fem. hand
        Ⲛ̄Ⲧ̄Ⲛ-, Ⲛ̄ⲦⲟⲟⲦ⸗ in, to, from 132,17; 138,8
          cp. ⲬⲒ, ⲌⲘⲟⲦ
         ⲈⲂⲟⲖ Ⲍ̄Ⲓ Ⲧ̄Ⲛ- by 132,22-133,1

(430b)   ⲦⲰϥ̄ⲛ carry
          138,5-6 ⲀⲨⲦⲰϥ̄ⲛ

(440b)   ⲦⲟⲟⲨ masc. mountain 133,14; 134,11

(441b)   ⲦⲀⲨⲟ, ⲦⲀⲨⲟ⸗ send
          137,30 ⲈⲀϥⲦⲀⲨⲟⲈⲒ

(445a)   ⲧⲱⲟⲩⲛ, ⲧⲱⲛ⸗ rise
                  ⲧⲱⲛ⸗ ⲉⲃⲟⲗ ⲍⲛ̄- rise from
                      139,20 ⲁϥⲧⲱⲛϥ ⲉⲃⲟⲗ ⲍⲛ̄-

(446b)   ⲧⲟⲩⲛⲟⲥ set up
                      135,14-15 ⲉⲧⲟⲩⲛⲟⲥ

(449b)   ⲧⲱϣ, ⲧⲟϣ⸗ orient, situate, assign
                      133,4 ⲉⲛⲁⲧⲟϣⲛ̄
                      136,11 ⲁϥⲧⲱϣ

(452b)   ⲧⲁϣⲟ, ⲧⲁϣⲉ- increase cp. ⲟⲉⲓϣ

(467b)   ⲟⲩ-, ⲩ-, ⲍⲉⲛ- (pl.) indefinite article
                  132,17.[19]; 133,3.11.18.27; 134,8.10.13;
                  135,3.15.17.20.22.23.24; 136,2.8.9.[9].
                  10(bis).12.14.22.26; 137,3.4.8.9.11.[18].
                  24.25; 138,4(bis).14.21.25.26; 139,7.[9].
                  14.17.18.19.20.21.25; 140,5(bis).7.9.11.
                  20.21(bis).27(bis)

(467b)   ⲟⲩ what?
                  ⲉⲧⲃⲉ ⲟⲩ why? 134,16; 135,2

(469a)   ⲟⲩⲁ masc. one
                  ⲡⲟⲩⲁ ⲡⲟⲩⲁ each one 140,10

(470a)   ⲟⲩⲁⲁ⸗, ⲟⲩⲁⲧ⸗ -self, alone
                      135,5 ⲟⲩⲁⲧⲧⲏⲩⲧⲛ̄

(480a)   ⲟⲩⲟⲉⲓⲛ masc. light 133,22; 134,6.10; 135,4;
                  138,12
                  ⲣ̄ ⲟⲩⲟⲉⲓⲛ shine
                      134,11 ⲛ̄ⲧⲉ- ⲣ̄ ⲟⲩⲟⲉⲓⲛ

(481a)   ⲟⲩⲟⲛ there is, ⲟⲩⲛ̄ⲧⲁ⸗ have, possess
                      133,22-23 ⲉⲧⲉⲩⲛ̄ⲧⲁϥ
                      134,26 ⲟⲩⲛ̄ⲧⲁⲛ
                  cp. also ⲙⲙ̄ⲛ-

(482a)   ⲟⲩⲟⲛ someone
                  ⲟⲩⲟⲛ ⲛⲓⲙ everyone 140,18

(482b)   ⲟⲩⲱⲛ open
                      139,9 ⲁϥⲟⲩⲱⲛ

(486a)   ⲟⲩⲱⲛⲍ̄, ⲟⲩⲟⲛⲍ̄⁺ reveal
                  ⲟⲩⲱⲛⲍ̄ ⲉⲃⲟⲗ appear, express
                      134,9-10 ⲁϥⲟⲩⲱⲛⲍ̄ ⲉⲃⲟⲗ
                      134,12-13 ⲉⲧⲁϥⲟⲩⲱⲛⲍ̄ ⲉⲃⲟⲗ
                      135,12 ⲉⲧⲁⲥⲟⲩⲱⲛⲍ̄ ⲉⲃⲟⲗ
                      137,19 ⲛⲉϥⲟⲩⲟⲛⲍ̄ ⲉⲃⲟⲗ

	137,27-28 ογωⲛ︤ⲍ︦ ⲉⲃⲟⲗ
	138,6 ⲡⲉⲧⲁϥⲟⲩⲱⲛ︤ⲍ︦ ⲉⲃⲟⲗ
	140,16 ⲁϥⲟⲩⲱⲛ︤ⲍ︦ ⲉⲃⲟⲗ

(487b)   ⲟⲩⲟⲡ, ⲟⲩⲁⲁⲃ† be holy

   133,25-26   ⲉⲧⲟⲩⲁⲁⲃ

   139,14   ⲉϥⲟⲩⲁⲁⲃ

   140,10   ⲉϥⲟⲩⲁⲁⲃ

(488b)   ⲟⲩⲏⲣ, ⲁⲟⲩⲏⲣ how much?

   138,16   ⲁⲟⲩⲏⲣ

(500a)   ⲟⲩⲱϣ want, would like

   132,16   ϯⲟⲩⲱϣ

   134,21   ⲧⲛⲟⲩⲱϣ

   135,14   ⲁⲥⲟⲩⲱϣ

   136,[8]   ⲁϥⲟⲩⲱϣ

   137,12   ⲥⲉⲟⲩⲱϣ

(502b)   ⲟⲩⲱϣ︤ⲃ︦ answer

   134,19   ⲁⲩⲟⲩⲱϣ︤ⲃ︦

   138,17   ⲁϥⲟⲩⲱϣ︤ⲃ︦

(504a)   ⲟⲩⲱϣ︤ⲧ︦ worship

   137,14   ⲁ- ⲟⲩⲱϣ︤ⲧ︦

(505b)   ⲟⲩⲱ︤ⲍ︦, ⲟⲩⲁ︤ⲍ︦- set, put

   ⲟⲩⲱ︤ⲍ︦ ⲉⲃⲟⲗ set down, bring down, follow

   135,16   ⲁϥⲟⲩⲱ︤ⲍ︦ ⲉⲃⲟⲗ

   ⲟⲩⲁ︤ⲍ︦ ⲥⲁ︤ⲍ︦ⲛⲉ cp. ⲥⲁ︤ⲍ︦ⲛⲉ

(511b)   ⲟⲩϫⲁⲓ̈ masc. salvation 132,21; 137,2.25; 139,7

(520a)   ⲱⲗ, ⲟⲗ⸗ hold, enclose

   ⲟⲗ⸗ ⲉ︤ⲍ︦ⲟⲩⲛ ⲉ- confine within

   135,25   ⲁϥⲟⲗ︤ϥ︦ ⲉ︤ⲍ︦ⲟⲩⲛ ⲉ-

(525a)   ⲱⲛ︤ⲍ︦ masc. life 134,4; 139,28

(533a)   ⲱϣ, ⲟϣ⸗ read, sound

   133,9-10   ⲛ︤ⲧ︦ⲉⲣⲉϥⲟϣⲟⲩ

   ⲱϣ ⲉⲃⲟⲗ cry out

   134,13-14   ⲁⲥⲱϣ ⲉⲃⲟⲗ

   137,18   ⲁⲥⲱϣ ⲉⲃⲟⲗ

(541b)   ϣⲁ-, ϣⲁⲣⲟ⸗ to 134,14; 137,18; 138,21; 140,13

   ϣⲁ ⲉⲛⲉ︤ⲍ︦ for ever 134,18; 140,23

(546a)   ϣⲉ masc. tree, cross 139,19

(547b)	ϣⲓ	measure

ⲁⲧϯ ϣⲓ   immeasurable   139,27

| (553a) | ϣⲃⲏⲣ | friend, fellow |

ϣⲃⲏⲣⲁⲡⲟⲥⲧⲟⲗⲟⲥ   fellow apostle   132,14

| (559a) | ϣⲗⲏⲗ | pray |

133,20 ⲁⲩϣⲗⲏⲗ

134,2-3 ⲁⲩϣⲗⲏⲗ

| (565b) | ϣⲙ̅ⲙⲟ | stranger (noun)   136,2-3; 139,21 |
| (567a) | ϣⲙ̅ϣⲉ | serve |

136,4 ⲁⲩϣ̅ⲙ̅ϣⲉ

| (569a) | ϣⲓⲛⲉ | seek |

134,16 ⲧⲉⲧⲛ̅ϣⲓⲛⲉ

ϣⲙ̅- news, ϣⲙ̅ⲛⲟⲩϥⲉ good news,
ϫⲓ ϣⲙ̅ⲛⲟⲩϥⲉ tell good news

133,5 ⲉⲛⲁϫⲓ ϣⲙ̅ⲛⲟⲩϥⲉ

| (573a) | ϣⲟⲛⲧⲉ | fem. thorn   139,<17> |
| (574b) | ϣⲱⲡ, ϣⲡ̅- | take |

ϣⲡ̅ ϩⲙⲟⲧ   ⲥⲡ. ϩⲙⲟⲧ

| (577b) | ϣⲱⲡⲉ | become, come into being, come forth, make ϣⲟⲟⲡ† be |

133,27 ⲁϥϣⲱⲡⲉ

134,5 ⲉⲧϣⲟⲟⲡ

134,17-18 ⲉⲧϣⲟⲟⲡ

135,19 ⲁϥϣⲱⲡⲉ

136,[7] ⲁϥϣⲱⲡⲉ

136,15 ⲉⲧⲉⲁⲥϣⲱⲡⲉ

137,3-4 ⲁϥϣⲱⲡⲉ

137,8 ⲉⲧⲉⲧⲛⲁϣⲱⲡⲉ

138,12-13 ⲉⲧⲉⲁϥϣⲱⲡⲉ

138,13 ⲁϥϣⲱⲡⲉ

140,19-20 ⲉϥⲉϣⲱⲡⲉ

ϣⲱⲡⲉ ⲉⲃⲟⲗ ϩⲛ̅- come from, come into being from

135,3-4 ⲁ- ϣⲱⲡⲉ ⲉⲃⲟⲗ ϩⲙ̅-

136,13-14 ⲁⲩϣⲱⲡⲉ ⲉⲃⲟⲗ ϩⲛ̅-

138,4-5 ⲁⲥϣⲱⲡⲉ ⲉⲃⲟⲗ ϩⲛ̅-

ϣⲱⲡⲉ ϣⲁⲣⲟ⸗ come unto

138,21 ⲁ- ϣⲱⲡⲉ ϣⲁⲣⲟⲟⲩ

ⲉϣⲱⲡⲉ when 137,6

ⲣ̅ ϣⲡ̅ⲛ̅ ⲛ̅ϣⲟⲟⲡ ⲥⲡ. ϣⲱⲣⲡ̅

ⲙⲁ ⲛ̅ϣⲱⲡⲉ ⲥⲡ. ⲙⲁ

(584a)   ϣηρε masc. son 134,3-4.4.6; 139,26
(586b)   ϣⲱⲣⲡ be early, ϣⲣⲡ first, before
                ⲣ̄ ϣⲣⲡ ⲛ̄ⲭⲟⲟⲥ say previously
                138,2 ⲉⲧⲁⲓ̈ⲣ̄ ϣⲣⲡ ⲛ̄ⲭⲟⲟⲥ
                ⲣ̄ ϣⲣⲡ ⲛ̄ϣⲟⲟⲡ be preexistent
                136,1-2 ⲉⲧⲣ̄ ϣⲣⲡ ⲛ̄ϣⲟⲟⲡ
(590b)   ϣⲱⲱⲧ masc. deficiency 134,21-22; 135,[9].10.
                20(bis); 137,3
(612b)   ϣⲁϫⲉ speak
                135,8 †ⲛⲁϣⲁϫⲉ
                135,15-16 ⲉⲧⲁⲥϣⲁϫⲉ
                ϣⲁϫⲉ ⲙ̄ⲛ̄- speak with
                136,22-23 ⲁⲓ̈ϣⲁϫⲉ ⲙ̄ⲛ̄-
                138,11 ⲛⲁⲩϣⲁϫⲉ ⲙ̄ⲛ̄-
                masc. word, statement, message 134,15;
                138,14; 140,25
(615b)   ϣⲟϫⲛⲉ take counsel, consider
                ⲙ̄ⲛ̄ⲧⲁⲧϣⲟϫⲛⲉ fem. foolishness 135,11
(616b)   ϣⲱϫⲡ̄ leave behind
                135,17 ⲉⲧⲁⲥϣⲱϫⲡ̄
(620a)   ϥⲓ take
                136,28 ⲁⲓ̈ϥⲓ
(625a)   ϥⲧⲟⲟⲩ four 140,25
(636b)   ϩⲁⲉⲓⲟ, ⲁⲉⲓⲟ yea
                ⲁⲉⲓⲟ 134,1
(637a)   ϩⲉ fall
                ϩⲉ ⲉⲃⲟⲗ fall away
                136,18 ⲉⲧⲉⲁϥϩⲉ ⲉⲃⲟⲗ
(638b)   ϩⲉ fem. way, manner 137,16
                ⲛ̄ⲁϣ ⲛ̄ϩⲉ how? 133,4-5
                ⲛ̄†ϩⲉ in this way, thus 133,20; 137,21.23;
                139,15
                ⲕⲁⲧⲁ ⲑⲉ, -ϩⲉ as, just as, like 133,24;
                136,24; 137,11-12; 138,2
(643b)   ϩⲓ- cp. ϩⲓⲟⲩⲉ
(643b)   ϩⲓ-, ϩⲓⲱⲱⲥ on, in 139,[17-18] (cp. †)
                ϩⲓⲧⲉϩⲓⲏ on the way 138,12
(645b)   ϩⲓⲉ cp. ⲉⲓⲉ
(646a)   ϩⲓⲏ fem. road, way
                ϩⲓⲧⲉϩⲓⲏ on the way 138,12

(651b)   ⲍⲱⲱⲉ too, also, self 138,19; 140,6

    ⲍⲱⲉ 136,24-25

(653a)   ⲍⲱⲃ masc. thing 139,12.24

(661b)   ⲍⲱⲱⲕ, ⲍⲱⲕⲉ gird

    ⲍⲱⲕⲉ ⲛ̄ⲍⲣⲁⲓ̈ ⲍⲛ̄- gird with

     137,26 ⲍⲱⲕⲧⲏⲩⲧⲛ̄ ⲛ̄ⲍⲣⲁⲓ̈ ⲍⲛ̄-

(681a)   ⲍⲙⲟⲧ masc. grace 140,21

    ϣⲡ̄ ⲍⲙⲟⲧ ⲛ̄ⲧ̄ⲛ̄- give thanks to

     138,8 ⲁⲩϣⲡ̄ ⲍⲙⲟⲧ ⲛ̄ⲧ̄ⲛ̄-

(683a)   ⲍⲛ̄-, ⲍⲙ̄- before ⲡ, ⲛ̄ⲍⲏⲧⲉ in, with, through
    133,11.17.25; 134,1.5.24; 137,9.24.25;
    138,3; 139,7.11.14.19.23; 140,[9].27(bis)

    ⲉⲃⲟⲗ ⲍⲛ̄- from, with, (out) of 134,12;
     135,3-4; 136,14.14-15; 137,18-19;
     138,5; 139,20

    ⲍ ⲣⲁⲓ̈ ⲍⲛ̄- in, with, within 132,21; 136,11;
     137,2; 138,9; 139,7.25.30

    ⲉ ⲍ ⲣⲁⲓ̈ ⲍⲛ̄- down in 136,17

    ⲛ̄ⲍ ⲣⲁⲓ̈ ⲍⲛ̄- with 137,26 (ⲥⲡ. ⲍⲱⲱⲕ)

(685b)   ⲍⲟⲩⲛ masc. inner

    ⲉ ⲍ ⲟⲩⲛ ⲉ- within, into 135,25; 136,27

    ⲥⲁ ⲍ ⲟⲩⲛ within, inner 137,22

(696a)   ⲍⲁⲡⲥ̄ it is necessary 138,19.23.24-25

(698a,700a)   ⲍ ⲣⲁⲓ̈ masc. upper part, ⲍ ⲣⲁⲓ̈ masc. lower part

    ⲍ ⲣⲁⲓ̈ ⲍⲛ̄- ⲥⲡ. ⲍⲛ̄-

    ⲉ ⲍ ⲣⲁⲓ̈ up, over, down

     ⲥⲡ. ⲉ ⲓ̄, ⲕⲱ, ⲧ̄ⲛ̄ⲛⲟⲟⲩ

    ⲉ ⲍ ⲣⲁⲓ̈ ⲉ- to, down to, up to 136,19;
     138,7.10; 139,5-6.6; 140,25

    ⲉ ⲍ ⲣⲁⲓ̈ ⲉ ⲭⲛ̄- ⲥⲡ. ⲭⲱ

    ⲛ̄ⲍ ⲣⲁⲓ̈ ⲍⲛ̄- ⲥⲡ. ⲍⲛ̄-

(704b)   ⲍ ⲣⲟⲟⲩ masc. voice, sound

    ⲍ ⲣⲟⲩⲛ̄ⲡⲉ masc. thunder 138,5

(714a)   ⲍⲏⲧ masc. heart

    ⲭⲓⲥⲉ ⲛ̄ⲍ ⲏⲧ ⲥⲡ. ⲭⲓⲥⲉ

    ⲣ̄ ϭ ⲁⲃ ⲍ ⲏⲧ ⲥⲡ. ϭⲃⲃⲉ

(719b)   ⲍⲏⲧⲉ ⲥⲡ. ⲉ ⲓ ⲥ

(723b)   ⲍⲱⲧ̄ⲃ, ⲍⲟⲧ̄ⲃⲉ kill

    134,9 ⲉ ⲍ ⲟⲧ̄ⲃⲛ̄

(724b)   ⲍ ⲓ ⲧ̄ⲛ̄- ⲥⲡ. ⲧⲱⲣⲉ

(730a) ₂ΟΟΥ masc. day

      Ⲙ̄ⲡⲟⲟⲩ today 136,25

(732b) ϩⲓⲟⲩⲉ, ϩⲓ- throw

      ϩⲓ ϣ̄ⲙⲛⲟⲩϥⲉ cp. ϣⲓⲛⲉ

(741b) ϩⲁϩ many

      Ⲛ̄ϩⲁϩ Ⲛ̄ⲥⲟⲡ many times, often 138,23

(746b) ϫⲉ that, so that, because; quotation indicator
      132,[16].19.20; 133,4.5.6.15.21; 134,3.
      14.15.20.23; 135,4.6.28; 136,12.21.26;
      137,3.5(bis).10.11.15(bis).20; 138,15.18.
      22.23; 139,10.15; 140,[3].6.12.15.17.25

(747b) ϫⲓ, ϫⲓⲧ⸗ receive, take

      133,8 Ⲛ̄ⲧⲉⲣⲉϥϫⲓⲧⲟⲩ

      135,22 ⲉⲧⲁϥϫⲓ

      ϫⲓ Ⲛ̄ⲧⲟⲟⲧ⸗ receive from

      132,17 ⲁⲛϫⲓ Ⲛ̄ⲧⲟⲟⲧϥ̄

      ϫⲓ Ⲙ̄ⲕⲁϩ cp. Ⲙ̄ⲕⲁϩ

      ϫⲓ ⲥⲙⲏ cp. ⲥⲙⲏ

(752a) ϫⲟ, ϫⲟ⸗ sow

      135,22 ⲁϥϫⲟϥ

(754a) ϫⲱ, ϫⲉ-, ϫⲟ⸗, ϫⲟⲟ⸗ say

      133,20-21 ⲉⲩϫⲱ

      134,3 ⲉⲩϫⲱ

      134,14 ⲉⲥϫⲱ

      134,15 ⲉϥ̄ⲉϫⲟⲥ

      134,20 ⲛⲁⲩϫⲱ

      135,4 ⲉⲥϫⲱ

      135,6 ⲁⲉⲓϫⲉ-

      137,14 ⲉⲩϫⲱ

      137,19 ⲉⲥϫⲱ

      138,14 ⲉⲩϫⲱ

      138,17 ⲉϥϫⲱ

      138,22 ⲉⲥϫⲱ

      138,22 ⲁⲓ̈ϫⲟⲥ

      140,3 ⲉϥϫⲱ

      140,14-15 ⲉⲩϫⲱ

      140,16 ⲉϥϫⲱ

      ⲣ̄ ϣⲟⲣⲡ̄ Ⲛ̄ϫⲟⲟ⸗ cp. ϣⲱⲣⲡ̄

(756a)   ⲭⲱⲟⲩ masc. head

       ⲉⲭⲛ̄-, ⲉⲭⲱⲟⲩ upon, on, over   133,13.19;
        135,24; 139,19

       ⲉ₂ⲣⲁⲓ̈ ⲉⲭⲛ̄-, ⲉⲭⲱⲟⲩ because of, over   136,6;
        135,23-24 (ⲥⲣ. ⲕⲱ).

(764a)   ⲭⲉⲕⲁⲁⲥ so that   139,3

(778b)   ⲭⲡⲟ, ⲭⲡⲟⲟⲩ bring forth

       135,28 ⲁⲩⲭⲡⲟⲟⲩ

(787b)   ⲭⲟⲉⲓⲥ masc. lord   132,18; 133,1; 134,20-21;
       137,15; 138,9.14.[15]; 139,8.11.25;
       140,[3].12-13

(788b)   ⲭⲓⲥⲉ exalt, be high

       ⲭⲓⲥⲉ ⲛ̄₂ⲏⲧ be high-hearted, become haughty

        136,6 ⲁϥⲭⲓⲥⲉ ⲛ̄₂ⲏⲧ

(790b)   ⲭⲟⲉⲓⲧ masc. olive

       ⲡⲁⲛⲓⲭⲟⲉⲓⲧ masc. the (Mount) of Olives,
        Olivet   133,15

(793a)   ⲭⲟⲟⲩ, ⲭⲟⲟⲩⲟ send

       132,10-11 ⲉⲧⲁϥⲭⲟⲟⲩⲥ

(800b)   ⲭⲱⲱϭⲉ be stained

       ⲭⲏϭⲉ purple   139,18

(802a)   -ϭⲉ so, then   135,22; 138,16

(805a)   ϭⲃⲃⲉ be weak

       ⲣ̄ ϭⲁⲃ₂ⲏⲧ be weak-hearted, afraid

       140,21-22 ⲙ̄ⲡⲣ̄ϥ̄ϭⲁⲃ₂ⲏⲧ

(815b)   ϭⲟⲙ fem. power, mighty deed   135,2.23.27;
       136,7.11; 137,10.26; 140,7.27

       ϭⲁⲙ 134,8; 140,21

       † ϭⲟⲙ give power

       136,3-4 ⲡⲉⲧⲉⲁⲩ† ϭⲟⲙ

       ⲥⲣ. also 134,8 † ⲛ̄ⲛⲟⲩϭⲁⲙ

CHAPTER III

GRAMMAR

Pages 132-40 of Codex VIII, preserved in a much better
state than most of the pages of this fragmentary codex,[1] present a tractate written in reasonably good Coptic. The Coptic
may be termed Sahidic, and conforms to standard Sahidic to a
large extent. This Coptic text, like the texts of the Nag
Hammadi library in general, appears to be written in transla-
tional Coptic. Such may be intimated by the Greek loan words,
which include certain important technical terms (for example
ⲁⲡⲟⲥⲧⲟⲗⲟⲥ, ⲉⲱⲛ, ⲡⲛⲁ̅, ⲭⲥ̅, and the like),[2] as well as a number
of more mundane words, such as particles (for example ⲁⲉ and
ⲙⲉⲛ), prepositions (for example ⲕⲁⲧⲁ), and conjunctions (for
example ⲁⲗⲗⲁ and ⲏ). This evidence is not conclusive, however,
since such loan words were widely used in Coptic literature.[3]
A Greek *Vorlage* to the Coptic tractate is not extant, as far
as we know; thus the Coptic translation of the *Ep. Pet. Phil.*
provides one of the many texts in the Nag Hammadi library which
were previously unavailable in the original Greek or in some
translation.

The focus of this section of our study is the Coptic text
of the *Ep. Pet. Phil.* In our brief grammatical analysis[4] we
shall discuss nonverbal elements, the verbal system, certain
scribal techniques, and dialectical variants.

In general, the nonverbal elements in the Coptic text of
the *Ep. Pet. Phil.* present few surprises. The nouns usually
conform in spelling to standard Sahidic. An exception to this
conformity is the noun ⲋⲟⲙ, which in two instances (134,8;
140,21) departs from the standard Sahidic spelling and is
copied as ⲋⲁⲙ. According to Crum (815b), ⲋⲁⲙ is the spelling
attested in the Achmimic, Subachmimic, and Fayyumic dialects.[5]
In addition, the tractate illustrates itacism, using ⲉ instead
of ⲁⲓ in ⲉⲱⲛ.[6] In this connection we might also note the
spelling of ⲉⲡⲓⲁⲏ (134,8; 136,2; 137,2.12.16), ⲃⲟⲏⲉⲓ (137,29.
29-30), and ⲭⲉ(ⲓⲣⲉ) (132,15). Special plural forms can be
utilized in the tractate: ⲥⲛⲏⲩ, plural of ⲥⲟⲛ, is used at

132,15; 139,13.21.28. In typical Coptic fashion, neuter Greek
nouns become masculine in the *Ep. Pet. Phil.*;[7] for example,
cωмλ is used with the masculine definite article at 136,17 and
138,3.

The tractate naturally makes extensive use of both definite and indefinite articles, and they are generally used in a
regular fashion. Among the definite articles, п-, т-, and н-
are the usual forms, though пι-, †-, and нι- are also attested.[8]
пι-, †-, and нι- may be utilized instead of пе-, те-, and не-
before words beginning with double consonants,[9] such as пιсмоγ
(136,7) and †мн̄татϣохне (135,11); †- may also be used with
ειрннн, hence †рннн (140,17).[10] Before р̄пе, however, a mere
п- is used, for the р̄ is sonant.[11] In the other cases where
the *Ep. Pet. Phil.* prefers пι-, †-, and нι-, it may very well
be that the definite article has more demonstrative force.[12]
пе- is used in two cases: те᷍ртн (138,12) and пехc̄ (passim).
In the former case, те is to be anticipated before a word beginning with double consonants or a consonant followed by a
semi-consonant (з̄ι), though as we have seen the *Ep. Pet. Phil.*
prefers пι-, †-, and нι- in such situations. In the latter
case, the use of пе- may have been established by the Christian
tradition in Egypt, where 'Ιησοῦς ὁ Χριστός was translated as
ῑc̄ пехc̄.[13] пе, те, and не are also used as copulas in nonverbal sentences;[14] and the definite article in general functions in a vocative manner.[15] A couple of times (133,17;
139,11) the phrase з̄н cωмλ is used without the definite
article--indeed, without any article at all--and seems to
function in an idiomatic fashion. This *artikellos* phrase may
be contrasted with the similar phrases making use of the definite article (136,17; 138,3), though no difference in nuance of
meaning can be detected.

The indefinite articles are used in an even more regular
manner. Only two features deserve special mention. The singular indefinite article oγ contracts to γ several times
(132,[19]; 133,3.18; 134,13; 135,3; 136,12; 137,[18].24;
138,21; 139,[9]); in each instance the contraction takes place,
in the usual fashion, after λ or е. A few times--six to be
precise--an initial н is doubled before the singular indefinite

article: ⲛ̄ⲛⲟⲩϭⲁⲙ (134,8), ⲛ̄ⲛⲟⲩⲍ̄ⲓ̄ⲕⲱⲛ (136,9), [ⲛ̄ⲛⲟⲩⲍ̄ⲓ̄ⲕⲱⲛ]
(136,[9], on the basis of 136,9-10), ⲛ̄ⲛⲟⲩⲙⲟⲣⲫⲏ (136,10-11),
ⲛ̄ⲛⲟⲩⲉⲓⲟⲩⲥⲓⲁ (136,26), and ⲛ̄ⲛⲟⲩⲥⲧⲟⲗⲏ (139,18). In each case
but one the root word before which the ⲛ is doubled is a Greek
loan word. Each doubled ⲛ functions as a *nota accusativi* with
† or ⲧⲁⲙⲓⲟ, except for 136,[9] and 136,10-11, where the ⲛ
functions as the genitive particle in the phrase ⲉⲡⲙⲁ ⲛ̄-.[16]
Yet it should be acknowledged that more often in this tractate
the ⲛ is not doubled before ⲟⲩ.[17]

Although the pronominal prefixes and suffixes of the *Ep.*
Pet. Phil. are used in a normal manner, and present no diffi-
culties, the independent pronouns merit a few additional comments. Sometimes a pronoun can be used as the subject of a
nonverbal clause (134,17; 135,4-5; 136,16.21; 137,5.10; 139,22),
with or without the copula, and often (135,4-5; 137,5.10;
139,22) with the relative in a cleft sentence. In the case of
ⲛ̄ⲧⲱⲧⲛ̄ at 137,5, the relative uses the plural ⲛ-; with the ⲁⲛⲟⲛ
at 139,22, the relative utilizes the masculine singular ⲡ-,
as we have already noted; in the other instances only ⲉⲧ- occurs. When the nonverbal clause includes the personal pronoun
ⲁⲛⲟⲕ, the resultant construction is reminiscent of ἐγώ εἰμι,
the self-declaration often termed an aretalogical statement;
the ⲁⲛⲟⲕ can be used with (134,17; 136,16) or without (136,21)
a copula. Often the personal pronouns of the *Ep. Pet. Phil.*
are used in order to emphasize the subject of the clause, frequently after a change in subjects or a contrast in moods.
Occasionally it has been possible to reflect this emphasis in
the translation itself (thus 133,1: "But as for you"; 136,20:
"But as for them"). Usually, however, such additions to the
translation constitute overtranslation (thus 137,26, where
ⲛ̄ⲧⲱⲧⲛ̄ is the emphatic subject of the imperative ⲍⲱⲕⲧⲏⲩⲧⲛ̄). In
three instances (136,5; 137,28; 138,15) ⲛ̄ⲧⲟϥ is utilized to
emphasize the noun functioning as subject of a clause, and
acts practically as a pronominal demonstrative; thus at 137,28
ⲛ̄ⲧⲟϥ is translated as "surely." At 138,16 the pronoun ⲁⲛⲟⲛ
functions as the subject of the elliptical verb.

The verbal system of the *Ep. Pet. Phil.* presents the
translator with certain difficult problems and unusual

constructions. Thus we shall briefly examine the verbs of the
tractate, and shall discuss the suffix conjugation, the infinitive, the imperative, the present system, the future system,
the perfect system, the habitude, the optative, the conjunctive, and the past temporal. We shall also add a few remarks
concerning the passive voice.

The Coptic suffix conjugation is represented in the *Ep.
Pet. Phil.* by only a few verbal forms. пєхλ⁰ is used upon two
occasions (пєхλϥ: 139,10.15), both times as part of a quotation
formula in the context of the speech of Peter. Elsewhere in
the tractate the use of a first perfect verb, with єϥ/с/ⲅхⲱ
ⲘⲘⲟⲥ хє, is a more customary quotation formula.[18] ⲟⲩⲛ- and
ⲘⲚⲚ- are not used in the *Ep. Pet. Phil.*, but ⲟⲩⲚⲧλ⁰ and ⲘⲚⲚⲧλ⁰
are; the former occurs as ⲟⲩⲚⲧλⲛ (134,26) and the relative
єⲧєⲩⲚⲧλϥ (133,22-23; the ⲟⲩ contracts to ⲅ after є), the latter
occurs as ⲘⲚⲚⲧλⲩ (137,11).

The infinitives of the *Ep. Pet. Phil.* are of two types,
simple and causative. The simple infinitives (134,9.21; 135,
14-15; 136,8-9) are all prefixed with the customary є-,[19] and
complement the main verb; at 134,9 the infinitive seems to
indicate purpose or objective. The main verb in the last three
of these cases is a form of ⲟⲩⲱⲱ, a verb which is complemented
by the conjunctive at 132,16, and by ⲍⲓⲛⲁ with the conjunctive
at 137,12-13. The causative infinitives (ⲡⲓⲧⲣєⲛєⲓ, 133,3;
єⲧⲣєⲛхⲓ, 138,19-20; єⲧⲣєⲧєⲧⲚхⲓ, 138,24; єⲧⲣєⲩⲚⲧⲏⲩⲧⲚ, 138,25)
also are introduced with є- in all but one of the examples; in
this case ⲡⲓⲧⲣєⲛєⲓ functions as a noun after Ⲙⲡєⲕⲙєⲣє, and consequently is prefixed with the masculine singular definite
article or demonstrative ⲡⲓ-.[20] The three causative infinitives introduced with є- all function in proper Coptic fashion,
as complements of the impersonal verbal form ⲍλⲡⲥ.[21]

The imperatives are used in a regular fashion. In most
instances, the imperative is expressed by means of the simple
infinitive, such as ⲥⲱⲧⲘ (133,24; 134,1), хⲓ (134,15; 139,13),
† (+ⲥⲃⲱ; 137,24), ⲍⲱⲕ⁰ (137,26), and ⲟⲩⲱⲚⲍ (137,27). In a few
cases certain of the special forms are used: ⲙλ† (134,8; 140,5),
the imperative prefix ⲙλ- along with the infinitive †, which is
used in the *Ep. Pet. Phil.* as well as † to express the

imperative of †;[22] ⲙⲁⲧⲁⲙⲟ⸗ (137,15), which uses the prefix ⲙⲁ-
to express the imperative of ⲧⲁⲙⲟ; and ⲁⲙⲏⲉⲓⲧⲛ (137,23-24),
which is used to express the plural imperative of ⲉⲓ. The
negative imperative is in evidence on one or two occasions in
the tractate: certainly at 140,21-22 (ⲙⲡⲣⲣⲅⲁⲃⲅⲏⲧ), and probably
also at 138,1 (ⲙⲡⲣ[.]ⲁⲃ[   ]).

The verbs of the present system are also regular in the
Ep. Pet. Phil. As would be anticipated, verbs of the present
system are frequent in the tractate, and include several constructions. The first present indicative is used nine times
(132,16; 134,8-9.16.21.23-24; 135,2; 136,1; 137,5.12), each
time in a regular fashion; two of those occurrences (136,1;
137,12) utilize the negative form of the ⲛ̄- prefix with ⲁⲛ.
In ten other instances the present relative[23] occurs (ⲉⲧⲟⲩⲁⲁⲃ,
133,25-26; ⲉⲧϣⲟⲟⲡ, 134,5; ⲉⲧϣⲟⲟⲡ, 134,17-18; ⲉⲧⲣ̄, 135,5;
ⲉⲧⲙⲟⲟⲩⲧ, 135,26; ⲉⲧⲣ̄, 136,[1]; ⲉⲧⲙⲟⲟⲩⲧ, 136,19-20; ⲉⲧⲧⲁⲕⲏⲟⲩⲧ,
137,7; ⲛⲉⲧⲙⲟⲟⲩⲧ, 139,20-21; ⲉⲧⲛⲁⲅⲧⲉ, 140,18); in several of
these cases the verb is a qualitative, and in one instance
(139,20-21) the relative is prefixed with the definite article
ⲛ- and functions as the object of the preposition. The relative is used adjectivally to modify definite nouns and pronouns, of course, and at 135,5 the relative is used with ⲛ̄ⲧⲱⲧⲛ̄
in a cleft sentence. The present circumstantial is the most
common of the constructions in the present system, and occurs
some twenty times in the *Ep. Pet. Phil.* (ⲉⲧⲃⲉⲗⲏⲗ, 133,11; ⲉⲩⲭⲱ,
133,20-21; ⲉⲩⲭⲱ, 134,3; ⲉⲥⲭⲱ, 134,14; ⲉⲥⲭⲱ, 135,4; ⲉⲩⲙⲟⲟⲩⲧ,
136,13; ⲉϥⲙⲟⲟⲩⲧ, 136,22; ⲉⲩⲙⲟⲟⲩⲧ, 137,9; ⲉⲩⲭⲱ, 137,14; ⲉⲥⲭⲱ,
137,19; ⲉⲩ†, 137,21; ⲉⲩⲛ̄ⲛⲏⲩ, 138,10-11; ⲉⲩⲭⲱ, 138,14; ⲉϥⲭⲱ,
138,17; ⲉⲥⲭⲱ, 138,22; ⲉϥⲟⲩⲁⲁⲃ, 139,14; ⲉϥⲭⲱ, 140,3; ⲉϥⲟⲩⲁⲁⲃ,
140,10; ⲉⲩⲭⲱ, 140,14-15; ⲉϥⲭⲱ, 140,16). These circumstantials
often function like the Greek participle, modifying a noun in
the sentence; the most common example of such a construction
utilizes a circumstantial form of ⲭⲱ in a quotation formula.[24]
A circumstantial is used instead of a relative to modify a noun
when the antecedent is indefinite;[25] thus a circumstantial form
of ⲙⲟⲟⲩⲧ is utilized instead of ⲉⲧⲙⲟⲟⲩⲧ after ⲅⲉⲛⲥⲱⲙⲁ (136,13),
ⲟⲩⲣⲱⲙⲉ (136,22), and ⲅⲉⲛⲣⲱⲙⲉ (137,9), and ⲉϥⲟⲩⲁⲁⲃ is used after
ⲟⲩⲡⲛ̄ⲁ̄ at 139,14 and 140,10. Furthermore, ⲉⲩ† (137,21) has an
almost independent character,[26] and seems to function with ⲅⲁⲣ

to communicate a causal meaning, while ⲉⲩⲛⲛⲏⲩ (138,10-11) has
more of a temporal meaning.[27]

The present is converted to the imperfect by means of a
prefixed ⲛⲉ- to form ⲛⲉⲩⲙⲉⲉⲩⲉ (136,21) and ⲛⲉϥⲟⲩⲟⲛϩ̄ (137,19).
In the latter case the imperfect is constructed as a relative.
On two occasions the verbal stem is converted with a prefixed
ⲛⲁ⸗ to form ⲛⲁⲩⲭⲱ (134,20) and ⲛⲁⲩϣⲁⲝⲉ (138,11); a precise
analysis of this form is difficult, since it could be described
as either an imperfect or a second perfect form.[28]   It is true
that ⲛⲉ- is used to form the imperfect in two other passages of
the tractate, but a diversity of forms for the imperfect is not
necessarily to be excluded in such a tractate as the *Ep. Pet.
Phil.*[29]   Furthermore, it is reasonable to surmise that these
two verbs with ⲛⲁ- are intended to emphasize the more continu-
ous action characteristic of the imperfect.   In the case of
134,20, the apostles are speaking in a manner which entails,
literarily, the stringing together of a series of separate
questions; and in the case of 138,11, the apostles are speaking
as they are in the process of traveling up to Jerusalem.   On
the other hand, although ⲛ̄ⲧⲁ- is the usual prefix for the second perfect in Sahidic, ⲉⲧⲁ- and ⲛⲁ- are attested as dialectical forms, and the prefix ⲉⲧⲁ- also occurs elsewhere in the
tractate, apparently as a second perfect form replacing the
past temporal.   It is not readily apparent why a second perfect
would be employed in 134,20, unless the scribe meant to emphasize the direct statement; in 138,11 it may be suggested that
the scribe could have intended to emphasize the adverbial element of the sentence, the introductory temporal clause or, more
probably, the concluding ⲉⲧⲃⲉ phrase.   Here we are suggesting
that the two verbal forms with ⲛⲁ- be understood as imperfects,
although the evidence is not decisive.   In either interpretation
these two verbs can be described as dialectical variants.

The future system is represented in the *Ep. Pet. Phil.* by
first, second, and third future forms.   The first future occurs
in the indicative (†ⲛⲁϣⲁⲝⲉ, 135,8; ϥⲛⲁⲣ̄ⲃⲟⲏⲑⲉⲓ, 137,29[30]), the
relative (ⲉⲧⲛⲁ†, 137,10, with ⲛ̄ⲧⲱⲧⲛ̄ in a cleft sentence; ⲉⲧⲛ̄ⲛⲁ†,
137,16, with ⲗⲱ ⲧⲉ ⲑⲉ; and in addition ⲉⲧⲉ ⲛ̄ϥⲛⲁⲝⲓ ⲁⲛ, 138,28,
with the negative prefix and particle), and the circumstantial

(ⲉⲧⲉⲧⲛⲁⲕⲁⲕ, 137,6, used with ⲉϣⲱⲡⲉ in a temporal or conditional
clause; ⲉⲧⲉⲧⲛⲁⲃⲱⲕ, 140,19, used in a temporal clause). Here
and elsewhere in the tractate, the scribe of the *Ep. Pet. Phil.*
shows a preference for shorter forms; the scribe chooses not to
double the ⲛ for the second person plural, and consequently
does not use a supralinear stroke in that connection, since the
ⲛ is followed by a vowel. The second future occurs when the
scribe wishes to emphasize an adverbial element in the sentence: the ⲉⲛⲁⲧⲟⲟⲩⲛ at 133,4 provides stress for ⲛ̄ⲁϣ ⲛ̄ⲍⲉ; the
use of ⲉⲛⲁⲃⲱⲕ at 134,25 places stress on the concluding interrogative phrase; the use of ⲉⲧⲉⲧⲛⲁϣⲱⲡⲉ at 137,8 may give added
emphasis to the ⲧⲟⲧⲉ or, more plausibly, to the concluding
prepositional phrase; and the ⲉⲧⲉⲧⲛⲁϯ at 137,20 emphasizes the
ⲛ̄ϯ ⲍⲉ. The scribe of the tractate can also utilize the second
future with ⲭⲉ in final clauses (so with ⲉⲛⲁϭⲛ̄, 132,19; ⲉⲛⲁϯ,
132,20; ⲉⲛⲁⲍ̄ⲛ̄, 133,5). Such a use of the second future with ⲭⲉ
is attested in Coptic literature, although, as in this tractate,
it is more customary to find a final clause utilizing ⲭⲉ with
the third future.[31] The third future occurs in a final clause
with ⲭ̄ⲉ at several places in the tractate (so with ⲉⲕⲉϭⲛ̄, 133,7;
ⲉϭⲛ̄ⲉⲭⲟⲥ, 134,15; ⲉⲩⲉⲡⲗⲁⲥⲥⲁ, 136,12; ⲉϥⲉϭⲛ̄, 136,27; ⲉⲩⲉⲧⲁϣⲉ,
140,12; ⲉⲩⲉⲧⲁϣⲉ, 140,25-26). In addition, the third future may be
used in a final sense with ⲭⲉⲕⲁⲁⲥ (ⲉϥ[ⲉ   ], 139,3) and, in one
instance, with both ϫ̄ⲓⲛⲁ and ⲭⲉ (ⲉⲛⲉⲉⲓⲣⲉ, 140,6-7).[32] In two
other instances the third future is also used (ⲉⲧⲉⲧⲛⲉϯ, 137,23;
ⲉϥⲉϣⲱⲡⲉ, 140,19-20); in both cases the sense of the future occurs in a much stronger fashion than with the first future.[33]
In the first case ⲉⲧⲉⲧⲛⲉϯ seems to strengthen the second future
form ⲉⲧⲉⲧⲛⲁϯ in 137,20, and thus places added emphasis upon the
statement, almost to the point of making it an order: "you shall
fight" or even "you must fight." In the second case ⲉϥⲉϣⲱⲡⲉ
also seems to provide added emphasis for the statement, and
gives the impression of a wish: "there shall be," even "may
there be."

        In the *Ep. Pet. Phil.* more verbs occur in the perfect than
in any other tense, as we would expect in a tractate dominated
in the framework and the revelation itself by narrative constructions. The first perfect indicative occurs some eighty

times in the tractate;[34] two of these times it is used in the
negative, which is constructed in the normal fashion in the
tractate, with ⲙ̄ⲡ(ⲉ)ⸯ prefixed to the verbal stem. When the
subject of the first perfect verb is a noun, the noun often is
prefixed with ⲁ-, though the verb sometimes has no prefixed
letters (135,3; 137,13-14; 138,21; 140,10-11). More often,
however (at 133,12; 134,13.19; 137,18; 138,8; 139,[4-5]; 140,
[1-2].7-8.23-24), both the subjects and the verbs possess all
the appropriate prefixes. We may also note that at 134,9-10;
135,16.18.26-27; 138,4.13-14.17; 139,9; 140,16, the verbs possess all the appropriate prefixes and the subjects are indicated by ⲛ̄ϭⲓ. In the speech of Peter at 139,11-12 and 15-16,
on the other hand, the nouns seem to function without the first
perfect prefixes, or ⲛ̄ϭⲓ, as subjects of the first perfect
verbs. The perfect relative occurs in two forms: more often
than not the prefix ⲉⲧⲁⸯ is attached to the verbal stem
(ⲉⲧⲁϥⲭⲟⲟⲩⲥ, 132,10-11; ⲉⲧⲁⲩⲉⲣⲏⲧ, 132,21-22; ⲉⲧⲁⲕⲛ̄ⲧⲱⲟⲩ, 133,
24-25; ⲉⲧⲁϥⲟⲩⲱⲛ̄ⲍ̄, 134,12-13; ⲉⲧⲁⲩⲥⲱⲧⲙ̄, 136,25; ⲉⲧⲁⲓ̈ⲣ, 138,2;
ⲡⲉⲧⲁϥⲟⲩⲱⲛ̄ⲍ̄, 138,6), but on five occasions the prefix ⲉⲧⲉⲁⸯ is
utilized (ⲡⲉⲧⲉⲁϥϯ, 136,3-4; ⲉⲧⲉⲁⲥϣⲱⲡⲉ, 136,15; ⲉⲧⲉⲁϥ₂ⲉ, 136,18;
ⲉⲧⲉⲁϥϣⲱⲡⲉ, 138,12-13; ⲡⲉⲧⲉⲁⲛⲭⲓ, 139,22-23). Both of these
forms differ from the usual Sahidic form. ⲉⲧⲁⸯ as a first
perfect relative prefix is a dialectical form attested in
Bohairic, Achmimic, and Fayyumic, and only occasionally in
Subachmimic, and ⲉⲧⲉⲁⸯ also represents a different dialect.[35]
Finally, the first perfect circumstantial occurs three times as
well in the tractate (ⲉⲁⲩⲥⲙⲟⲩ, 136,5; ⲉⲁϥⲅ̄ⲃⲟⲏⲑⲓ, 137,29-30;
ⲉⲁϥⲧⲁⲩⲟⲉⲓ, 137,30); in each of these instances the perfect
circumstantial may connote a sense of time prior to that of the
main verb.[36]

A precise identification of the two verbal forms prefixed
with ⲛⲁ- (ⲛⲁⲩⲭⲱ, 134,20; ⲛⲁⲩϣⲁⲭⲉ, 138,11) is, as we have seen,
not easy to make. The forms could conceivably indicate a dialectical form of either the imperfect or the second perfect.

Three verbs occur in the first habitude (*praesens consuetudinis*) in the *Ep. Pet. Phil.*, and these three verbal forms
are constructed in a regular manner. ⲛⲉϥϣⲁⲕⲡⲱϥⲭ̄ (133,2) is the
preterite form of the habitude, ⲉⲧⲉ ϣⲁⲩⲙⲟⲩⲧⲉ (133,14) is the

relative form, and ⲉⲧⲉ ϣⲁⲩⲥⲱⲟⲩ⳯ (133,15-16) is likewise the
relative form. In each case these verbs express, though perhaps somewhat subtly, the sort of action connoted by the habitude: the state of affairs with or typical posture of Philip
(133,2), or the usual or habitual action on the part of the
people or the apostles (133,14.15-16).

The optative is utilized only once in the tractate, and
there it is found in the negative. ⲙⲡ̅ⲧ̅ⲣⲉⲛⲥⲱⲧⲙ̅ occurs at 139,
28-29, and is constructed in the usual manner, with ⲙⲡⲣ̅- prefixed to the causative infinitive form ⲧⲣⲉ⳽.

Seven conjunctive verbal forms are observed in the *Ep.
Pet. Phil.*, and they are used in a regular manner. They can be
used after the second future (ⲛ̅ⲧ̅ⲛ̅ⲧⲁϣⲉ, 132,20-21), after the
causative infinitive (ⲛ̅ⲧ̅ⲛⲉⲓⲙⲉ, 133,4), and after the negative
optative (ⲛ̅ⲧ̅ⲛⲙⲟⲟϣⲉ, 139,30). In addition, the conjunctive is
used twice after the Greek conjunction ⳅⲱⲥⲧⲉ in a result clause
(ⲛ̅ⲧⲉ- ⲅ̅, 134,11; ⲛ̅ⲧⲉⲛⲝⲓ, 138,27). Two other times the conjunctive functions as a verbal complement after ⲟⲩⲱϣ (ⲛ̅ⲕⲓⲙⲉ,
132,16; ⲛ̅ⲧⲉⲛ̅ⲛⲟⲩ⳯ⲙ̅, 137,13).[37] In the first instance the ⲛ̅ⲕ-
is of interest, since this prefix is used frequently in Fayyumic, ⲛ̅ⲣ- being the more usual form in Sahidic.[38] In the second
instance, the conjunctive is introduced by the Greek loan word
ⳅⲓⲛⲁ.

The seven past temporal (*temporalis*) verbal forms deserve
particular attention. Three times (ⲛ̅ⲧⲉⲣⲉϥϫⲓⲧⲟⲩ, 133,8;
ⲛ̅ⲧⲉⲣⲉϥⲟϣⲟⲩ, 133,9-10; ⲛ̅ⲧⲉⲣⲟⲩⲉ̅ⲓ, 133,18) the past temporal conforms to standard Sahidic, but on four other occasions the dialectical form ⲉⲧⲁ⳽ is utilized (ⲉⲧⲁⲥⲟⲩⲱⲛ̅⳯, 135,12, with the
ⲉⲧⲁ- prefixing the subject partly emended at 135,10; ⲉⲧⲁⲥϣⲁⲝⲉ,
135,15-16; ⲉⲧⲁⲥϣⲱⲝⲛ̅, 135,17; ⲉⲧⲁϥⲝⲓ, 135,22, with ⲉⲧⲁ- prefixing the subject). The context makes it clear that past temporal forms are desired here, and the Bohairic ⲉⲧⲁ⳽ is utilized in
these four instances.[39]

A few words should be devoted to the use of the passive
voice in the *Ep. Pet. Phil.* The passive may be formed when a
third person plural pronominal subject is utilized with a verb
whose object is the one acted upon. This circumlocutory construction is used several times in this tractate, though it is

not always clear whether a passive construction or a somewhat
ambiguous subject is the intention of the author. It may be
suggested that the passive is intended at 132,21-22 (ⲉⲧⲁⲩⲉⲣⲏⲧ
ⲙ̄ⲙⲟϥ), 133,14 (ϣⲁⲩⲙⲟⲩⲧⲉ ⲉⲣⲟϥ), 134,23-24 (ⲥⲉⲁⲙⲁ₂ⲧⲉ ⲙ̄ⲙⲟⲛ),
135,28 (ⲁⲩⲭⲡⲟⲟⲩ), apparently 136,3-4 (ⲡⲉⲧⲉⲁⲩϯ ϭⲟⲙ ⲛⲁϥ), 136,17
(ⲁⲩⲧ̄ⲛ̄ⲛⲟⲟⲩⲧ), possibly 137,1 (ⲁⲩⲙⲟⲩ₂ ⲉⲃⲟⲗ [　　]), most likely
137,5 (ⲥⲉⲁⲙⲁ₂ⲧⲉ ⲙ̄ⲙⲱⲧⲛ̄), 138,5-6 (ⲁⲩⲧⲱϥⲛ̄ ⲙ̄-), probably 138,25
(ⲉⲧⲣⲉⲩⲛ̄ⲧⲏⲩⲧⲛ̄), 139,16 (ⲁⲩⲗⲱϥϥ), 139,18-19 (ⲁⲩⲗⲱϥϥ), and 139,19
(ⲁⲩⲧⲟⲙⲥϥ).

　　When we examine the peculiar techniques of the scribe of
the *Ep. Pet. Phil.*, we discover some important matters of style.
To begin with, we should note that the scribal hand of Codex
VIII--the so-called "majority hand"[40]--is a clear and attrac-
tive hand; the letters are formed with considerable consistency
and grace. Such a scribal hand--in contrast to the scribal
hand of, for example, the first two tractates of Codex XI--
allows for some confidence in the restoration of letters where
only a portion of the letter now remains.[41] The scribe of
Codex VIII also made use of a system of decoration and punctuation. Not only are the title, the opening, and the conclusion
of the tractate set off by clear scribal marks. The scribe
also utilized indentation or *eisthesis* (for the title, 132,10-
11); extra space between lines (between 132,11, the conclusion
of the title, and 132,12, the opening of the tractate itself);
perhaps *ekthesis* (132,16, a possible "paragraph" designation);
supralinear dots (passim, used to separate sentences and sense
units) and *dicola* (132,11, at the end of the title where it is
followed by a *diple obelismene*, or "forked *paragraphus*";
136,15, at the end of the myth of the mother; probably at
138,16, at the end of the question on suffering; 139,21, at
the end of the traditional kerygmatic formulae; 140,15, after
the liturgical "Amen"; and 140,27, at the conclusion of the
tractate, where it is also followed by a *diple obelismene*);
scribal strokes like the *coronis* or *paragraphus* in the margin
(after 132,11; 136,15; 138,16; and 140,15--always, it seems, in
conjunction with the *dicola*); and extra space on the line itself (139,21.28; 140,15--after the *dicolon*, or after a supralinear dot at a clear break in the text of the speech of

Peter).[42] Again, the scribe also made extensive use of abbreviations, particularly of common *nomina sacra*: ⲓ̅ⲥ̅ for ιⲏⲥⲟⲩⲥ,
ⲭ̅ⲥ̅ for ⲭⲣⲓⲥⲧⲟⲥ, ⲡⲛ̅ⲁ̅ for ⲡⲛⲉⲩⲙⲁ, ⲑⲓ̅ⲏ̅ⲙ̅ for ⲑⲓⲉⲣⲟⲩⲥⲁⲗⲏⲙ, and perhaps ⲭⲉ for ⲭⲁⲓⲣⲉⲓⲛ.

     Furthermore, in at least two instances a scribe (or a la-
ter reader) emended the text that was first written. At 134,
22 a ⲕ apparently has been corrected to an ⲩ, and at 138,14 an
ⲩ seemingly has been corrected over a ϥ. In both instances the
apparent mistake was reasonable enough, and the correction was
accomplished by utilizing the ink already present and adding
additional strokes for the desired emendation; in the latter
instance some attempt may also have been made to erase part
of the ϥ.

     Particular mention should be made of the word divisions at
the ends of the Coptic lines. It is obvious that the scribe
did not divide the words in an arbitrary manner, but was careful to divide words in a manner approaching our division on the
basis of syllables. A cursory examination of the text would
suggest that the scribe preferred to end a line with a completed
word, if possible, but also was able to divide a word between
consonants, or after a vowel and before a consonant. In numerous instances it seems as if the scribe divided a word according
to the separable components, for example by separating prefixed
elements from the verbal or substantival base. Apparently the
scribe felt less confident in dividing Greek words, and clearly
wished to finish a Greek word on a line, even if it meant ex-
tending the line noticeably into the right margin. Such an obvious tendency allows us to suggest the unusually long line at
136,9, and could also provide an argument for ⲭⲉ[ⲓⲣⲉ] rather
than ⲭⲉ at 132,15.

     Finally, a few comments should be made on the matter of
dialectical variants in the *Ep. Pet. Phil.*, a topic already
discussed in a number of contexts in the preceding pages. As
we have seen, in two instances the noun ϭⲁⲙ does not conform to
the standard Sahidic spelling ϭⲟⲙ, the imperfects (or second
perfects) represent forms attested in dialects other than
Sahidic, the ⲉⲧⲁϥ perfect relative and past temporal verbs are
forms known in the dialects, and the conjunctive prefix ⲛ̅ⲕ- is

also found in Fayyumic. In addition, it may be noted that the
interjection ⲗⲉ̄ⲟ (134,1) is attested in this form in Bohairic,
and ⲗⲓ̈ⲟ is also to be found in Fayyumic, but the usual form in
standard Sahidic is ⲁ̀ⲗⲓ̈ⲟ or ⲁ̀ⲗⲉ̄ⲟ; the forms ⲗⲉ̄ⲟ and ⲗⲓ̈ⲟ, however, are also known in Sahidic and old idiomatic Coptic.[43] The
interrogative pronoun ⲗⲟⲩⲏⲣ (138,16) is to be found in Bohairic
manuscripts, ⲟⲩⲏⲣ being the usual form in Sahidic; here too,
however, the form ⲗⲟⲩⲏⲣ is also used in both Sahidic and Bohairic manuscripts, and sometimes in the sense of a *qal wa-homer*.[44]
Again, the prepositional form ⲛⲉⲙⲏ⸗ with the second plural suffix (140,22) is found in Fayyumic, though with the second plural
suffix ⲛⲉⲙⲉ⸗ (Achmimic and Subachmimic)[45] ought also to lengthen
the second ⲉ to ⲏ.[46] According to Crum (169b), the form ⲛⲉⲙⲉ⸗
is also known in "Sᵃ"[47] and Fayyumic. ⲧⲁⲕⲛⲟⲩⲧ (137,7) is described by Crum (405a) as the Bohairic form of the qualitative
of ⲧⲁⲕⲟ, the standard Sahidic form being ⲧⲁⲕⲏⲩ(ⲧ).[48] ⲧⲏⲛⲉ occurs at 137,7 as the pronominal suffix of the verb, in the form
known in Achmimic and Subachmimic rather than the more usual
Sahidic form ⲧⲏⲩⲧⲛ̄.[49] ⲟⲩⲁⲍ- (135,13) has been identified as an
Achmimic, Bohairic, and Fayyumic form of ⲟⲩⲉⲍ- (ⲟⲩⲱⲍ) in the
expression ⲟⲩⲁⲍ ⲥⲁⲍⲛⲉ, though ⲟⲩⲁⲍ is attested in certain Sahidic constructions as well.[50] Again, ϫⲓ ϣ̄ⲙⲛⲟⲩϭⲉ (133,5) makes
use of the Sahidic and Subachmimic form of ϣ̄ⲙⲛⲟⲩϭⲉ, the Bohairic
and Fayyumic form being ϣⲉⲛⲛⲟⲩϥⲓ; yet, as Crum (570a) points
out, the Bohairic seems to prefer this expression, while the
Sahidic often utilizes the Greek or some other Coptic expression.[51] Once again, the particle ϫ̄ⲉ (138,16) is utilized in
the usual Subachmimic form; but although the standard Sahidic
form is ϭⲉ, Crum (645b) cites one instance where ϫ̄ⲉ is also
attested in Sahidic.[52] Finally, the pronominal form ⲭⲟ⸗ (138,
22; probably also at 134,15) is known as a Subachmimic and Bohairic pronominal form of ⲭⲱ, the Sahidic (and also the Subachmimic) being attested as ⲭⲟⲟ⸗.[53]

Furthermore, Hans-Martin Schenke and Orval Wintermute have
also contributed some additional observations on dialectical
matters. Schenke[54] has suggested that 133,24-26 be restored as
ⲉⲧⲁ[ⲕ]ⲛ̄ⲧⲱ[ⲟ]ⲩ ϩⲙ̄ ⲡⲉⲕⲁⲗⲟⲩ ⲉⲧⲟⲩⲁⲁⲃ ⲓ̄ⲥ̄ ⲡⲉⲭ̄ⲥ̄, and thus has solved
the dilemma of this lacuna. It has been known, of course, that

ᴍᴀᴛⲱⲟⲩ is the Sahidic form of the qualitative of ᴍᴀᴛⲉ, and already at the end of June of 1967, H. J. Polotsky suggested that
he expected some form of the verb for "to be pleased" in this
passage.[55]   In the Oxyrhynchite text of Acts 9:22 a clause occurs which is not to be found in either the Sahidic or the Bohairic: ⲉⲧⲉ ⳬⲁⲛⲛⲧ ᴍⲧⲟⲟⲩ ⳬⲣⲏⲓ ⲛ̇ⳬⲏⲧϥ, "in whom God has taken
pleasure." This clause, which is also found in Old Latin as
"in quo deus bene sensit," bears a striking resemblance to the
restored passage at 133,24-26. Not only are both clauses perfect relatives, but also both utilize a form of ⳬⲛ̄-, ⲛ̄ⳬⲏⲧ⸱.
Wolf-Peter Funk[56] has thus suggested that ᴍⲧⲟⲟⲩ is an Oxyrhynchite and ⲛ̄ⲧⲱⲟⲩ a Sahidic form of the infinitive of ᴍᴀⲧⲉ.

Orval Wintermute has provided a couple of additional suggestions on some constructions in our tractate. According to
him, the difference in form between ⲛ̄ⲁⲱ ⲛ̄ⳬⲉ (133,4-5) and ⲛ̄ⲁⲱ
ⲛ̄ⲣⲏⲧⲉ (134,26) may be due to dialectical influence, the former
being Sahidic and the latter perhaps Bohairic.[57] Again,
Wintermute suggests that the use of the relative with the
demonstrative ⲡⲏ (134,12; 137,19; 138,27-28) illustrates the
Bohairic type of relative substantive, without the aspirated
stops of true Bohairic.[58] Indeed, as we have seen, elsewhere
in the *Ep. Pet. Phil.* the relative substantive may be found
with the definite article, for example ⲡⲉⲧⲁϥⲟⲩⲱⲛ̄ⳬ at 138,6.

Hence, although the Coptic of our tractate may be designated as Sahidic, a considerable number of dialectical variants
may also be noted. Besides the dialectical forms which may be
described as Subachmimic, to which the Nag Hammadi tractates in
general bear ample witness, additional variants in the *Ep. Pet.
Phil.* also suggest particularly Bohairic forms. How are we to
interpret this data relating to dialectical peculiarities?
Although our present knowledge of the character and development
of Coptic dialects is incomplete and imperfect, we may suggest
three possible answers.

First of all, it could be suggested that the dialectical
variants provide hints of sources which reflect the dialectical
peculiarities of the Delta (Bohairic) or some other area to the
north of Chenoboskeia and Pabau. Such a suggestion might be
supported by the observation that certain dialectical forms

occur exclusively in particular sections of the *Ep. Pet. Phil.*
which on other grounds may be identified as unique units. Thus
the Bohairic past temporal form ∊ⲧⲁ- is used four times in the
tractate (135,12.15-16.17.22), each time within the context of
the Savior's first revelatory answer (135,8-136,15),[59] which
constitutes a section set off from the tractate by means of its
opening subtitle (∊ⲧⲃ∊ ⲡⲓϣⲱⲣⲡ ⲙ∊ⲛ ⲛ̄ⲧ∊ ⲛ∊ⲱⲛ, 135,8-9), its un-
christianized character, and the concluding punctuation marks.[60]

        This source theory, however, assumes that sections of the
tractate had an independent history as Coptic traditions, within areas of Egypt where certain dialects were dominant. Subsequently, this theory suggests, dialectically divergent materials
were brought together and combined into a single tractate, with
their dialectical peculiarities still evident. Such a theory,
we would judge, cannot be maintained on the basis of the evidence in the *Ep. Pet. Phil.* To begin with, this theory calls
into question the usual assumption about the literary history
of the Coptic materials in the Nag Hammadi library, namely that
they were initially composed in Greek and later translated into
Coptic, with only minor editorial work being done at the Coptic
level. The dialectical evidence of the *Ep. Pet. Phil.* does not
suffice to contradict this supposition. Our tractate is too
short to provide numerous examples, and the dialectical variants which can be observed do not usually cluster as neatly as
the examples of the past temporal forms just noted.[61]

        Two other possible explanations for the dialectical vari-
ants are more reasonable. On the one hand, it is conceivable
that the scribe, with a native dialect other than Sahidic, was
able to conform to standard Sahidic in only an imperfect and
somewhat inconsistent manner. Such an explanation may be made
more complex by the suggestion that a plurality of translators,
scribes, and copyists may have turned their attention, at one
time or another, to the *Ep. Pet. Phil.*, and may have approached
the text with different philological standards and abilities.
On the other hand, it may also be proposed that it is misleading even to suggest a truly standard Sahidic for the early
Coptic of the Nag Hammadi library. Perhaps such early Coptic
had not yet been sufficiently standardized and identified with

particular regions, but rather existed in a "mixed" state.
According to this explanation, "standard Sahidic" is a term
which is meaningful only at a later stage of the Coptic
language.[62]

Whatever may be the case with the dialectical variants,
the philological peculiarities of our tractate remain, and
provide a variegated texture for the *Ep. Pet. Phil.*

NOTES

CHAPTER III

[1]In addition to the minor lacunae, which can be filled
with considerable confidence, the *Ep. Pet. Phil.* presents us
with only four major lacunae, all at the top of the latter
pages of the codex: 137,1-2; 138,1; 139,1-4; 140,1-2.

[2]See the indices of proper names and Greek loan words
above, pp. 47-49. These Greek loan words include terms which
themselves have come into Greek as Semitic loan words: ἀμήν
(אָמֵן), ʼΙερουσαλήμ (יְרוּשָׁלֵם), ʼΙησοῦς (יֵשׁוּעַ).

[3]More conclusive would be the evidence of a Greek title,
or Greek endings, or Greek idioms translated into clumsy Coptic;
such evidence proves helpful in the analysis of other Coptic
tractates. In the *Ep. Pet. Phil.* the title utilizes Greek loan
words, but the syntax is Coptic. Similarly, the nominal forms
among the Greek loan words uniformly use the nominative singular
endings, and the verbal forms imperatival endings (see Till,
Koptische Grammatik, §280). Greek idioms (for example ἐν (τῷ)
σώματι) are represented in our tractate, and certain difficult
passages could conceivably be explained by referring to a suggested Greek *Vorlage* (see below, p. 188 n. 237).

[4]This grammatical analysis is based, in part, on discus-
sions and unpublished studies by members of the Coptic Gnostic
Library Project of the Institute for Antiquity and Christianity.
These studies are available in the Nag Hammadi Archive of the
Institute; the most significant study for the following dis-
cussion is the paper of Orval Wintermute ("The Verbal System of
VIII,*2*").

[5]For a brief introduction (with bibliography) to the
Coptic dialects and the Coptic language in general, see Bentley
Layton, "Coptic Language," IDBSup, 174-79.

[6]ⲉⲱⲛ occurs at 134,22; 135,9.15.21.25; ⲁⲓⲱⲛ is never used
in the tractate. Note also ⲍ̄ⲕⲱⲛ at 136,9. On the other hand,
ⲉⲓⲣⲏⲛⲏ is used at 140,27, and ⲉⲓⲁⲉⲁ at 136,15. On itacism in
the Greek of the period see BDF, §§22-25. Here it may also be
observed that the *Ep. Pet. Phil.* tends to prefer the ⲓ alone
instead of ⲉⲓ in Coptic words. Thus ⲓⲱⲣ̄ⲍ̄ rather than ⲉⲓⲱⲣ̄ⲍ̄ occurs at 134,12. ⲓⲱⲧ is used consistently except for 136,28;
137,27: in the former instance the use of the abstract form may
account for the retention of the ⲉⲓ, and in the latter instance
the prefixed possessive adjective ⲡⲁ- (with its concluding ⲁ)
may account for the spelling ⲉⲓⲱⲧ. (Though still likely, the ⲉ
of ⲉⲓⲱⲧ is visually uncertain, since only a trace of ink is
visible in this damaged section of papyrus.)

[7]See Till, *Koptische Grammatik*, §76.

[8] ⲡⲓ-: 132,21; 133,3; 134,11; 135,[9].10.16.18.21; 136,5.
7.16.18; 137,22.25; 138,12; 139,27; 140,25. ϯ-: 134,4.7;
135,[1].1.10.11.13; 136,15.27; 137,26; 140,17. ⲛⲓ-: 133,15.23;
135,2.21.25.27; 136,7.11; 137,10.16.[17].21; 140,8.

[9] On ⲡⲉ-, ⲧⲉ-, and ⲛⲉ- before words beginning with double
consonants, see Till (*Koptische Grammatik*, §88) and Crum (258b).

[10] See Till, *Koptische Grammatik*, §87: ϯⲣⲏⲛⲏ, when ⲧ is
often written as ϯ before an introductory ⲉⲓ.

[11] See Walters, *An Elementary Coptic Grammar* (§20), where
ϯⲛⲉ is cited as an example.

[12] The definite article is, after all, a demonstrative,
albeit a weak demonstrative. Hence it becomes somewhat arbitrary to distinguish between ⲡⲓ-, ϯ-, and ⲛⲓ- as comparable to
our definite article on the one hand, and to our demonstrative
on the other.

[13] Cp. Till, *Koptische Grammatik*, §96.

[14] Note ⲡⲉ as a copula at 134,17; 135,[10].20; 136,16;
137,3; 139,22.27; ⲧⲉ at 137,16; ⲛⲉ at 136,3. ⲡ- is used with
a relative clause in a cleft sentence at 136,3 and 139,22, and
ⲛ- at 137,6; see Till, *Koptische Grammatik*, §247; H. J. Polotsky,
"Nominalsatz und Cleft Sentence im Koptischen," *Or* 31 (1962)
413-30; more examples above, p. 71. ⲡⲉⲧⲉ with ⲁⲛⲟⲛ at 139,22
presents no real difficulty, and is attested in Coptic (Till,
Koptische Grammatik, §246; Polotsky, "Nominalsatz," 419-20). ⲡⲉ
can also be used with the feminine ⲏⲥⲓ (Isis) in line 94 of the
great magical papyrus of Paris (Bibl. Nat. suppl. gr. 574); see
PGM 1.70.

[15] See 133,21(bis).22; 134,3.4.6(bis).20; 137,15; 140,4.
Possessive adjectives also function in a vocative fashion at
132,16; 133,6; 134,7; 139,13.21.28; 140,[3].

[16] See Crum, 154a.

[17] See 133,27; 135,17.19-20.22; 136,7-8; 137,4.11;
139,[17]; 140,5.

[18] Note the entries in the index of Coptic words, s.v. "ⲭⲱ."

[19] The ⲉ of ⲉⲧⲁⲙⲓⲟ at 136,8 is in a lacuna, but may be
restored with total confidence.

[20] See Till, *Koptische Grammatik*, §348.

[21] Crum, 696a.

[22] See Till, *Koptische Grammatik*, §298; Crum, 392b. Perhaps ϯ is utilized as the imperative in 137,24 because of the
idiomatic phrase ϯ ⲥⲃⲱ; note also the opinion of Lefort cited
in Till, *Koptische Grammatik* (§298 n. 11).

[23]The relative prefix can also be used in a nonverbal manner, as at 132,15; 136,23; 137,6.22; 138,7.

[24]The same sort of quotation formula can be used in the Coptic (Sahidic) NT. Note, for example, Acts 8:24: ⲁϥⲟⲩⲱϣ̅ⲃ̅ ⲛ̅ϭⲓ ⲥⲓⲙⲟⲛ ⲉϥϫⲱ ⲙ̅ⲙⲟⲥ ϫⲉ; or again, Luke 19:16: ⲁⲡϣⲟⲣⲡ̅ ⲇⲉ ⲉⲓ ⲉϥϫⲱ ⲙ̅ⲙⲟⲥ ϫⲉ.

[25]See Till, *Koptische Grammatik*, §475: "Der unechte Relativsatz."

[26]On the independent use of such verbal forms, see ibid., §334. ⲉⲩϯ could be understood as a second present form, in which case the ⲛ̅ⲛ phrase of 137,22 could be stressed.

[27]On the nonverbal use of the circumstantial prefix ⲉ- with a preposition, note 133,17; 138,3; 139,11.

[28]See W. Till, *Koptische Dialektgrammatik* (Munich: Beck, 1961) §264 (ⲛⲁ- for second perfect in Achmimic), §270 (ⲛⲁ- for imperfect in Bohairic, Achmimic, and Fayyumic).

[29]No neat pattern can be seen in the use of ⲛⲉ- and ⲛⲁ- in our tractate. Although the imperfects with ⲛⲉ- occur within the general context of the revelatory answers of Christ, the second occurrence is in the quotation formula of the additional revelatory answer. ⲛⲁ- occurs once within the quotation formula introducing the questions raised by the apostles, and once in the description of the apostles discussing matters on the road to Jerusalem.

[30]On the use of ⲣ̅- with Greek verbs in Sahidic and the dialects, see Crum (84a) and Till (*Koptische Dialektgrammatik*, §187). In the *Ep. Pet. Phil.*, ⲣ̅- is used with a Greek verb at 137,29.29-30; 139,16-17; 140,14; a Greek verb is used without ⲣ̅- at 136,12.

[31]See Marvin R. Wilson, *Coptic Future Tenses: Syntactical Studies in Sahidic* (The Hague: Mouton, 1970) 25-27, 48-51; Till, *Koptische Grammatik*, §361. In the *Ep. Pet. Phil.*, ϫⲉ with the second future occurs only at the very beginning of the tractate, in the letter itself.

[32]ϩⲓⲛⲁ with the conjunctive at 137,13 is discussed below.

[33]See Till, *Koptische Grammatik*, §308; Wilson, *Coptic Future Tenses*, 52-64.

[34]First perfect: 132,17; 133,6.10.12.13.19.20.27; 134,2. 2-3.9-10.13.19.25; 135,3.6.14.16.18.19.22.23.25.26.28; 136,4.6. [7].8.11.13-14.17.19.22-23.23-24.26.28; 137,1(?).3-4.13-14.18; 138,4.5-6.8.10.13.16.17.18.21.22; 139,[5].5.6(bis).8.9.[12]. 13.14.[16].16.16-17.17.18-19.19.20.24; 140,[2].8.9.10-11.11. 13.14.16.24.26. First perfect negative: 133,3; 136,20-21.

[35]See Till, *Koptische Dialektgrammatik*, §347. For both
ⲉⲧⲁ⸗ and ⲉⲧⲉⲁ⸗ note may be taken of the discussion and references in Wintermute ("The Verbal System of VIII,2," 8-9) where
he attempts to suggest a possible Middle Egyptian origin of the
form ⲉⲧⲉⲁ⸗, in a setting where the ⲁ̄ⲁ- prefix was utilized to
form the perfect and ⲉⲧⲉ ⲁ̄ⲁ- was used for the relative; see
also the example above, p. 81. In this connection, note Till
(*Koptische Dialektgrammatik*, §262) on the Subachmimic and Fayyumic forms.

[36]In the case of ⲉⲁⲩⲥⲙⲟⲩ at 136,5 it is also possible that
the circumstantial functions in a manner analogous to the conjunctive (see Till, *Koptische Grammatik*, §331), and could be
understood as a coordinate clause parallel to ⲁⲩⲱ̄ⲙ̄ϣⲉ ⲙ̄ⲙⲟ⸗. In
this interpretation the two clauses could be translated as
follows: "they served him and praised him." Cp. the similar
use of the Greek participle (BDF, §§419-20). Our interpretation, however, an interpretation which fits very well the use
of the Coptic circumstantial as well as the Greek participle,
seems to function better in the context: after the powers
praised the Arrogant One (cp. also 135,26-28), they assumed
their stance as his servants. Other adverbial ideas than the
temporal are also possible, for example the instrumental: "they
served him by praising him."

[37]On ⲟⲩⲱϣ with the conjunctive, see Crum (500b). As we
have seen, ⲟⲩⲱϣ may be complemented by the infinitive elsewhere
in the tractate. Wintermute ("The Verbal System of VIII,2,"
4-5) may be consulted for his suggestions concerning the use of
the conjunctive after ⲟⲩⲱϣ. Among other things, he suggests
that the conjunctive is used with ⲟⲩⲱϣ much more frequently in
Bohairic than in Sahidic. Such a tendency is also apparent
from the few examples cited by Crum.

[38]See Till, *Koptische Dialektgrammatik*, §267; *Koptische
Grammatik*, §321.

[39]As Till claims (*Koptische Dialektgrammatik*, §265) with
regard to the *temporalis*, "Im *B* (ist es) durch Perf. II (= ⲉⲧⲁ-)
ersetzt" (parenthetical insertions mine).

[40]Cp. James M. Robinson, "On the Codicology of the Nag
Hammadi Codices," pp. 17-18 in *Les textes de Nag Hammadi*
(NHS 7; ed. J.-E. Ménard; Leiden: Brill, 1975).

[41]For example, the mere presence of the tail of a letter
at 138,1 makes ⲁ a very likely restoration, for the scribe
writes ⲁ's in a consistent way.

[42]For a discussion of these scribal conventions, see Eric
Turner, *Greek Manuscripts of the Ancient World* (London: Oxford
University, 1971) 9-15.

[43]See Crum, 2a, 636b.

[44]See Crum, 21b, 488b. In both Matt 7:11 and Heb 9:14, a
qal wa-homer is utilized. In both instances the Bohairic has
ιε ⲁⲩⲏⲣ ⲙⲁⲗⲗⲟⲛ, but the Sahidic uses the Greek loan words
ⲡⲟⲥⲱ ⲙⲁⲗⲗⲟⲛ.

[45]So with Till, *Koptische Dialektgrammatik*, §153.

[46]So also ⲛ̄-, ⲙ̄ⲙⲟ⸗, at 137,5: ⲙ̄ⲙⲱⲧⲛ̄; ⲛ̄-, ⲛⲁ⸗, at 134,16:
ⲛⲏⲧⲛ̄; ⲉ-, ⲉⲣⲟ⸗, at 138,23: ⲉⲣⲱⲧⲛ̄ (also consider ⲉⲣⲱϥ at 139,9).

[47]"Sa'idic with Achmimic tendency (mostly Theban)"; Crum,
xiii b.

[48]See also Till, *Koptische Dialektgrammatik*, §218.

[49]Ibid., §120. Elsewhere, the *Ep. Pet. Phil.* can make use
of ⲑⲏⲧⲛ̄, for example at 137,26.

[50]According to Crum (505b), ⲟⲩⲁ₂ occurs as a standard
spelling in several dialects, Sahidic included, of the pronominal form and conjunctive participle of ⲟⲩⲱ₂. Also see
Crum, 385b, s.v. "ⲥⲁ₂ⲛⲉ."

[51]Consider, for example, Acts 8:4, where the Bohairic has
ⲉⲩⲍ ι ϣⲉⲛⲛⲟⲩϥι ⲙ̄ⲡⲓⲥⲁⲭⲓ and the Sahidic ⲉⲩⲧⲁϣⲉ ⲟⲉⲓϣ ⲙ̄ⲡϣⲁϫⲉ; or
1 Cor 15:2, where the Bohairic reads ⲁⲓ̈ⲍ ι ϣⲉⲛⲛⲟⲩϥι and the
Sahidic ⲛ̄ⲧⲁⲓ̈ⲉⲩⲁⲅⲅⲉⲗⲓⲍⲉ. Also see Crum, 257b, s.v. "ⲧⲁϣⲉ ⲟⲉⲓϣ."

[52]Also note Till, *Koptische Dialektgrammatik*, §§322, 341.

[53]See Crum, 754a; Till, *Koptische Dialektgrammatik*, §§193,
200. Till classifies ⲭⲟⲟ⸗ as a Sahidic, Achmimic, and Subachmimic form, and ⲭⲟ⸗ as a Bohairic form. The sole example
of ⲭⲟⲟ⸗ in the *Ep. Pet. Phil.* occurs at 138,2, where there is
considerable uncertainty about the restoration.

[54]Schenke, "On the Middle Egyptian Dialect of the
Coptic Language," 58*(104); also see Bethge, col. 168 n. 8.
Schenke has advised me privately, in letters of 11 May and
21 September 1978, of an additional occurrence of the verb
ⲛ̄ⲧⲱⲟⲩ in a Coptic fragment (to be published by Dr. Bernd Jörg
Diebner).

[55]Notes of Frederik Wisse's consultation with Prof.
Polotsky, on file at the Institute for Antiquity and Christianity (p. 1).

[56]W.-P. Funk, "Zur Syntax des koptischen Qualitativs,"
Zeitschrift für Ägyptische Sprache und Altertumskunde 104 (1977)
31-32.

[57]Wintermute, "The Verbal System of VIII,*2*," 3. Note the
examples cited by Crum at 305a; (ⲛ̄)ⲗⲱ ⲛ̄ⲣⲏⲧⲉ is often used in
Bohairic, and a construction utilizing ⲍⲉ or the Greek in
Sahidic.

[58]Wintermute, "The Verbal System of VIII,2," 14-15, where an additional example from the Gospel of John is given. See also Till, *Koptische Dialektgrammatik*, §§358-60.

[59]Note also the use of ⲉⲧ<ⲁ>ϯⲙⲛⲧⲁⲧⲥⲱⲧⲙ, 135,10-11. This section is discussed below, pp. 121-28.

[60]In three other instances (133,8.9-10.18) the past temporal conforms to standard Sahidic, and these three forms occur in the narrative framework of the tractate.

[61]Here we may also note that the evidence of the grammatical peculiarities is similarly inconclusive as evidence for the independent transmission of particular Coptic sections of the *Ep. Pet. Phil.* In most cases where certain sections show grammatical peculiarities, this situation may be traced to the character of the Greek *Vorlage*; see below, p. 190 (with the notes). But also see the use of ⲭⲉ with the second future in a final clause, discussed above, p. 75, and esp. n. 31.

[62]For a general discussion of these issues, see Layton, "Coptic Language," IDBSup, 175-77.

Title (132,10-11)

The *Ep. Pet. Phil.* opens with a superscribed title:
τ∈πιϲτολη ⲛⲡⲉⲧⲣⲟⲥ ⲉⲧⲁϥϫⲟⲟⲩⲥ ⲛ̄ⲫⲓⲗⲓⲡⲡⲟⲥ, "The letter of Peter
which he sent to Philip," usually shortened and simplified in
the secondary literature to "The Letter of Peter to Philip." That
these two lines are intended to designate the tractate title
cannot be doubted. The use of *eisthesis*, the extra space between 132,11 and 132,12, the *dicolon* and *diple obelismene* at
the end of 132,11, and the marginal punctuation after 132,11
and decoration at 132,13 all point to the fact that the scribe
considered 132,10-11 to function as the tractate title. The
superscription is the only indication of a title for the *Ep.
Pet. Phil.*, for no titular *incipit* and no subscription appear.[1]

According to its title, then, the *Ep. Pet. Phil.* is an
∈πιϲτολη, and like a few other tractates in the Nag Hammadi
library the *Ep. Pet. Phil.* has some relationship to this popular *Gattung* of the letter.[2] The *Ap. Jas.* takes the form of a
letter from James to a certain unknown addressee ([...]ⲉⲟⲥ,
I 1,2); James claims that he has written this work ⲍ̄ⲛ̄ ⲍⲉⲛⲥⲍⲉⲉⲓ
ⲙⲙⲛ̄ⲧⲍ∈ⲃⲣⲁⲓⲟⲓⲥ, "in Hebrew characters" (1,15-16), and can use
the terms ⲁⲡⲟⲕⲣⲩⲫⲟⲛ (1,10.30-31) and ⲗⲟⲅⲟⲥ (1,28) to describe
his letter. Again, the *Treat. Res.* claims to be written by
some teacher to a certain Rheginos, and although no opening of
the letter is given, a closing is provided at 50,11-16.
Eugnostos, too, is in the form of a letter, apparently with the
appropriate opening and closing elements.[3] In addition to
these letters in the Nag Hammadi library, we know of other letters which were in use among the Gnostics; besides Ptolemy's
Letter to Flora, we can cite letters of Valentinus, Monoimus
the Arabian, and Marcion.

Furthermore, just as a magnificent epistolary tradition
developed around Paul and the Pauline school, so also a more
modest collection of letters came to be ascribed to Peter.
These Petrine or pseudo-Petrine letters include, in addition to

the *Ep. Pet. Phil.*, the two catholic letters of Peter in the
NT, the *Epistula Petri* at the opening of the Pseudo-Clementines,
and perhaps another letter of Peter known only from a brief
quotation in Optatus.[4]   Of these letters the *Epistula Petri* is
of particular interest, since it shares a number of features
with our tractate. Not only is it prefixed to the beginning of
a collection of materials relating to Peter; it also is intended
to attest the authority of Peter, and as it concludes the *Contestatio* begins by referring to the recipient--here James the
Just--reading and responding to the letter in a manner reminiscent of 133,8-11 in our tractate.[5]   The *Ep. Pet. Phil.*, however, is not identical with any of these letters of Peter. It
must represent a newly discovered work in the Petrine corpus,
and it constitutes an additional witness to the popularity of
the epistolary genre in the early church.[6]

     A problem emerges, however, when we compare the title of
this tractate with the actual contents. Though the tractate is
entitled ⲦⲈⲠⲒⲤⲦⲞⲖⲎ ⲘⲠⲈⲦⲢⲞⲤ, this letter of Peter actually constitutes only a small part of the entire tractate; clearly the
letter itself concludes at 133,8, and the remainder of the tractate is of a genre quite different from that of the letter.
Much of the balance of the *Ep. Pet. Phil.* may be described, with
certain qualifications, as a "dialogue" between the resurrected
Christ and the apostles, and thus may represent yet another example of the use of this famous and popular *Gattung* among Gnostic Christians.[7]   In the *Ep. Pet. Phil.*, however, the setting
provided and the questions presented bring some unique features
to the tractate, and should caution us against a facile classification of the *Ep. Pet. Phil.*

     What is the relationship, then, between the title and the
letter, on the one hand, and the nonepistolary remainder of the
tractate on the other hand? Though for the scribe of the *Ep.
Pet. Phil.*, 132,10-11 functions as the tractate title, we may
assume that at some prior point in the literary history of the
materials in our tractate the situation may have been quite
different. It seems probable that something similar to 132,10-
11 once functioned as an *incipit* or title for only the letter
itself. As the literary materials were reworked, however, the

title was utilized not only for the letter but also for additional materials from the traditions relating to Peter. In
this way a somewhat misleading title was appropriated for the
tractate.

Letter (132,12-133,8)

Following the tractate title, the tractate begins with the
prefixed letter of Peter. The letter opens (132,12-15) in
typical Greek epistolary fashion, and provides an identification
of the sender (by name and description), an identification of
the principal addressee (by name and twofold description) as
well as his companions, and a typical greeting. Unfortunately,
the greeting cannot be restored with complete confidence.
Clearly a form of the Greek χαίρειν is utilized, but the lacuna
at 132,15 does not allow us to ascertain precisely which form
it is. The extraordinary length required for the line if
ϫε[ιρε] is to be read would suggest that an abbreviated greeting, perhaps followed by a punctuation mark, is to be preferred; extant Greek letters illustrate that the greeting can
be abbreviated as χ, χα, χαι, or χαιρ.[8] On the other hand,
unusually long lines, particularly with Greek loan words, are
by no means unknown in the *Ep. Pet. Phil.*, so that ϫε[(ι)ρ] and
ϫε[(ι)ρε] must remain at least possible readings. After the
greeting, the body of the letter begins, in good epistolary
fashion, with †ογωϣ.[9] At the conclusion of the body of the
letter, however, no closing elements are to be found; except
for this lack the letter of Peter resembles private Hellenistic
letters in form and content.[10]

The descriptions of Peter and Philip deserve special mention.[11] Peter is described as ⲡⲁⲡⲟⲥⲧⲟⲗⲟⲥ ⲛⲧⲉ ⲓ̅ⲥ̅ ⲡⲉⲭ̅ⲥ̅, a description which is in no way a surprise, considering the universal testimony in early Christian literature that Peter is
not only an apostle but often the first of the apostles.
The depiction of Philip is somewhat more problematic. He is
termed ⲡⲉⲛⲥⲟⲛ ⲙⲙⲉⲣⲓⲧ, a common and appropriate enough phrase
for Philip,[12] but he is also described as ⲡⲉⲛϣⲃⲏⲣⲁⲡⲟⲥⲧⲟⲗⲟⲥ.
When we note that the particular Philip here addressed seems to

be none other than the Philip of Acts 6:5, 8:4-40, and 21:8,
we may be surprised by the title ϣвнрапостолос. After all, in
the NT Acts this Philip is described as one of the seven "dea-
cons," and is called ὁ εὐαγγελιστής (21:8). Philip the apostle
is one of the Twelve, and is also listed as one of this group
in Acts (1:13). For the author of Acts, who goes to such
lengths to provide apostolic sanction for the Hellenistic mission of Philip in Samaria, there is a clear distinction between
these two Philips. Furthermore, Luke is somewhat jealous in
his use of the term ἀπόστολος in Acts; in general it is re-
served for the exclusive group of the Twelve, though in at
least two instances (14:4, 14) Paul and Barnabas can be described as οἱ ἀπόστολοι, Christian missionaries in a rather
wide sense.[13] Other sources, however, some as early as the
second century C.E., tend to identify these two Philips; such
seems to be the case with the Bishop Polycrates of Ephesus as
well as Clement of Alexandria,[14] and may also be the case in
our tractate. In other words, just as the various women named
Mary may merge at times into a "universal Mary," particularly
in certain tractates within the Nag Hammadi corpus, so also
Philip the apostle and Philip the evangelist may no longer be
distinguished in certain documents from the second century and
on.

The body of the letter of Peter presents the request of
Peter that Philip join the gathering of the apostles. Peter
begins with a reminder of the previous instructions from
пенхоеіс ᾶᴎ псωтнр ᾶτе пкосмос тнрϥ (132,18-19), whom Peter can
also identify as пеннογτе τϲ (133,7-8).[15] In a manner reminiscent of the end of Luke and the beginning of Acts, the apostles
have been instructed to come together before going forth to
preach. In Luke 24:49 Jesus issues the command, "ὑμεῖς δὲ
καθίσατε ἐν τῇ πόλει ἕως οὗ ἐνδύσησθε ἐξ ὕψους δύναμιν," a command also mentioned in Acts 1:4, where Jesus alludes to the
ἐπαγγελία τοῦ πατρός. Similarly in the letter of Peter, the
promise is mentioned as characteristic of the salvation to be
preached and taught.[16] Philip, however, had kept himself separate from the apostles, and was unwilling to participate in
the apostolic gathering. Hence Peter now reiterates the request that Philip and the others come together.

The theme of the separation of Philip is also to be found
in Acts 8:4-40, and especially the account of the mission to
the Samaritans in 8:4-25. According to Luke, Philip the evangelist, one of the Seven, flees from Jerusalem on account of
the persecution, and in Samaria preaches the gospel to the
people there. The official ministry to the Gentiles has not
yet begun. That ministry is to begin through the apostles,
especially Peter (Acts 10:1-11:18) and Paul (Acts 9:1-31; chapters 13 and following, and especially 15:1-35). Apparently,
Luke suggests later (Acts 11:19), this mission abroad was re-
stricted to Jews; but Luke must qualify this statement by ac-
knowledging that τινες ἐξ αὐτῶν ἄνδρες Κύπριοι καὶ Κυρηναῖοι
did indeed speak to Gentiles as well (11:20)--hence the origin
of the church at Antioch. In other words, Luke wishes to emphasize the primary role and authority of the apostles: it is
from the apostles that the ministry to the Gentiles must begin.
While Philip, then, is a successful preacher and magician, and
even moves Simon Magus to belief and baptism, he cannot confer
the crucial gift of the Holy Spirit. That gift requires the
attention of οἱ ἐν Ἱεροσολύμοις ἀπόστολοι (8:14). Thus Peter
and John travel to Samaria so that the believers there might
receive the Spirit; οὐδέπω γὰρ ἦν ἐπ' οὐδενὶ αὐτῶν ἐπιπεπτωκός,
μόνον δὲ βεβαπτισμένοι ὑπῆρχον εἰς τὸ ὄνομα τοῦ κυρίου Ἰησοῦ
(8:16). In this way Luke portrays the mission of Philip as
subordinate to the central authority of the apostles: his
separation is due to persecution, and his mission is dependent
on that of the apostles.

In this connection we must remember that Luke's portrayal
of life in the early church is, as Ernst Haenchen has convinc-
ingly demonstrated, a portrayal characterized by specific theological, historical, apologetic, and dramatic concerns.[17] Luke
as historian traces the "ideal curve"[18] of the primitive Christian mission: "Everything that might interfere with its
straightforward movement is smoothed out or omitted."[19] As a
result, the prominent place of Peter and the apostles in the
first half of Acts, and the development of the Christian mission from Jerusalem with the apostles to the ends of the earth
with Paul, leave little room for a dynamic and autonomous

mission on the part of missionaries like Philip. On the one
hand, Philip must be subservient to the apostles, and particularly Peter; on the other hand, any real friction or disagreement between Philip and Peter must be smoothed over. Thus Luke
provides a placid portrayal of the innovative mission of the
pre-Pauline Hellenistic Christians, and presents us with rather
domesticated pictures of Stephen, Philip, and Nicolaus.[20]

The opening letter of Peter in the *Ep. Pet. Phil.*, however,
acknowledges the separation and disagreement between Peter and
Philip. As Peter writes, Philip not only remained separated
from the apostolic group, but also was initially unwilling to
join the others (133,1-5). Thus, whether through insight into
the text of Acts, or through exposure to additional sources of
information, the author of this pseudo-apostolic letter indicates more clearly than Luke the independence of Philip and his
mission. It is tantalizing to speculate that perhaps the author of this letter of Peter was aware of additional traditions
regarding Philip and the emergence of Samaritan Christianity.
Even in Acts, the positive association between Philip and Simon
Magus in Samaria, along with the character of Philip himself,
may suggest that the historical Philip was involved in some way
with an esoteric and perhaps proto-Gnostic Samaritan Christian
movement. Yet it must also be admitted that the place of
Philip in our tractate is less that of the assertive founder of
a religious movement than that of the repentant and submissive
apostle. As in Acts, so also here Philip ultimately is submissive to the will of the apostle Peter; he returns from his
separation, and gathers with the other apostles. Hence in the
Ep. Pet. Phil., as in Acts, the day belongs to Peter. His is
the preeminent authority, and the letter and tractate champion
his cause.

Our tractate, then, opens with a pseudonymous letter attributed to Peter. Philip occupies a place in the plot only at
the very opening of the tractate. In fact, after the reference
to his willing submission to the authority of Peter at 133,9,
Philip disappears from the scene, and is only implicitly present as an anonymous member of the apostolic group. Thus Philip
provides the occasion for the manifestation of the authority of

Peter, and the letter of Peter bears witness to that authority
in a manner not unlike the *Epistula Petri* at the beginning of
the *Kerygmata Petrou*.[21]

Hans-Gebhard Bethge has suggested that the curious role of
Philip, limited as it is to the first part of the *Ep. Pet.
Phil.*, reflects the nature of the tractate. The *Ep. Pet. Phil.*,
he proposes, "ist gar kein Text, sondern nur ein Textfragment
und 'Buchfüller.'"[22] Bethge entitled the earlier typescript of
his article "Der sogenannte 'Brief des Petrus an Philippus,'
oder: Die Einleitung gnostischer Acta Philippi." For, Bethge
suggests,

> Es ist nur der Anfang einer Schrift. Und da, wo der
> Codex VIII zu Ende ist, müsste man sich vorstellen,
> dass diese Schrift weiterging etwa mit den Worten:
> "Philippus aber wurde ausgesandt und ging in das Land
> der Phrygier." Kurzum, wir hätten hier eine Art
> erstes Kapitel von gnostischen Philippus-Akten vor
> uns.[23]

Bethge's theory is an exciting hypothesis. The evidence
of the apocryphal Acts of the Apostles indicates that portions
of these works were frequently copied in the form of a single
Act; even the manuscript BG 8502 contains, as its fourth and
final tractate, a work with the subscribed title ⲦⲈⲚⲠⲢⲀⲜⲓⲤ
ⲘⲠⲈⲦⲢⲞⲤ (141,7). Yet this theory seems too clever and too in-
genious. If we accept this proposal, we must be willing to
assume that this "Textfragment" just happens not to mention
Philip except at the beginning, and is about to turn back to
Philip again as the Act conveniently comes to a close. In
other words, Bethge's suggestion is certainly not impossible,
but requires the supposition of an extremely interesting co-
incidence. Furthermore, Bethge's hypothesis implies that
Philip is the leading actor in the tractate, or at least in the
document of which the tractate is only the first part, or introduction. Our analysis of the tractate, however, leads us to
conclude that Peter is clearly the protagonist throughout the
document, even at the very beginning.

Hence we prefer to think of the *Ep. Pet. Phil.* as a complete document in its own right, with an integrity of its own.
Indeed, it has a rather definite focus: a Christian Gnostic

interpretation of traditional Christian and Gnostic materials,
particularly materials resembling those in the NT Acts and the
Gnostic Sophia myths.

Account of the Gathering (133,8-17)

     Peter the chief apostle gathers the apostles together.
After receiving the letter, Philip becomes properly submissive
to the authority of Peter and the orders of Jesus, and gladly
joins in the gathering. In fact, 133,8-11 functions as the
conclusion of the Philip scene; we may even detect a seam at
this point in the tractate, as the author resets the stage by
having Peter gather the rest of the apostles as well (133,12-
13). In any event, with the ⲧⲟⲧⲉ of 133,12 the focus turns to
Peter and the anonymous apostolic group gathering together.[24]
This motif of gathering together, reminiscent of the closing
verses of Luke 24 and the opening verses of Acts 1,[25] occurs a
number of times in the *Ep. Pet. Phil.*, and constitutes a major
theme in the tractate. Thus the verb ⲥⲱⲟⲩⲍ is utilized four
times in our tractate (133,12.15-16; 140,[2].13), while the
similar phrase ⲉ̄ⲓ ⲉⲩⲙⲁ occurs an additional four times (132,
19-20; 133,3.18; 137,23-24).

     The first meeting takes place on the Mount of Olives, de-
picted as a customary place for gathering.[26] Acts 1:12 provides a close parallel for this scene and its conclusion; the
apostles return to Jerusalem ἀπὸ ὄρους τοῦ καλουμένου ἐλαιῶ-
νος.[27] In addition, as the *Ep. Pet. Phil.* intimates in 133,
15-17, the Mount of Olives is described in the NT and early
Christian literature as a favorite gathering place for Jesus
and the disciples. Thus elsewhere the Mount of Olives is
designated as the place where Jesus and his followers gather
for the sake of apocalyptic revelations (Mark 13:3; Matt 24:3),
prophetic utterances (Mark 14:26 par. Matt 26:30, also Luke
22:39), perhaps prayer and solace (Luke 21:37; John 8:1), and
the final revelatory dialogue with the risen Christ before the
ascension (Acts 1:12). In other Christian literature, too, the
Mount of Olives is noted as a place of revelatory utterances,
dialogue, and marvelous disclosures,[28] a place appropriate for

apocalyptic revelations.[29]   To be sure, in the ancient world in
general, mountains figure as holy places, perfectly fitting for
the disclosure of divinity in hierophanies.   The sacred becomes
manifest on the holy mountain, whether that be Fuji, Olympus,
Saphon, Sinai, Carmel, Zion, or Olivet.[30]   Prophecy, prayer,
sacrifice, and cultic activities are most appropriate on a
mountain, for there God is present.   Hence the mountain becomes
the scene, in the OT, NT, and especially apocryphal and pseude-
pigraphal literature, for prophetic and apocalyptic disclosures
of various sorts; and Jesus is depicted as withdrawing, praying,
preaching his so-called "Sermon on the Mount," teaching his
disciples, and appearing in transfigured glory upon one mountain or another.[31]

   It is hardly surprising, then, that Gnostic documents
which include revelatory dialogues and disclosures of the
resurrected Christ frequently take place, as with the *Ep. Pet.
Phil.*, on mountains. *Pistis Sophia* describes the disciples and
a glorious Jesus upon the Mount of Olives.   The *Soph. Jes. Chr.*
depicts a gathering of the twelve disciples and the seven women
on a mountain in Galilee called "Place of Harvesttime (and) Joy"
(III 91,1-2), where the resurrected Savior appears in glorious
light; reference is also made to teachings on Olivet, which is
said to be in Galilee.   The *Apoc. Paul* has Paul standing on
"the mountain of Jericho" (V 19,12-13), perhaps the Mount of
Olives, about to learn of hidden mysteries.[32]   And thus the *Ep.
Pet. Phil.*, reflecting the Christian traditions and anticipating the revelation which is to follow, also has the apostles
assembled on that favorite mountain, Olivet.

   The locale is described as the place where the apostles
used to assemble when "the blessed Christ"[33] was in the body.
Such a statement is important for its reference back to the
bodily life of Jesus before his death.   Indeed, the *Ep. Pet.
Phil.* provides a positive evaluation of previous traditions
regarding Jesus, and consciously seeks to build upon and rein-
terpret these traditions.   Also interesting in this present
context is the phrase ϩⲛ ⲥⲱⲙⲁ.   This phrase is utilized in two
forms in our tractate: with the definite article (136,17; ⸱
138,3) and without any article (133,17; 139,11).[34]   Obviously

a Greek phrase lies behind the Coptic of our tractate, but the
precise meaning of this phrase is not immediately apparent.
How docetic is this phrase, and how literally are we to understand ϩⲛ̄ (ⲡ)ⲥⲱⲙⲁ?

Greek phrases of a very similar sort are well attested,
and provide some aid in clarifying the meaning of our text.
The phrase ἐν σώματι and similar phrases are used in the NT
upon several occasions. In 2 Corinthians 5, where Paul speaks
about the nature of τὸ οἰκητήριον τὸ ἐξ οὐρανοῦ (5:2), he declares that now our life is lived ἐν τῷ σώματι (5:6), and we
are responsible for what we do διὰ τοῦ σώματος (5:10); yet he
admits to a desire to be away ἐκ τοῦ σώματος (5:8). Later, in
the section depicting the ecstatic experience, Paul states that
he was not sure whether he was ἐν σώματι or ἐκτὸς τοῦ σώματος--
οὐκ οἶδα, ὁ θεὸς οἶδεν (12:2). Again, the author of Hebrews
recommends compassion, ὡς καὶ αὐτοὶ (viz. ὑμεῖς) ὄντες ἐν
σώματι (13:3). In the *Acts of Thomas*, too, the apostle Thomas
states that certain things cannot be declared ἐφ' ὅσον ἐν
σώματί ἐσμεν (36). Later, in chapter 66, Thomas expresses the
same thought a bit differently when he emphasizes that he also
is a man σῶμα ἐνδεδυμένος. Near the end of the *Acts*, in the
section on the μαρτύριον of the apostle, Thomas realizes that
henceforth he will speak no more ἐν σώματι (159); soon he will
experience an apparent death which is actually release from
τοῦ σώματος (160).

The examples could be multiplied,[35] but the matter has by
now become clear. The phrases ἐν σώματι and ἐν τῷ σώματι seem
to refer most often to mortal life, earthly existence in a
mortal body. This existence ἐν (τῷ) σώματι can be transcended,
however, in ecstacy and death, when one may experience a reality
ἐκτὸς τοῦ σώματος. This new reality may be described as a disembodied existence, at least in the sense of no longer being in
this mortal body.

In such a manner the *Ep. Pet. Phil.* can also utilize the
phrases ϩⲛ̄ ⲥⲱⲙⲁ and ϩⲙ̄ ⲡⲥⲱⲙⲁ. The references back to the time
when Jesus was ϩⲛ̄ (ⲡ)ⲥⲱⲙⲁ refer to his life in relation to an
earthly body. The precise relationship between the heavenly
Christ and the earthly body is not made clear by the phrase

ⲉ̄ⲛ (ⲛ)ⲥⲱⲙⲁ; the author will attempt to clarify this matter
later in the tractate (136,16-137,4; 139,15-28). It is obvious
from the parallels cited, however, that this phrase need not be
taken in a docetic sense, but simply may refer to the time when
Jesus was alive on the earth, and subject to a physical body.

Account of the Two Prayers (133,17-134,9)

Introduced by ⲧⲟⲧⲉ, the account of the two prayers opens
(133,17-21) with a reiteration of the gathering theme and proceeds to offer a brief description of the preparation of the
apostles for prayer. Their posture for prayer is the well-
known, respectful posture of genuflection. This posture of
humility in the presence of an honorable person or a divine being has been utilized from ancient times, particularly in the
Near East, and was a significant part of Jewish and Christian
piety. Such a posture must have been used in the church from
the earliest days, since even the NT reflects such genuflection.
Thus not only does the NT present scenes where genuflection
suggests homage to a worthy person, especially Jesus (for example Mark 1:40, Matt 17:14, and the like); frequently genuflection also accompanies prayer and thus reflects the emerging
custom in the early church. Such a description of the appropriate posture for prayer is especially common in Luke-Acts
(Luke 22:41; Acts 9:40, 20:36, 21:5, and apparently 7:60), and
is also used rather extensively in the later Christian sources.[36]
The *Ep. Pet. Phil.* reflects such a Christian custom, and may
suggest that some Christian Gnostic believers also practiced
genuflection in their communal prayers.[37]

Two prayers are presented by the kneeling apostles. In
structure these two prayers are remarkably similar, and may reflect the prayers in use among the Christians behind the tractate. The first prayer (133,21-134,1) is directed to the
Father, the second (134,3-9) to the Son; their similar structure and complementary forms would suggest that they may also
have had a complementary function in a Christian community.
Both prayers open with a compound statement of address, utilizing appropriate vocatives and descriptive clauses.[38]   In the

first case a triple vocative is used; the third vocative in the
series is expanded, and a descriptive clause is appended. In
the second case more vocatives are used, and the third element
functions as a descriptive clause; the vocatives in this case
seem to reflect some of the favorite titles in use for Christ.
Following the statement of address, both prayers present a petition;[39] in each case the request itself is simple, consisting
of a very short imperatival clause, with additional elements
added for the sake of substantiation or reiteration. In the
first case reference is made to ⲓⲥ ⲛⲉⲭⲥ, and the petition is
reiterated at the conclusion of the prayer. The emphasis upon
ⲓⲥ ⲛⲉⲭⲥ in the first prayer not only suggests that Jesus functioned in a mediatorial role, but also indicates that the first
prayer could lead quite naturally into the second. In the second case the ⲉⲡⲓⲁⲏ clause attached to the petition provides the
grounds for the request, and suggests that the prayer is literally a matter of life and death;[40] the theme of suffering and
persecution, so prevalent particularly near the conclusion of
the *Ep. Pet. Phil.*, thus plays a significant role in the prayer
as well.

The themes and terms utilized in the two prayers provide
important hints for our understanding of the origin and function of the prayers. "Father" (ⲡⲓⲱⲧ, πάτερ) is such a common
term used to describe and address God in Jewish and Christian
prayers that it serves practically as a universal term of address; it is to be found in the so-called Lord's Prayer, but it
is also used in numerous other early Christian prayers. "Father
of the light" is a more specific phrase. It is reminiscent of
Johannine themes, and reminds us of the statement that ὁ θεὸς
φῶς ἐστιν καὶ σκοτία ἐν αὐτῷ οὐκ ἔστιν οὐδεμία (1 John 1:5).[41]
Furthermore, τὸ φῶς τὸ ἀληθινόν is now shining in the world
(1 John 2:8; John 1:9), and that light is Christ (John 3:19;
8:12); hence God is τὸ φῶς and the Father of τὸ φῶς. John apparently reflects Gnostic usage of "light," a term which is
dearly loved by most Gnostics and is used to designate what is
characteristic of and derived from the heavenly realm: God is
light, his world is light, his Christ is light, his seeds are
light.[42]

This Father, the apostles in the *Ep. Pet. Phil.* confess,
possesses ⲛⲓⲁⲫⲑⲁⲣⲥⲓⲁ. Elsewhere God can be called ἄφθαρτος
(Rom 1:23; 1 Tim 1:17; *Kerygma Petrou* 2), and it can be said
that ἀφθαρσία is characteristic of the new life of the future
(for example, 1 Cor 15:42-54); in *2 Clem.* 20.5 Jesus can even
be termed ἀρχηγὸς τῆς ἀφθαρσίας. In the *Epistola Apostolorum*
Jesus also speaks in a similar manner of "the incorruptibility
of my Father."[43] In the Gnostic sources ⲛⲓⲁⲫⲑⲁⲣⲥⲓⲁ functions
particularly as a descriptive term for the powers, the glories,
and the aeons of heaven. The *Gos. Eg.*, for example, depicts
heaven filled with the pleroma of the glories, the lights, the
thrones, and ⲛⲓⲁⲫⲑⲁⲣⲥⲓⲁ; included in the description is a discussion of how ⲛⲓⲁⲫⲑⲁⲣⲥⲓⲁ are established (III 55,1) and how
the praise of ⲛⲓⲁⲫⲑⲁⲣⲥⲓⲁ is offered (III 50,8).[44]

The first prayer in the *Ep. Pet. Phil.*proceeds to refer to
Jesus as ⲡⲉⲕⲁⲗⲟⲩ ⲉⲧⲟⲩⲁⲁⲃ ⲓ̅ⲥ̅ ⲡⲉⲭ̅ⲥ̅ (ὁ ἅγιος παῖς σου 'Ιησοῦς ὁ
Χριστός).[45] This phrase was a primitive element in Christian
confession and prayer; it occurs in similar form and in the
context of prayer in Acts 4:27 and 4:30, as well as *Did.* 9.2,
9.3, 10.2, and 10.3.[46] It is derived from OT discussions on
the παῖς θεοῦ (for example in Deutero-Isaiah) and was apparently utilized in the earliest Palestinian Christian community as
a Christological title. The meaning of παῖς θεοῦ seems to have
shifted, however, from "servant of God" to "child of God," particularly in Gentile communities; we can see this latter meaning clearly reflected in the Coptic ⲁⲗⲟⲩ.[47] It should be noted
that the relevant phrases in Acts 4:27 and 4:30, utilizing
forms of ὁ ἅγιος παῖς σου 'Ιησοῦς, come extremely close to the
phrase in the *Ep. Pet. Phil.*; the Sahidic NT uses ⲡⲉⲕϣⲏⲣⲉ in
both instances, but the Bohairic resembles our tractate in using ⲡⲉⲕⲁⲗⲟⲩ. Furthermore, it is said that the Father takes
pleasure in or is well pleased with (ⲛ̅ⲧⲱⲟⲩ ⲉ̅ⲛ̅; εὐδοκεῖν ἐν)[48]
Jesus Christ. Such a statement recalls the declaration of God
on the occasion of the baptism or transfiguration of Jesus. In
Mark 1:11, Matt 3:17, and Luke 3:22 the heavenly φωνή of God
utters the decree of election at the time of the baptism of
Jesus; in Matt 17:5 and 2 Pet 1:17 the heavenly voice makes a
similar utterance on the occasion of the transfiguration.[49]

The *Gos. Eb.* fragment 3 also uses an εὐδοκεῖν clause in its
account of Jesus' baptism, and adds that a great light accompanied this marvelous occurrence. In addition, in Isa 42:1-4,
quoted in Matt 12:18-20, use is made of παῖς in conjunction
with an εὐδοκεῖν clause, as apparently was also the case in the
Greek *Vorlage* to the Coptic *Ep. Pet. Phil.* It may also be
noted that in each of these instances εὐδοκεῖν is used in the
aorist, and the sense is comparable to the English present perfect; these aorist verbs may account for the first perfect
verbs utilized in the Coptic NT as well as in our tractate. To
complete the picture we should also recall that in some Latin
and Coptic (Oxyrhynchite) texts of Acts 9:22 a similar phrase
is introduced, and forms of *sentio bene* and ⲙⲧⲟⲟⲩ are employed.

Several additional terms and phrases are used to describe
Christ. He is called ⲫⲱⲥⲧⲏⲣ, a term used occasionally in the
NT (Phil 2:15;[50] Rev 21:11), but never to depict Christ--
although, as we have seen, NT traditions can indeed link Christ
and τὸ φῶς. ⲫⲱⲥⲧⲏⲣ and φωστήρ are commonly utilized within
Gnosticism, however, where these terms can function in a dualistic way, just as φῶς can function over against σκοτία in John;
hence in our tractate, at 133,27-134,1 the ⲫⲱⲥⲧⲏⲣ is contrasted
with the ⲕⲁⲕⲉ. In Gnostic documents ⲫⲱⲥⲧⲏⲣ can be used to describe the heavenly lights, as in the *Ap. John*, or the Gnostic
illuminator or revealer, whether that be Christ or some other
illuminator.[51]

Certain other titles and epithets are provided for Christ
in the second prayer. Some of these titles are very familiar
from the NT and other early Christian literature, titles such
as ⲡϣⲏⲣⲉ (ὁ υἱός) and ⲡⲉⲭⲥ (ὁ Χριστός). These titles, however,
are qualified by such terms as ⲡⲱⲛϩ and ⲧⲙⲛⲧⲁⲧⲙⲟⲩ; in addition,
the descriptive clause makes mention of ⲡⲟⲩⲟⲉⲓⲛ. Roughly
similar phrases can be found in the NT, to be sure. We need
only think of υἱὸς εἰρήνης (Luke 10:6), υἱοὶ (τοῦ) φωτός (Luke
16:8; John 12:36; 1 Thess 5:5), τέκνα φωτός (Eph 5:8), υἱοὶ τῆς
ἀναστάσεως (Luke 20:36), υἱὸς παρακλησέως (Acts 4:36), and the
like, which may be Hebraisms.[52] Furthermore, they are not used
to depict Jesus, who is more frequently described in the NT as
υἱὸς Δαυίδ, υἱὸς (τοῦ) θεοῦ, or υἱὸς (τοῦ) ἀνθρώπου. Such

phrases as are used in the *Ep. Pet. Phil.* are also to be found
in other Gnostic sources, which can use these titles indepen-
dently or with abstract qualifiers; and the particular qualify-
ing terms utilized in the *Ep. Pet. Phil.*--ⲡⲱⲛϩ, †ⲙⲛ̅ⲧⲁⲧⲙⲟⲩ,
ⲡⲟⲩⲟⲉⲓⲛ--constitute some of the favorite terms of the
Gnostics.[53]

A final title depicting Christ is ⲣⲉϥⲥⲱⲧⲉ (λυτρωτής), a
term which is employed only once in the NT, at Acts 7:35, where
it is used of Moses. The term ⲥⲱⲧⲉ, however, is more common in
the NT, and can be utilized as both a noun and a verb. In the
Nag Hammadi corpus ⲣⲉϥⲥⲱⲧⲉ is to be found in several other contexts. In the *Tri. Trac.*, for example, ⲣⲉϥⲥⲱⲧⲉ is used as a
title of Christ the Logos at I 81,17 and particularly 87,7.[54]

The two prayers of 133,17-134,9 thus are complementary
prayers preserving primitive Christian elements. The terms
employed and the perspective taken are not indisputably Gnostic, to be sure. In fact, as we have seen, the prayers illustrate traditional Christian features to be found in a number of
diverse sources. Yet it cannot be denied that the particular
constellation of terms in these prayers is especially appropriate for Christian Gnostics, who frequently emphasize the glorious and luminous nature of God and Christ. This observation
suggests that the various elements within the prayers may have
been selected and shaped by such Christian Gnostics. They pray
in a more general manner to the glorious Father to be heard,
and in a more specific manner to the glorious Son to be given
power in the midst of adversity. The request for power is
especially important in the *Ep. Pet. Phil.*, for such power will
enable the believers to combat the archons (137,25-28) by going
forth to preach (140,19-21.26-27). It is in response to these
prayers, then, that Christ comes forth to speak.

Account of the First Appearance (134,9-18)

After the two prayers have been offered, then (ⲧⲟⲧⲉ: 134,9)
a theophany occurs: ⲟⲩⲛⲟϭ ⲛ̅ⲟⲩⲟⲉⲓⲛ and ⲟⲩⲥⲙⲏ come in answer to
the prayers of the apostles. This theophany constitutes the
first appearance of the resurrected Christ recorded in our

tractate, though the oblique references to the orders received
from Christ (132,17-133,1; 133,7-8) could conceivably refer to
some earlier appearance or appearances of the resurrected
Christ.[55]

The appearance of the resurrected Christ as a light and a
voice represents a common way of speaking about the resurrection
appearances in Gnostic circles. Such a portrayal of a glorious
resurrection appearance constitutes an extremely early portrayal, apparently going back to the very early days of the primitive church. Paul, after all, uses similar terms to present
his understanding of the resurrection of believers and, by
analogy, the resurrection of Christ in 1 Corinthians 15; Christ
has risen from the dead, ἀπαρχὴ τῶν κεκοιμημένων (15:20). On
the question of the nature of the resurrected σῶμα, Paul emphasizes that it is a σῶμα πνευματικόν (15:44), raised in ἀφθαρσία
(15:42), δόξα, and δύναμις (15:43). Indeed, τὸ φθαρτόν must be
clothed with ἀφθαρσία, and τὸ θνητόν with ἀθανασία (15:54). The
last Adam, the ἐπουράνιος Man, became a πνεῦμα ζωοποιοῦν (15:45);
for σάρξ καὶ αἷμα βασιλείαν θεοῦ κληρονομῆσαι οὐ δύναται, οὐδὲ
ἡ φθορὰ τὴν ἀφθαρσίαν κληρονομεῖ (15:50). Hence the resurrected
person must be changed; and the resurrected σῶμα, the new form,
self, personality, or individuality,[56] is described by Paul as
something heavenly, spiritual, glorious, bright. Paul even enters into an appropriate discussion of the varieties of δόξα
(15:41).[57]

Elsewhere in the NT glorious resurrection appearances can
be described in a similar fashion. In Rev 1:12-16 John hears a
φωνή and sees the resurrected, exalted Christ, who appears as a
glorious and luminous being with a pure white head and pure
white hair, fiery eyes, and a face shining like ὁ ἥλιος ἐν τῇ
δυνάμει αὐτοῦ (1:16), shining as his face shone on the occasion
of the so-called transfiguration. This portrait of the resurrected Christ is painted with the colors prescribed by passages
dealing with apocalyptic materials and the heavenly מֶרְכָּבָה
(Daniel, Ezekiel), and the brightness, glory, and transcendent
nature of the portrait cannot be missed. Likewise the face of
the transfigured Christ can be described as shining ὡς ὁ ἥλιος
(Matt 17:2)--and just as the face of Moses shone after he had

spoken with God on Mount Sinai (Exod 34:29-35), so that
ἐπέθηκεν ἐπὶ τὸ πρόσωπον αὐτοῦ κάλυμμα (34:33).

The transfiguration story (Mark 9:2-8; Matt 17:1-8; Luke
9:28-36) has frequently been recognized as a narrative which
originally may have been a resurrection story.[58] Like a resurrection account, it functions as an epiphany story on a mountain, it discloses the divine δόξα of Christ, it has a heavenly
φωνή declare that Jesus is God's Son, and in general it reflects the triumph of faith in the crucified one who becomes
the glorious one. In fact, the commands to secrecy at the con-
clusions of the accounts and the additional references to the
coming resurrection of Christ further suggest that belief in
this transfigured Christ was closely linked to the resurrection;[59] after the resurrection the earthly Jesus could be proclaimed from the viewpoint of post-resurrection faith. Furthermore, 2 Pet 1:16-19 describes an epiphany scene very similar to
the transfiguration accounts. It makes no mention of the transfiguration, however, and seems to function as an account of a
resurrection appearance.[60] Peter states that when he and the
others were on the holy mountain, they were ἐπόπται τῆς ἐκείνου
(viz. Ἰησοῦ Χριστοῦ) μεγαλειότητος (1:16); Christ received
τιμή and δόξα from God, and the φωνή spoke out from heaven.
Hence, it is said, take heed to this ὡς λύχνῳ φαίνοντι ἐν
αὐχμηρῷ τόπῳ (1:19).[61] Thus, whether we consider the transfiguration accounts to function as narratives proclaiming the
glory revealed in the life of the earthly Jesus, or as resurrection stories placed back into the lifetime of Jesus, it is
clear that these accounts anticipate the exaltation of Jesus
in the post-Easter faith of the believers.

Glorious resurrection appearances of Christ are also included in the Lucan Acts. As we shall see, Luke polemicizes
extensively against docetic accounts of the risen Christ; but
in his depictions of the appearance of the risen Christ to
Paul, he allows the glorious light and the heavenly voice to
describe the resurrected Christ. This appearance, however, in
the Lucan scenario, occurs after the ascension, and thus does
not need to have the same emphasis as the appearances which
took place between the resurrection and the ascension. In Acts

9:1-9, 22:4-11, and 26:9-18, Luke provides similar accounts of
this appearance. In all three accounts a heavenly φῶς flashes
forth from heaven; in 22:6 it is designated a φῶς ἱκανόν, and
in 26:13 it is described as being even brighter than the sun.
Along with the heavenly φῶς comes a φωνή, which identifies the
source of this glorious vision (ἐγώ εἰμι 'Ἰησοῦς, with varia-
tions) and orders Paul to respond with obedience. In the accounts of the appearance of the risen Christ to Paul, then,
Luke is willing to include a description of a glory appearance
after the ascension.[62]

These accounts of glorious appearances of the resurrected
Christ, commonly with a light and a voice, mean to display the
divine majesty of the exalted Jesus before mortals. Hence it
is not at all surprising that they resemble the accounts of
theophanies in various religious sources, and especially the OT.
Phenomenologically, the appearance of the divine as light and
voice is closely related to the experience of lightning and
thunder, as is clear even from the OT and NT.[63]   Like sky and
storm gods such as Baal, Hadad, and Zeus, the OT God also can
become manifest in a glorious and awesome manner, flashing forth
in the lightning and uttering his voice in the thunder. Thus,
for example, at Mount Sinai the revelation of the Torah is given
in the context of thunder and lightning (Exod 19:16, 20:18);
Moses speaks to God, and God answers him φωνῇ, בְּקוֹל (19:19). In
Deuteronomy the numinous character of the theophany is even more
striking. Yahweh speaks from the middle of the fire with a φωνὴ
μεγάλη, קוֹל גָּדוֹל (5:22); though the sound of words (φωνὴ ῥημάτων,
קוֹל דְּבָרִים) was heard, no form could be observed, ἀλλ' ἢ φωνήν,
זוּלָתִי קוֹל (4:12). The voice, then, functions in a central way
in the theophany, though other developments in the religion of
Israel also brought an emphasis upon the revealing presence of
God in φωνὴ αὔρας λεπτῆς (1 Kgs 19:12), the quiet inspiration
in contrast to the roaring thunder. Along with the voice of God
on Sinai there is also the smoke, fire, and cloud--the δόξα, the
כָּבוֹד of God which came down upon the mountain (Exod 24:15) and
looked like a roaring fire. Moses asked to see God's δόξα (Exod
33:18); and though he only caught a glimpse of God from behind,
still Moses' face was aglow with a holy luminosity from this
mountaintop experience.

To return, then, to the *Ep. Pet. Phil.*: it is to this
theophany tradition that the account of the glorious appearances of the resurrected Christ, often as φῶς and φωνή, belongs.
As we have seen, this tradition is an exceedingly old tradition,
and appears very early within Christian circles. This early
tradition is preferred by the *Ep. Pet. Phil.*, and indeed by many
Gnostic Christians, who in general emphasize the heavenly light
and the revelatory divine voice.[64] Christ appears gloriously,
for example, in the *Gos. Truth*, where Jesus the heavenly revealer comes to reveal the Father to the world; as the believers can confess, using parallelism, ⲉⲁϥϣⲉϫⲉ ⲁⲃⲁⲗ ϩⲛ ⲣⲱϥ ⲛϭⲓ
ⲡⲟⲩⲁⲉⲓⲛ ⲟⲩⲁϩⲛ ϯⲥⲙⲏ ⲛⲧⲟⲟⲧϥ ⲛⲧⲁⲥⲙⲓⲥⲉ ⲛⲡⲓⲱⲛϩⲉ, "Light spoke through
his mouth, and his voice brought forth life" (I 31,13-16). In
the *Ap. John*, a divine light shines, and the resurrected Christ
appears[65] ϩⲙ ⲡⲟⲩⲟⲉⲓⲛ, "in the light" (II 2,1-2.7), in a variety
of forms, as a youth, an old man, and a servant. As the risen
Christ, he reveals to John that he is indeed the light: ⲁⲛⲟⲕ ⲡⲉ
ⲡⲟⲩⲟⲉⲓⲛ ⲉⲧϣⲟⲟⲡ ϩⲙ ⲡⲟⲩⲟⲉⲓⲛ ⲁⲛⲟⲕ ⲡⲉ ⲡⲣⲡⲙⲉⲉⲩⲉ ⲛⲧⲡⲣⲟⲛⲟⲓⲁ, "I am
the light which is in the light; I am the remembrance of the
forethought" (II 30,33-35)--the light which speaks out to call
the forgetful to remembrance. In the *Soph. Jes. Chr.* the
resurrected Christ also appears in glory on a mountain; he appears not in "his first form" (ⲧⲉϥϣⲟⲣⲡ ⲙⲙⲟⲣⲫⲏ), but rather in
"invisible spirit" (ⲡⲉⲡⲛⲁ ⲛⲁϩⲟⲣⲁⲧⲟⲛ), thus resembling "a great
angel of light" (ⲟⲩⲛⲟϭ ⲛⲁⲅⲅⲉⲗⲟⲥ ⲛⲧⲉ ⲡⲟⲩⲟⲉⲓⲛ; III 91,10-13). In
this glorious form he proceeds to provide revelatory answers to
the queries of the twelve disciples and the seven women. Again,
in the *Apoc. Pet.* the heavenly Savior shows and tells Peter that
the living, laughing Jesus is a being of light, with a ⲥⲱⲙⲁ ⲛⲧⲉ
ⲡⲣⲟⲩⲟⲉⲓⲛ (VII 71,32-33), a ⲥⲱⲙⲁ ⲛⲁⲧⲥⲱⲙⲁ (83,7-8). For, the
Savior declares, ⲁⲛⲟⲕ ⲡⲓⲛⲟⲉⲣⲟⲛ ⲙⲡⲛⲁ ⲡⲁⲓ ⲉⲧⲙⲉϩ ⲉⲃⲟⲗ ⲛⲟⲩⲟⲉⲓⲛ
ⲉϥⲡⲣⲉⲓⲱⲟⲩ ⲉⲃⲟⲗ, "I am the noetic spirit, he who is full of
radiating light" (83,8-10). We might also observe that in the
Trim. Prot. the heavenly redeemer ·Protennoia reveals itself as
Father, or voice (ϩⲣⲟⲟⲩ), as Mother, or sound (ⲥⲙⲏ), and as
Son, or word (ⲗⲟⲅⲟⲥ). Perhaps anticipating the Logos hymn in
John 1,[66] where Christ the Son is depicted as λόγος and φῶς,
this tractate describes the heavenly redeemer as a glorious and

radiant being from the realm of light, and emphasizes that the
Word dwells in the Light and communicates the Light. As Protennoia says, ⲁ[ⲛⲟⲕ] ⲡⲉ ⲡⲟⲩⲟⲉⲓⲛ ⲉⲧ⳨ ⲟⲩⲟⲉⲓⲛⲉ ⲛⲡⲧⲏ[ⲣϥ], "[I] am
the light which illumines the All" (XIII 47,28-29). Again,
according to the *Pistis Sophia*, after the resurrection Christ
appears to the disciples, on the Mount of Olives, a great light
(ⲟⲩⲛⲟϭ ⲛⲁⲩⲛⲁⲙⲓⲥ ⲛⲟⲩⲟⲉⲓⲛ) from heaven surrounds Jesus, and he
ascends to heaven. When he descends again, he has a brilliance,
an indescribable light, which is truly breathtaking in its awesome splendor, and he proceeds to reassure the disciples and
relate the mysteries to them (2-5). Finally, in the *Acts of
Thomas* the apostle addresses the risen Lord, who has spoken
through a wild ass. Using *parallelismus membrorum*, Thomas addresses Christ as ὁ ἐπουράνιος λόγος τοῦ πατρός and τὸ ἀπόκρυ-
φον φῶς τοῦ λογισμοῦ (80). In addition, the "Hymn of the
Pearl" embedded within the *Acts of Thomas* proclaims how the
marvelous heavenly letter, like a Gnostic redeemer, calls upon
the slumbering human and awakens him. It gives forth a φωνή
and a φῶς; with its φωνή it rouses him, and with its φῶς it
guides him (111).

More examples of glorious appearances of the risen Christ,
or the heavenly revealer, in Gnostic literature could be cited,[67]
but the matter is now evident. The *Ep. Pet. Phil.* and numerous
other Christian Gnostic sources portray the resurrected Christ
in glorious light, and describe his appearance as a theophany,
with a heavenly light and a revealing voice. Furthermore,
these sources frequently have the voice disclose itself in aretalogical utterances, in the self-predications of the revealer.[68]

These accounts of glorious appearances of Christ were often
opposed, however, by authors and heresiologists who feared the
specter of docetism. Such tendencies can be seen already in the
NT. Luke is emphatic in his insistence upon the physical reality of the body of the resurrected Christ, at least during the
vital period between the resurrection and ascension. The first
known Christian author to distinguish specifically between the
resurrection and the ascension, Luke maintains that during the
period before the ascension and exaltation the risen Christ appears in a mundane rather than a pneumatic manner. For Luke,

who has his feet firmly planted upon the ground and wishes
likewise to plant the church firmly in history, the physical
reality and the "real presence" of the resurrected Christ are
of paramount importance. Luke cannot tolerate the possibility
of the risen Christ as only πνεῦμα, as simply one of the disembodied spirits with which the Hellenistic world was familiar,
as the exalted Savior who appears as a heavenly φῶς and φωνή.
Hence during this "sacred period between the times,"[69] before
the outpouring of the Spirit, Luke has Jesus appear as a trav-
eler on the Emmaus road (Luke 24:13-35), eat and drink with the
disciples (Luke 24:41-43; Acts 10:41), and function in many
ways as an ordinary, physical being. Clearly Luke is polemi-
cizing against Christians suggesting appearances of a pneumatic
sort. In Luke 24:37 he even refers to the claim brought forward by these pneumatic Christians: ἐδόκουν πνεῦμα θεωρεῖν![70]
In opposition to such a claim, the Lucan Jesus quickly points
to his hands and feet, and invites the disciples to observe his
σάρξ and ὀστέα (24:39). Yet, in spite of his opposition to
this primitive Christian position on the spiritual resurrection
and appearances, Luke cannot totally deny the glorious nature
of the resurrection appearances; Christ has attained to δόξα
αὐτοῦ (24:26), he seems to come and go in a supernatural manner
(24:31, 36-37), and he even has his glorious heavenly companions by the tomb (24:4).[71]

      The situation is somewhat similar in the Gospel of John.
It has long been suggested that John writes in the context of
Gnostic or gnosticizing thinking; his intellectual setting seems
to reflect Gnostic sorts of styles, concerns, and terms.[72] But
John and especially the Johannine school stand firm in their
emphasis upon the physical reality of the Christ: ὁ λόγος σάρξ
ἐγένετο (John 1:14). 1 John 4:3 even provides a test for whether
or not a person confesses Christ in the true manner; the true
confession is that Ἰησοῦν Χριστὸν ἐν σαρκὶ ἐληλυθότα, and whoever does not make this confession is not of God. If 1 John 4:1-3
thus can polemicize against ψευδοπροφῆται (4:1), those who reflect the spirit τοῦ ἀντιχρίστου (4:3), 2 John 7 can decry those
deceiving docetists who will not confess that Ἰησοῦν Χριστὸν
ἐρχόμενον ἐν σαρκί. Hence, considering the Johannine stance

against a docetic Christology, John's statements about the appearances of the resurrected Christ may be anticipated. Christ
can be mistaken for the gardener (John 20:14-15) or a passer-by
(21:4), show the disciples his hands and his side (20:20), in-
vite doubting Thomas to touch his wounds (20:24-29), and make a
cultic breakfast for his disciples (21:9-14). Yet the risen
Christ also has his heavenly angels in white (20:12), an abili-
ty to move about supernaturally (20:19, 26) and know things
miraculously (21:6), and the πνεῦμα ἅγιον to bestow on the Johannine "Pentecost" (20:22).

     In the *Epistula Apostolorum*, a document which bears some
resemblance to the *Ep. Pet. Phil.* in genre, general outline,
and certain themes, the doubting Thomas story of John is also
used, with a few modifications intensifying its stance,[73] to
polemicize against Gnostic docetism. The *Epistula* thus seems
to participate, at a later day, in this continuing battle with
docetism, and may in fact reflect and oppose, among other traditions, a tradition similar to that which is represented by
the *Ep. Pet. Phil.*[74]

     The *Ep. Pet. Phil.*, then, presents a glorious appearance
of the risen Christ as ογνοϭ ⲛ̄ογοειν and ογϭⲙⲏ; the mountain
on which the appearance takes place shines from the glory of
the theophany. The voice cries out (134,15-18) with a command,
a question, and a declaration. The introductory command provides a natural opening for a discourse by commanding the attention of the listeners.[75] The question, practically a rhetorical question,[76] and the declaration, appropriately given as
an aretalogical self-predication, tie in nicely with the prayers
that have been offered, particularly the second prayer; the
declaration identifies the φῶς and φωνή as Christ, and includes
a promise. Given here and reiterated at 140,22-23, the promise
functions like the promise given by the risen Savior in a similar context in Matt 28:20, a promise to the apostles--the
church: ἰδοὺ ἐγὼ μεθ' ὑμῶν εἰμι πάσας τὰς ἡμέρας ἕως τῆς συντε-
λείας τοῦ αἰῶνος. In the *Ep. Pet. Phil.*, however, the concluding apocalyptic reference would hardly be appropriate, and was
not part of the tradition utilized by our tractate.

The stage is prepared, then, for a climactic portion of
the *Ep. Pet. Phil.*: the revelatory words of the risen Christ
for his followers.

Account of the Questions Raised by the Apostles (134,18-135,2)

Following the quotation formula, which utilizes the customary ⲧⲟⲧⲉ, several questions are raised by the apostles for the
resurrected Christ to answer. The syntax of these questions is
somewhat unusual, and suggests the juxtaposition of several
questions for the sake of the revelatory answers that are to
follow. The first question is given as an indirect question,
and the next five questions are presented as direct questions,
each introduced by the conjunction ⲏ except for the first
direct question.[77] The first direct question is introduced by
ⲁⲩⲱ ⲝⲉ, so that the grammatical construction suggests, though
in an elliptical fashion, that the questions of the apostles
are resumed with a series of direct questions.[78]

Furthermore, the correspondence between the questions
asked and the answers provided--particularly the opening formulae of the answers--is not uniformly close. The indirect question is of two parts, and corresponds quite closely to the
first two answers provided by the Savior (135,8-136,15; 136,16-
137,4). These two parts naturally complement each other very
well; in the *Dial. Sav.* the same two queries similarly can be
linked together, where the disciples ask, ⲟⲩ ⲡⲉ ⲡⲉⲡⲗⲏⲣⲱⲙⲁ ⲁⲩⲱ
ⲟⲩ ⲡⲉ ⲡϭⲱⲱⲧ, "What is the fullness and what is the deficiency?"
(III 139,14-15). In the second part of the indirect question a
scribe or a reader apparently emended the text from "your fullness" to "their fullness." Indeed, either reading is quite
appropriate for the answer which is to follow;[79] the orienta-
tion of the question was merely changed from the Savior to the
aeons, or from Christology to soteriology. The first of the
series of direct questions relates quite well to the formula
introducing the third answer (137,4-9), although the formula is
rather abbreviated. In our text the third answer provides
something of a response to the third direct question as well.
In fact, it could be concluded that the third answer may, in a

very general way, speak to the issues of the first four direct
questions, for the fourth and concluding answer in the series
(137,10-13) clearly responds to the fifth direct question. In
spite of the fact that the Coptic syntax differs a bit, the
fifth direct question and the fourth response both have to do
with the war being waged between the powers and the Gnostic
Christians. It is also feasible that in fact a discrepancy
exists between the questions listed and the answers provided;
the list of questions and the suggested answers may have been
brought together into their present form secondarily. In any
case, several of the questions raised illustrate the typical
fears and hopes of Gnostics, and also show the fundamental concern for the origin and resolution of the unhappy human condition. In addition, it should be noted that the fourth direct
question reflects a concern for ⲡⲁⲣϩⲏⲥⲓⲁ, particularly, it
seems, boldness and power in speaking and preaching, and perhaps also in performing mighty deeds. Such a concern may reflect the use of παρρησία and related terms in the NT Acts and
the apocryphal Acts of the Apostles.[80]

      Such a list of questions is by no means unknown in Gnostic
documents. In fact, it seems as if the Gnostics had a special
appreciation for particular questions grouped in different
ways, and frequently included lists of questions in their literature. A variety of lists can be observed. At times a list
of questions can appear near the beginning of a discourse or
dialogue, and can provide, as in our tractate, something approaching a table of contents for what is to follow. Thus in
the *Hyp. Arch.* Norea asks the great angel Eleleth several questions about the origin of ⲛⲉϩⲟⲩⲥⲓⲁ (II 93,32-94,2), and Eleleth
responds with an account of the fall of Sophia. Again, *Zost.*
has its protagonist ponder a number of troubling and vital
questions concerning existence (VIII 2,24-3,13). These questions have to do with the origin, nature, and character of existence, and constitute the matters to be revealed in the ecstatic heavenly journey which follows. Similarly, the *Ap. John*
also opens with a troubled John asking himself difficult questions concerning matters of ultimate concern to Christian Gnostics: the origin, person, and work of the Savior, and the

nature of the aeon that is the destiny of the Savior and of all
Gnostics (II 1,17-29). Immediately after these questions are
posed, the vision of the risen Christ occurs, and the revelation ensues. Likewise, the *Soph. Jes. Chr.* also utilizes introductory indirect questions near the opening of the tractate;
the twelve disciples and the seven women were troubled, it is
said, ⲉⲧⲃⲉ ⲧⲍⲩⲡⲟⲥⲧⲁⲥⲓⲥ ⲛ̄ⲡⲧⲏⲣϥ, ⲧⲉⲡⲣⲟⲛⲟⲓⲁ, ⲛⲉⲭⲟⲩⲥⲓⲁ, ⲡⲥⲱⲧⲏⲣ, and
so on (III 91,2-9).

At other times a series of questions can appear within the
body of a text. In the rather fragmentary *Testim. Truth* a long
series of questions appears (IX 41,21[?]-42,16[?]) within a
homily for the Gnostic Christian. These questions have to do
with numerous themes of a cosmological and soteriological sort,
and the answers to these questions constitute true wisdom.
Furthermore, in the *Excerpta ex Theodoto* 78.2 it is emphatically stated that we are liberated not only through baptism but
also through knowledge (γνῶσις): τίνες ἦμεν, τί γεγόναμεν· ποῦ
ἦμεν, ἢ ποῦ ἐνεβλήθημεν· ποῦ σπεύδομεν, πόθεν λυτρούμεθα· τί
γέννησις, τί ἀναγέννησις.[81]

Such passages as these illustrate how significantly questions and lists of questions function in Gnostic self-
understanding. Gnosticism is a religion of knowledge, of an
insightful illumination which breaks through the categories of
mundane existence. For the Gnostics true liberation necessi-
tates the transmission of true knowledge. This knowledge is
passed from the heavenly revealer, the risen Christ, to his
disciples, and from the knower, the bearer of the tradition, to
the inquiring person or group. The lists of questions passed
down within the tradition thus represent the key issues which
must be truly understood if salvation is to occur. Sometimes,
as with the *Excerpta ex Theodoto*, the questions can stand alone,
as abbreviations for the essential knowledge to be embraced. At
other times, as with *Ep. Pet. Phil.*, the questions are followed
with revelatory answers which provide the essential knowledge,
practically like a Gnostic catechism.

Consequently, we are not surprised to observe how frequently Gnostics made use of the literary genre of the dialogue, of
questions and answers presented within the framework of a

conversation between a master and the students, and often between the risen Christ and his disciples. As questers for di-
vinely revealed truth, the Gnostics eagerly adopted the dialogue as a most appropriate format for the presentation of
truth as they perceived it. Kurt Rudolph defines the dialogue
as "eine bekannte antike Literaturform, in der ein wirkliches
oder fiktives Gespräch zwischen zwei oder mehr Personen liter-
arisch gestaltet ist."[82] Utilized in classical times for philosophical dialogues, dramatic comedies, and the like, the dialogue was widely used in Hellenistic times by such people as
the Gnostics, who found some variety of this *Gattung* of the
dialogue to be an excellent means of presenting their message.
The Gnostic teacher, often depicted as the resurrected Christ
discoursing on a mountain, communicates divine truths to the
followers. Thus the Gnostics stress the revelatory character
of the teachings, and employ a form of the dialogue which differs considerably from the classical dialogue: indeed, their
dialogues often resemble the "question and answer" (*Erotapokriseis*) literature in significant ways.[83] Hence the Gnostic
dialogue is an adapted dialogue, which proved suitable for the
mediation of revelatory knowledge.

To what extent, then, does the *Ep. Pet. Phil.* conform to
the style of the Gnostic dialogue? To begin with, we should
observe that only a portion of our tractate is actually any-
thing like a dialogue between the risen Christ and the apostles.
133,8-138,10 provides the setting, the questions, the revelatory
answers, and the dismissal typical of the Gnostic dialogue. In
addition, 138,21-139,4 provides another revelation imparted by
the voice to the disciples as they are discussing matters together, and 140,15-23 has the appearing Jesus provide words of
reassurance to the apostles as they are going forth. These
latter utterances, however, are authoritative and supportive
declarations that function as elements in a dialogue only in a
very oblique fashion. Again, as we have seen, the tractate
opens with a passage representing the letter genre of literature (132,10-133,8). Furthermore, the tractate concludes with
a description of the return to Jerusalem, the speech of Peter,
the reception of the spirit, and the divine commission to

preach (138,10-140,27). Thus the *Ep. Pet. Phil.* includes a
number of different literary forms. As a whole it resembles
in genre the NT Acts to a considerable extent, with a similar
diversity and a similar progression.

But even when we consider the climactic series of questions and answers within our tractate, we note that it differs
rather markedly from more typical Gnostic dialogues. Indeed,
certain features suggest that 133,8-138,10 is not really a dialogue at all! After all, the only verbal response of the disciples to the revelatory answers of the Savior occurs at 137,
13-17, where an additional question and answer is juxtaposed
to the first set of questions and answers. Here a different
tradition may even be reflected, as we shall see later. Hence
in some ways 133,8-138,10 resembles a revelatory discourse
(given in two parts) more than a revelatory dialogue.

To understand better what is transpiring here, we might
consider the relationship between *Eugnostos* and the *Soph. Jes.
Chr.* It has been proposed[84] that the *Soph. Jes. Chr.* is a
Christian tractate which was composed as a Christian version of
a non-Christian document very much like *Eugnostos*. Formally
Eugnostos is a letter, complete with an epistolary opening and
closing; it claims to have been written by a Gnostic teacher to
his followers. Some version of this philosophical epistle, an
epistle with no clear Christian motifs,[85] was apparently transformed by a Gnostic Christian into the *Soph. Jes. Chr.*, a Gnostic dialogue between the resurrected Christ and his disciples.
By means of various interpolations a Christian framework for
the tractate was established. The truths of Eugnostos the
Blessed[86] were adopted and slightly adapted to become the truths
of the risen Christ, who now provides revelatory answers to the
queries of the disciples on the mountain. As a part of the
Christian framework twelve questions are addressed to Jesus;
and although these questions are inserted into the text in a
somewhat artificial manner, such a loose relationship between
the questions and the answers of a Gnostic dialogue is by no
means rare. Thus the tractate *Eugnostos* is appropriated by
Gnostic Christians, and Christ becomes the revealer of Gnostic
truths.

The situation is somewhat analogous in the *Ep. Pet. Phil.*
Several mythological descriptions and soteriological statements
have been used as the revelatory utterances of the resurrected
Christ. Although the framework of the *Ep. Pet. Phil.* is thoroughly Christian, the utterances of Christ are not uniformly
Christianized. In fact, the first answer offered by the Savior
(135,8-136,15) shows no discernable Christian elements, while
the other answers are perhaps only marginally Christian. Unlike the *Soph. Jes. Chr.*, however, the *Ep. Pet. Phil.* does not
have the questions of the apostles interrupt the discourses of
the Savior, except in the case of the additional question (137,
13-17); and the questions that are raised in the *Ep. Pet. Phil.*
relate rather closely to the answers that are given, with the
exception of certain of the direct questions.

Thus the *Ep. Pet. Phil.*, particularly 133,8-138,10, illustrates another way in which traditional Gnostic materials can
be integrated into the authoritative teaching of the risen
Christ. If Gnostic dialogues in general are adapted dialogues,
the series of questions and answers in the *Ep. Pet. Phil.* functions even less as a true dialogue. Rather, this series of
questions and answers provides the occasion for Christ to present a revelatory discourse on Gnostic themes. The resultant
"dialogue" provides a summation of essential Gnostic Christian
doctrine, as perceived by the author and the community: a revelation for those who would truly know.

Introduction to the Revelatory Answers Given by the Savior
(135,3-8)

After the questions have been presented by the apostles,
then (ⲧⲟⲧⲉ) the revelatory response may begin. Once again mention is made of the voice and the light, here described as
ⲟⲩⲥⲙⲏ coming to the apostles ⲉⲃⲟⲗ ⲍ̄ⲛ̄ ⲡⲟⲩⲟⲉⲓⲛ (135,3-4). Before
the questions are answered seriatim, the voice of the resurrected Christ provides an introductory statement to put his
answers in proper perspective. This statement refers back to
previous disclosures and ahead to the impending revelation.

The reference to previous disclosures is particularly note-
worthy. The apostles themselves, Christ the glorious voice

declares, are witnesses to the fact that he had told them all
of these things previously, that he had already given them all
the answers to these most vital questions which the apostles
had just asked. Presumably the risen Christ is referring to
revelations given when he was "in the body"; such reminders of
previous declarations while "in the body" occur several times
in the *Ep. Pet. Phil.*[87] Yet, in spite of these previous revelations, the apostles did not believe. Other Christian literature can also refer to the unbelief of the followers of
Jesus while he was still alive, before Easter faith came alive
in their hearts. Here in the *Ep. Pet. Phil.*, however, the unbelief of the apostles may be interpreted more precisely. For
it is these apostles who are the witnesses, the bearers of the
tradition, the guarantors of the authenticity of the tradition
since primitive times. It is these apostles who establish the
oral and the written traditions, and to them the church looks
for guidance. And their unbelief may be taken as the unbelief
of the Great Church, which has not acknowledged the spiritual
truths of Christian Gnosis.

In other words, the affirmation of the traditions and the
charge of unbelief reflect the self-understanding of the people
behind the *Ep. Pet. Phil.* The author and community represented
by the *Ep. Pet. Phil.* do not deny or reject their heritage, the
Christian tradition handed down to the church. Christ has provided words of revelation, written words, spoken words--if only
the apostles would believe! The revelatory words are present--
if only the Christians would apply the proper interpretation!
The *Ep. Pet. Phil.* affirms its heritage, understood and interpreted in accordance with the theological guidelines of Gnostic
Christian belief, and thus looks to the new revelation of the
risen Christ to bring, at last, a faithful presentation of
spiritual truths.

Seeking thus to legitimate its message by maintaining continuity between the teachings of Jesus and those of the Gnostic
community, the *Ep. Pet. Phil.* offers a latter-day revelation of
the risen Christ to transcend the unbelief of the Great Church.
Elsewhere in Gnostic literature revelatory utterances can function in a similar fashion by presenting the authoritative words

of the risen Christ to his followers for a considerable time
after the resurrection. In the *Ap. Jas.*, for example, Christ
remains five hundred fifty days after the resurrection, and
then appears to the disciples as they are writing their memoirs
or gospels (ϫⲱⲱⲙⲉ, "books," I 2,15); consequently, before returning to heaven, Christ takes James and Peter aside and fills
them with revelatory knowledge. In addition, the Savior claims
that the disciples have compelled him to stay another eighteen
days ⲉⲧⲃⲉ ⲛ̄ⲡⲁⲣⲁⲃⲟⲗⲏ, "on account of the parables" (8,2-3). In
a similar fashion Irenaeus claims that other Gnostics, apparently Ophites and Valentinians, maintain that Jesus lingered
for eighteen months (five hundred forty days) after the resurrection, and taught great mysteries to the few followers who
could assimilate such marvelous teachings.[88] This period of
time also corresponds rather closely to the five hundred forty-
five days between the resurrection and ascension in the *Ascension of Isaiah* 9.16. Later, it seems, the period of resurrection appearances can be prolonged even further. The *Pistis
Sophia* and the two *Books of Jeu* have the resurrected Jesus con-
versing and discoursing with his disciples for twelve years
after the resurrection;[89] the former work discloses the revelation of the supreme mysteries during the twelfth year of Jesus'
resurrection sojourn, after the luminous and glorious journey
of Jesus through the aeons. Thus Gnostic sources can appeal to
authoritative appearances of the resurrected Christ which occur
much later than many of those recorded in the NT; certainly
such appearances would not be acceptable to Luke, whose periodization of history allows only forty days for "canonical" appearances of the risen Christ before his ascension.[90]

    The *Ep. Pet. Phil.* does not make use of a precise periodi-
zation of the resurrection appearances of Jesus. In fact, the
Ep. Pet. Phil. does not really propose a single ascension account at all.[91] Unlike Luke-Acts, *Ep. Pet. Phil.* merely portrays the coming and going of the heavenly light and voice,
which can appear when necessary in order to bring the apostles
and followers of the light to knowledge. Yet our tractate,
like the other Gnostic documents, utilizes the appearances of
the risen Christ to speak against unbelief and for the true

presentation and interpretation of Gnostic Christian beliefs.
In the *Ep. Pet. Phil.* the Gnostic Jesus speaks forth with
clarity to provide revelatory answers to questions of ultimate
concern.

The First Revelatory Answer (135,8-136,15)

The revelatory discourse of Jesus in answer to the questions posed by the apostles begins with an answer to the first
part of the indirect question; the disciples have asked about
ⲡⲓϣⲱⲧ ⲛ̄ⲧⲉ ⲕⲉⲱⲛ (134,21-22). In answering this question Jesus
utters an abbreviated version of the myth of the mother, who
remains otherwise unnamed in the tractate. This first revelatory answer is constructed in a careful manner, and its structure parallels that of the other answers in this set of four
answers. In particular the first two answers are very similar
to each other; just as the two parts of the indirect question
are linked together, so also the first two answers complement
each other nicely. Both are fairly long; both correspond
closely to the two parts of the indirect question; both are
introduced by subtitles and summary statements; both close with
a final statement intended to bring the answer to a reasonable
conclusion. The last two answers are quite similar to the
first two, but are even more similar to each other. Both of
these last two answers are very brief; both tend to paraphrase
somewhat the direct questions that have been raised; both are
introduced by similar subtitles[92] and terse causal statements
introduced by ⲭⲉ; both close with short explanatory statements.
Hence we may see these four questions as paralleling each other,
with the first two and last two sharing particular features of
structure.

The Savior's first revelatory answer contains no clearly
Christian features. Such an observation is especially remarkable when we consider how overwhelmingly Christian the framework of the *Ep. Pet. Phil.* is. Furthermore, the other three
answers in the series also are only vaguely Christian at best;
the Christian character of these three answers can be disputed,
though the best case for Christian motifs can be made for the

second answer ᴇᴛʙᴇ ᴨɪᴨʟʜᴘⲱᴍʌ. Thus we observe that the author
of the *Ep. Pet. Phil.* has taken non-Christian or marginally
Christian traditions, has woven them into the Christian framework of the tractate, and thus has baptized these traditions
as revelatory utterances of the risen Christ.

Like the other three answers in this series, the first
answer opens with a subtitle referring back to the original
question: ᴇᴛʙᴇ ᴨɪϣⲱⲱᴛ ᴍᴇɴ ⲛ̄ᴛᴇ ɴᴇⲱɴ (135,8-9).[93] Such a title
or subtitle is very common in the literature of antiquity; Paul,
for example, can utilize similar subtitles in 1 Corinthians,
where he also seems to be referring back to questions raised by
the Corinthians.[94] After the subtitle comes a very brief and
somewhat enigmatic statement: ᴨʌï ᴨᴇ ᴨɪϣⲱⲱᴛ (135,9-10). The
meaning of this statement is not obvious, though it does seem
to function as an introductory or summary statement; particularly ambiguous is the antecedent of the demonstrative pronoun
ᴨʌï. On the one hand, ᴨʌï could easily refer to the words and
sentences which follow, and which attempt to describe the origin and nature of ᴨɪϣⲱⲱᴛ. In this case ᴨʌï could point ahead
to the revelatory answer which is just beginning: "The deficiency is as follows." On the other hand, ᴨʌï could also refer
to this world around us, this mortal creation which is the
tragic result of the fall of the mother. This interpretation
of ᴨʌï is more difficult and provocative, and suggests that ᴨʌï
could point to the evidence of deficiency all around: "This
world illustrates the deficiency."[95] Although we cannot be
entirely certain, a comparison with the parallel statement in
the second answer (ʌɴoᴋ ᴨᴇ, 136,16) encourages us to opt for
the latter interpretation.

The body of the answer begins with the Savior presenting
a brief account of the origin of the deficiency (135,10-21).
The mother, who is named Sophia in most versions of the myth,[96]
is the one whose tragic blunder has led to the deficiency. It
is said that this blunder can be traced back to her disobedience and foolishness (ᴍⲛ̄ᴛʌᴛᴄⲱᴛᴍ̄ and ᴍⲛ̄ᴛʌᴛϣoxɴᴇ), for apart from
the command and will of the Father's greatness[97] she wished to
create aeons.[98] In certain versions of the myth Sophia is said
to be motivated by desire (ἐνθύμησις) and passion (πάθος);

festering for a while in the Pleroma, this πάθος burst forth in
the transgression of Sophia. Supposedly motivated by love
(ἀγάπη) for the Father, a love which in reality was audacity
(τολμά), Sophia searched for the Father in order, if possible,
to embrace the greatness of his inscrutable, incomprehensible
divinity. Of course, she was doomed to failure, and destined
for distress and grief.[99] Other versions of the myth, which
may resemble more closely the description of the mother's creative actions in the *Ep. Pet. Phil.* (135,10-17), claim that
Sophia wanted to imitate the mighty, unbegotten Father: ἠθέλησε
μιμήσασθαι τὸν Πατέρα καὶ γεννῆσαι καθ' ἑαυτὴν δίχα τοῦ συζύγου,
ἵνα μηδὲν ᾖ ἔργον ὑποδεέστερον τοῦ Πατρὸς εἰργασμένη.[100] According to the *Ap. John*, she wanted to create or procreate ⲀⲭⲘ
[ⲡⲟⲅⲱ]ⲱ ⲘⲡⲉⲡⲚⲀ, "without [the consent] of the Spirit" (II 9,29;
also see II 9,34), and without her consort,[101] and the result
was a ⲍⲟⲨⲌⲉ ⲘⲠⲔⲀⲕⲉ, an "abortion of darkness."[102] The ⲘⲚⲦⲀⲦⲤⲱⲧⲘ
and ⲘⲚⲦⲀⲦⲱⲟⲭⲚⲉ of the mother in the *Ep. Pet. Phil.* is reminiscent of the transgression and fall of Eve as depicted in Genesis
and early Christian literature.[103] To be sure, elsewhere in
Gnostic literature Sophia and Eve can be brought together in
some significant ways.[104] Other sources also can refer to this
fall of Sophia as the fall of this erring aeon (τοῦτον τὸν
παρατραπέντα),[105] of the transgressing aeon (ὁ παρελθὼν αἰών).[106]

It is reasonable to see how the mother's blunder could be
termed disobedience, foolishness, and even a transgression
(ⲠⲀⲢⲀⲂⲀⲤ ⲓ ⲥ, 139,23). After all, she did passionately exceed
the bounds of propriety, and impulsively desired to do what was
quite inappropriate in the realm of the Pleroma; in other words,
she transgressed the law of the Pleroma.[107] As a result of her
passion and ignorance, this fallen world of mortality came into
being.[108]

From the misdeed of the mother, the *Ep. Pet. Phil.* continues, emerges the Arrogant One, ⲀⲨⲐⲀⲗⲀⲎⲤ. ⲀⲨⲐⲀⲗⲀⲎⲤ seems to
function practically as a proper noun in our tractate; a Greek
loan word, this adjective is taken over and used in a substantival manner. Of course, there is an exceedingly fine line in
such mythological literature between a proper noun per se and a
key epithet. ⲀⲨⲐⲀⲗⲀⲎⲤ is used elsewhere in the literature of

and about the Gnostics,[109] but in the *Ap. John* the usage of
this technical term is especially close to its use in our tractate. At II 13,27, as well as IV 21,16 and BG 46,1, ⲡⲁⲩⲑⲁⲇⲏⲥ
is utilized, as in the *Ep. Pet. Phil.*, in a substantival manner,
and it is said that ignorant ⲡⲁⲩⲑⲁⲇⲏⲥ took power from his
mother. According to the simple and similar myth of the Barbelognostics of Irenaeus, *mater* Sophia "generavit opus, in quo
erat ignorantia et audacia" ("Αγνοια καὶ 'Αυθάδεια)--namely,
the Proarchon, the demiurge who stole a "virtutem magnam" from
the mother.[110] In numerous Gnostic sources the arrogance of
the chief archon is made abundantly clear. It is he who is so
ignorant and blind[111] that he boasts that he is God, and God
alone. Thus in the *Hyp. Arch.*, for example, it is said that
ⲁϥⲣ̄ (viz. ⲡⲁⲣⲭⲱⲛ) ϩⲁⲥⲓ ϩⲏⲧ ⲉϥϫⲱ ⲙ̄ⲙⲟⲥ ϫⲉ ⲁⲛⲟⲕ ⲡⲉ ⲡⲛⲟⲩⲧⲉ ⲁⲩⲱ ⲙ̄ⲛ
ϭⲉ ⲁⲝⲛ̄ⲧ, "he (viz. the archon) became haughty, saying, 'I am
God, and there is no other besides me'" (II 94,21-22).[112]

   In the *Ep. Pet. Phil.* the author seems to suggest that
ⲁⲩⲑⲁⲇⲏⲥ emerged when the mother spoke, just as Yaldaboath appeared (ⲁ- ⲟⲩⲱⲛ₂) as ⲧⲁⲣⲭⲏ ⲙ̄ⲡⲕⲟⲁⲭⲉ, "the first principle of the
word," when Pistis Sophia spoke to him and uttered his name,
according to the mythological account in *Orig. World*.[113] This
passage in our tractate, however, remains difficult to interpret; it is said of ⲁⲩⲑⲁⲇⲏⲥ that ⲁϥⲟⲩⲱ̈ϩ ⲉⲃⲟⲗ. According to
Crum (505b-508b), ⲟⲩⲱ̈ϩ has the general meaning of "put," "set,"
or "be (there)," on the one hand, and the intransitive meaning
of "be placed" or "dwell" on the other. With the adverb ⲉⲃⲟⲗ
this verb ordinarily can be translated as "set down," "pause,"
or (transitively) "let, bring down." It is conceivable, though
very unlikely, that this passage in the *Ep. Pet. Phil.* could
state that ⲁⲩⲑⲁⲇⲏⲥ "paused" or "halted in his tracks" when the
mother spoke; such an understanding could then reflect the
shock and consternation in the realm of the chief archon when
the mother spoke forth from heaven in response to his bold,
ignorant claims.[114] On the other hand, ⲟⲩⲱ̈ϩ with the preposition ⲛ̄ⲥⲁ- can mean "follow," and it seems reasonable to suggest
a similar sort of meaning for ⲟⲩⲱ̈ϩ ⲉⲃⲟⲗ: "set forth," "set out,"
"emerge," "follow."[115] Yet, as we have noted, it remains tempting to follow the scholars who have suggested that a ⲛ has been

omitted by the scribe, and that consequently this passage
should be emended to ογω<ν>ς εβολ.

How, then, did the deficiency come to be? The *Ep. Pet.
Phil.* states that the mother left behind a мєрос, which was
taken by λγθλλнс and became a ϣϫωτ; and πλϊ, the concluding
summary statement of our tractate says, пє пϣϫωτ ῆτє νιєωη
(135,20-21). The Greek loan word мєрос is used to denote the
portion of light or spirit which has fallen out of the world
of the Pleroma and has been imprisoned in this world of
darkness.[116]

As we have already seen, the *Ap. John* explains this by
describing how λϥχι ῆϭι πλγθλλнс ῆογϭοм εβολ ςιτῆ тєϥмλλγ, "the
Arrogant One took power from his mother" (II 13,26-28).[117]
Mother Sophia was aware of the fact that part of her heavenly
brightness was gone. She was aware of this defect or deficiency (ϣτλ),[118] for the glowing of her light (πρριє ῆπєсογοєιν)
lessened (13,14-15), and she began to darken with the darkness
of ignorance (пкλкє ῆтмῆῆτλτсοογη, 13,24-25). Not only did the
mother transgress against the divine Pleroma; she also lost a
portion of her spiritual power. In some versions of the myth
this loss can be described as the expulsion of the passions of
erring Sophia, or of the ἔκτρωμα that she had produced. According to Irenaeus' account of the Valentinian teacher Ptolemaeus, Sophia was purified and restored, τὴν δὲ ἐνθύμησιν αὐτῆς
σὺν τῷ πάθει ὑπὸ τοῦ Ὅρου ἀφορισθῆναι καὶ ἀποστερηθῆναι (Latin:
crucifixam), καὶ ἐκτὸς αὐτοῦ (viz. τοῦ Πληρώματος) γενομένην
(*Adv. Haer.* 1.2.4). Though this desire and passion was shapeless, formless, and frail, yet it was a πνευματικὴ οὐσία, since
it emerged from one of the aeons; and this spiritual substance
was destined to be lost and imprisoned in the lower world of
the demiurge. In the account of Hippolytus, too, the shapeless
and formless ἔκτρωμα of Sophia is left behind, abandoned outside the Pleroma (*Ref.* 6.31.4); and steps must be taken to en-
sure that this substance, this deficiency (ὑστέρημα), does not
approach the heavenly aeons of the Pleroma (6.31.6). In the
Ap. John it is said that the mother threw away from herself
(λсноχϥ ςιсλ νβολ ῆμοс) the monstrous lion-headed product of
her desire, Yaltabaoth, and put him away from that place, the
Pleroma (II 10,7-19).

Thus the mother Sophia has left behind a portion that came
from herself, and is in need of healing, of wholeness. According to the *Ap. John*, the mother prays fervently and repents
with tears, and consequently her deficiency is healed and her
wholeness is restored through the action of the Pleroma. The
whole Pleroma hears her prayer, the invisible Spirit gives his
consent, and the holy Spirit anoints her from ⲡⲉⲩⲡⲗⲏⲣⲱⲙⲁ ⲧⲏⲣϥ,
"all their fullness" (II 14,6). Meanwhile, her consort also
comes down to her ϩⲓⲧⲛ̄ ⲡⲡⲗⲏⲣⲱⲙⲁ ϫⲉⲕⲗⲁⲥ ⲉϥⲛⲁⲥⲱϩⲉ ⲙ̄ⲡⲉⲥϣⲧⲁ,
"through the Pleroma, so that he might correct her deficiency"
(II 14,8-9).

It should also be noted that the wholeness of the heavenly
aeons will not really be restored until the ⲙⲉⲣⲟⲥ of divine
light is reclaimed from the wicked ⲁⲅⲑⲁⲗⲁⲏⲥ. The deficiency has
become firmly entrenched in the realm outside the Pleroma;
hence this world below is also caught up in the cosmic drama of
restoration. The world below is characterized by deficiency;
as Hippolytus notes, that is why Horos, the limit, cross, and
guardian of the Pleroma, ἀφορίζει ἀπὸ τοῦ πληρώματος ἔξω τὸ
ὑστέρημα...ὡς μὴ δύνασθαι μηδὲν τοῦ ὑστερήματος καταγενέσθαι
ἐγγὺς τῶν ἐντὸς πληρώματος αἰώνων (6.31.6). In contrast to the
divine Pleroma, this world of ignorance and all that is con-
nected with it—the passion of Sophia, the demiurge, the frag-
mented existence—can be described as defective and deficient,
in need of restoration to the unity and fullness of the One.[119]

The Arrogant One is now on center stage in the *Ep. Pet.
Phil.* It remains for him to organize a cosmic bureaucracy by
setting up powers, and to erect a prison by creating a mortal
world. ⲁⲅⲑⲁⲗⲁⲏⲥ begins by setting up his empire. Just as the
first archon of the *Ap. John* takes a great power (ⲟⲩⲛⲟϭ ⲛ̄ⲁⲩⲛⲁ-
ⲙⲓⲥ, II 10,20-21) from his mother and, with a fiery light-flame
(ϩⲛ̄ⲕⲉⲗⲓⲱⲛ ϩⲛ̄ ⲟⲩϣⲁϩ ⲛ̄ⲕⲱϩⲧ ⲛ̄ⲟⲩⲟⲉⲓⲛ, 10,24-25), creates other
aeons as well as additional authorities (ϩⲉⲛⲉⲝⲟⲩⲥⲓⲁ, 10,28), so
also ⲁⲅⲑⲁⲗⲁⲏⲥ in the *Ep. Pet. Phil.* establishes powers (ϩⲉⲛϭⲟⲙ)
and authorities (ϩⲉⲛⲉⲝⲟⲩⲥⲓⲁ) for the governance of the world.
ⲁⲅⲑⲁⲗⲁⲏⲥ sows the ⲙⲉⲣⲟⲥ from the mother, the spiritual seed from
heaven, "the seed (ⲡⲓⲥⲡⲉⲣⲙⲁ) that had fallen away" (136,18).
This image of the heavenly seed on earth is a common motif among

the Gnostics, and epitomizes the Gnostic sense of estrangement
from this world and identification with the world above, the
divine world of light; thus the heavenly race of Seth can refer
to themselves as the imperishable and holy seed.[120] The actual
sowing of the seed can be attributed to the demiurge, though
sometimes he and his cohorts function as lackeys for the higher
beings. Thus, among the Valentinians some suggested that Acha-
moth, the lower Sophia, as the real power behind the throne of
the demiurge, secretly prompted and enabled him to sow the
spiritual seed of the mother.[121] For such Gnostics, as for the
author of the *Ep. Pet. Phil.*, the divine origin of the seed is
of utmost importance; the мерос or сперма has come ultimately
from the mother.

The Arrogant One proceeds with the construction of aeons
of death, "mortal aeons," which are modeled after the immortal
aeons above. As the *Ap. John* explains, the creator made everything κατα πιnε ññϣορπ ñαιωn εnταϩϣωπε ϩωϲτε ατρεϥταμιοου
ñпсмат ñαττεκο, "after the likeness of the first aeons which
had appeared, that he might create them like the imperishable
ones" (II 12,34-13,1). Created in ignorance--he had not
actually seen the imperishable aeons, but was moved by the
power (τ6ομ) within him, which he got from his mother--, the
lower aeons are but a dim and deadly reflection of the glory of
the heavenly aeons.

The prison of the κοϲμος has been constructed, and the
petty powers are elated. They rejoice at their status,[122]
though they are ignorant. Like many of the accounts about
Yaldabaoth, this account about nι6ομ illustrates how foolish
they are; they are quite oblivious of the great preexistent
Father in heaven,[123] and offer their service to little αγθαληϲ.
The powers, after all, are ϩεnϣ̄нмо (136,2-3) to the great
Father; according to the *Hyp. Arch.*, when the divine image appeared on the waters, nεγϲοογn αn ñτε4бομ xε nιм пε, "they did
not know whose power it was" (II 88,9-10). Just as elsewhere
the children of light can be considered as strangers with respect to the world of darkness, so also here the powers of this
darkened world are presented as strangers with respect to the
Father of light.[124]

ⲁⲅⲑⲁⲁⲏⲥ, haughty of heart, becomes a ⲣⲉϥⲕⲱⲍ (136,8).[125]
According to Marcus and other Valentinians, the demiurge wished
τῆς ἄνω ὀγδοάδος τὸ ἀπέραντον, καὶ αἰώνιον, καὶ ἀόριστον, καὶ
ἄχρονον μιμήσασθαι; but he was doomed to failure because he is
the fruit of ὑστέρημα. Hence his imitation is a bastardization,
a falsehood.[126] In one way of conceptualizing this imitation,
the creator and his comrades can be said to model their mortal
creation after the reflection that appears in the water. An
exalted divine being--the first Man,[127] or Pistis Sophia,[128] or
Incorruptibility[129]--peers down, and its image reflects upon
the water. Seen by the demiurge, this fascinating image or
form becomes the model for the human being that is to be produced. ⲁⲅⲑⲁⲁⲏⲥ thus creates in the image of God (Gen 1:26-27);
and as a substitute for the image which appeared he makes an
inferior copy, ⲟⲩⲋⲓ̄ⲕⲱⲛ ⲉⲡⲙⲁ ⲛ̄ⲛⲟⲩⲋ̄ⲓ̄ⲕⲱⲛ ⲙ̄ⲛ ⲟⲩⲙⲟⲣⲫⲏ ⲉⲡⲙⲁ ⲛ̄ⲕⲟⲩⲙⲟⲣⲫⲏ
(VIII 136,9-11).[130]

The powers begin to mold mortal bodies. Some tractates
give detailed descriptions of the powers, procedures, and parts
involved in the assembling of these bodies. The *Ap. John*, for
instance, provides an exotic picture of the precise powers involved in the creation of the psychic form (II 15,1-29) and
particularly the material body (15,29-19,14); a total of three
hundred sixty-five powers work on this chore, ⲟⲩⲁⲛⲧϥϫⲱⲕ ⲉⲃⲟⲗ
ⲋⲓⲧⲟⲟⲧⲟⲩ ⲕⲁⲧⲁ ⲙⲉⲗⲟⲥ ⲛ̄ϭⲓ ⲯⲩⲭⲓⲕⲟⲛ ⲁⲩⲱ ⲡⲋⲅⲗⲓⲕⲟⲛ ⲛ̄ⲥⲱⲙⲁ, "until the
psychic and the material body was finished, limb by limb, by
them" (19,4-6). Similarly, in *Orig. World* the authorities are
depicted as enslavers producing models or molded bodies
(ⲙⲡⲗⲁⲥⲙⲁ) in order to entrap the souls, which then are imprisoned within these models; each of the seven ⲛ̄ⲁⲣⲭⲱⲛ contribute a portion to the ⲡⲗⲁⲥⲙⲁ of this Adam (II 114,15-115,3).
Thus is the ⲡⲗⲁⲥⲙⲁ ⲉⲧⲙⲟⲟⲩⲧ (VIII 136,19-20) of ⲁⲅⲑⲁⲁⲏⲥ and the
powers completed. Yet the mortal bodies are only poor imita-
tions of the ⲉⲓⲕⲱⲛ or ⲓⲁⲉⲁ which had appeared, and veritable
prisons of death.[131]

The Second Revelatory Answer (136,16-137,4)

Without going into further detail in the account of the
fall of the mother and the origin of the deficiency, the author

of the *Ep. Pet. Phil.* allows the risen Christ to provide a
revelatory answer to the second portion of the indirect question raised by the apostles. If the first answer analyzes the
human and cosmic dilemma, the second proclaims how this broken
existence can attain to fullness. Following the section subtitle (ⲉⲧⲃⲉ ⲡⲓⲡⲗⲏⲣⲱⲙⲁ, 136,16), a concise statement of the
resurrected Christ summarizes the answer in the briefest of
aretalogies: ⲁⲛⲟⲕ ⲡⲉ.[132] Thus the author of our tractate has
Christ claim identity with the fullness.

Such a statement is reminiscent of similar statements in
the NT. In Col 1:19 the Paulinist presents part of the Christ-
hymn which states that ἐν αὐτῷ (viz. Χριστῷ) εὐδόκησεν πᾶν τὸ
πλήρωμα κατοικῆσαι, while in 2:9 it is said that ἐν αὐτῷ κατοικεῖ πᾶν τὸ πλήρωμα τῆς θεότητος σωματικῶς. Similarly in Eph
1:22-23 the Paulinist says that the Father has made Christ head
over all things for the ἐκκλησία, which is τὸ σῶμα αὐτοῦ, τὸ
πλήρωμα τοῦ τὰ πάντα ἐν πᾶσιν πληρουμένου, and in 3:19 a prayer
is offered for the readers, that πληρωθῆτε εἰς πᾶν τὸ πλήρωμα
τοῦ θεοῦ. In these passages, God can be referred to as the
πλήρωμα that fills Christ with divine power; Christ can also be
intimately related to the πλήρωμα that fills and empowers him;
and the church, the saved people of God, is also saved by being
filled with all the πλήρωμα of God. Hence in such passages of
the NT, πλήρωμα can function in a theological, Christological,
and soteriological manner, and can approach the Gnostic usage
of the term.[133]

Among the Gnostics πλήρωμα is a favorite term to depict
the world of the divine. Often the divine realm is termed the
Pleroma, and then the term functions in a spatial manner: the
Pleroma is the divine world of light, inhabited by the aeons of
light, over which the Father of all dwells, a world which can
be separated and insulated by Ὅρος, "Limit," from this lower
fallen realm. Yet πλήρωμα can also function in a more qualitative fashion, as in our passage: the fullness is the quality
of life enjoyed by spiritual beings, perfect beings of light,
particularly the divine aeons of heaven, and such spiritual beings can be termed πληρώματα.[134] Thus, as Irenaeus has Ptolemaeus explain, Jesus as redeemer comes forth from the Pleroma,

as the perfect representative, star, and fruit of the Pleroma
(*Adv. Haer*. 1.2.6); but, as the *Ep. Pet. Phil*. makes abundantly
clear, he also is to be characterized by fullness. Coming from
the πλήρωμα, filled with the light and spirit of the divine, he
comes down to the cosmos lost in deficiency.[135]

As the divine fullness, Christ was sent down from the
world above to the cosmos below, ϩⲙ ⲡⲥⲱⲙⲁ, for the sake of the
fallen light-seed. It is said that Christ descended to
ⲡⲉⲩⲡⲗⲁⲥⲙⲁ ⲉⲧⲙⲟⲟⲩⲧ, "their mortal model" (136,19-20). While
this phrase could be a reference to this world, with its mortal
aeons and deadly features, the parallel at 136,12-13 would suggest that mortal bodies are of particular interest here. Christ
descended to their mortal bodies, that is, to the bodies molded
by the powers; and presumably he clothed himself in ⲡⲉⲩⲡⲗⲁⲥⲙⲁ
ⲉⲧⲙⲟⲟⲩⲧ. For the sake of this descent the redeemer apparently
put on a body as a disguise, and went unrecognized by the cosmic powers.

Such a salvific ploy is described in greater detail in
other Gnostic sources. In the *Ap. John*, for example, the revealer states that he entered the region of darkness, and even
went into ⲧⲙⲏⲧⲉ ⲙⲡⲉϣⲧⲉⲕⲟ, "the middle of the prison" (II 30,
18-19). This phrase is picked up again a few lines later and
is explained very clearly: ⲧⲙⲏⲧⲉ ⲙⲡⲟⲩϣⲧⲉⲕⲟ ⲉⲧⲉ ⲡⲁⲓ ⲡⲉ ⲡⲉϣⲧⲉⲕⲟ
ⲡⲥⲱⲙⲁ, "the middle of their prison, which is the prison of the
body" (31,3-4). Thus the heavenly redeemer was hidden from the
powers of this world, ⲁⲩⲱ ⲙⲡⲟⲩⲥⲟⲩⲱⲛⲧ, "and they did not recognize me" (30,21). Again, in the *Treat. Seth* Jesus Christ
claims that he visited ⲟⲩⲏⲉⲓ ⲛ̄ⲥⲱⲙⲁⲧⲓⲕⲟⲛ, "a bodily house" (VII
51,20-21); after throwing out the previous inhabitant, the
Savior himself entered and occupied it. The Savior, however,
does not resemble that first occupant, ⲡⲏ ⲅⲁⲣ ⲛⲉⲩⲣⲱⲙⲉ ⲛ̄ⲕⲟⲥⲙⲓⲕⲟⲥ
ⲡⲉ· ⲁⲛⲟⲕ ⲇⲉ ⲉⲁⲛⲟⲕ ⲟⲩⲉⲃⲟⲗ ⲙ̄ⲡⲥⲁⲛⲧⲡⲉ ⲛ̄ⲛⲙ̄ⲡⲏⲩⲉ, "for he was a man of
the cosmos, but as for me, I am from above the heavens" (51,34-
52,3). Hence, says the Savior, ⲛⲉⲓⲟⲩⲟⲛ̄ϩ ⲉⲃⲟⲗ ϫⲉ ⲁⲛⲟⲕ ⲟⲩϣⲙ̄ⲙⲟ
ⲛ̄ⲧⲉ ⲛⲓⲙⲉⲣⲟⲥ ⲉⲧⲥⲁⲡⲉⲥⲏⲧ, "I revealed that I am a stranger to the
regions which are below" (52,8-10). Later the Savior explains
how no one saw him as he descended, ⲛⲉⲉⲓϣⲓⲃⲉ ⲅⲁⲣ ⲙ̄ⲡⲓⲙⲟⲣⲫⲏ ⲛ̄ϩⲣⲁⲓ
ⲛ̄ϩⲏⲧ· ⲉⲓⲟⲩⲱⲧⲃ̄ ⲉⲃⲟⲗ ⲛ̄ⲟⲩⲉⲓⲇⲉⲁ ⲉⲩⲉⲓⲇⲉⲁ, "for I was changing my

forms, going from semblance to semblance" (56,23-25). While
at the various gates (ⲡⲩⲗⲏ) of the powers, the descending
Savior took on their likeness (ⲛⲉⲓ̈ⲭⲓ ⲉⲓⲛⲉ ⲙ̄ⲙⲟⲟⲩ), and thus
passed by them quietly and unobtrusively.[136] In fact, the ignorant and blind powers did not even recognize that they were
not crucifying the Savior at all! Once again, the so-called
Docetists depicted by Hippolytus are said to suggest that the
heavenly Son, wishing to save the souls trapped in cosmic
darkness, came down from above in a peculiar manner; ὁ μονογενὴς
παῖς ἄνωθεν αἰώνιος ἐπενδυσάμενος κατὰ ἕνα ἕκαστον τοῦ τρίτου
αἰῶνος αἰῶνα καὶ γενόμενος ἐν τριακοντάδι αἰώνων εἰσῆλθεν εἰς
τόνδε τὸν κόσμον (Ref. 8.10.5). The Son was not recognized: he
was ἀφανής, ἄγνωστος, ἄδοξος, ἀπιστούμενος. Finally the Son
from on high clothed himself with τὸ σκότος τὸ ἐξώτερον, τὴν
σάρκα φησίν (8.10.6), and thus he put on the offspring of Mary.

Although the Ep. Pet. Phil. does not proclaim the radical
docetism of some of the texts cited here, two themes are shared
among all the examples: in some way the Savior puts on a mortal
body; and thus he is able to travel incognito within the cosmos,
as ⲟⲩⲣⲱⲙⲉ ⲉϥⲙⲟⲟⲩⲧ (136,22).

The question of the origin of this account of the descending Christ has prompted Klaus Koschorke to provide certain suggestions in his recent article "Eine gnostische Paraphrase des
johanneischen Prologs." As his title intimates, Koschorke ar-
gues that this section of the Ep. Pet. Phil. illustrates the
Gnostic use and interpretation of the Gospel of John, the NT
authority who, along with Paul, was especially beloved by
Gnostic thinkers. Koschorke terms the Ep. Pet. Phil. "eine
gnostische Paraphrase der Apostelgeschichte (v.a. Lk 24-Act 8)."
Furthermore,

> Weniger offensichtlich als diese Abhängigkeit vom
> lukanischen Werk ist der Bezug des im Folgenden er-
> örterten Abschnittes 136,16-137,4 auf Joh 1. Doch
> dürften die hier bestehenden Übereinstimmungen kaum
> zufällig sein; und sie gewinnen doppeltes Gewicht
> dadurch, dass sie sich in einem Traktat finden, der--
> wie der Vergleich mit der Apostelgeschichte zeigt--
> ja ohnehin in seiner ganzen Anlage geprägt ist durch
> den Bezug auf eine neutestamentliche Schrift.[137]

Thus, Koschorke proceeds to illumine this suggested dependency
of our tractate upon the prologue to the Gospel of John. He
sees the phrase "sent down in the body" (136,17) as reflecting
σὰρξ ἐγένετο of John 1:14, and suggests that the reference to
the "fallen" seed (136,18) may reflect ἐρχόμενον εἰς τὸν κόσμον
(1:9). Furthermore, both documents refer to the nonrecognition
of the Savior ("they did not recognize me," 136,20-21; ὁ κόσμος
αὐτὸν οὐκ ἔγνω, 1:10), the word ("I spoke," 136,22; ὁ λόγος,
1:1, 14), coming to one's own ("him who is mine" [sing.], 136,
23; οἱ ἴδιοι [pl.], 1:11), the reception of the word ("he
hearkened to me just as you also who hearkened today," 136,
23-25; ὅσοι δὲ ἔλαβον αὐτόν, 1:12), the bestowal of authoritative power ("I gave him authority (ἐξουσία)," 136,26; ἔδωκεν
αὐτοῖς ἐξουσίαν, 1:12), and the eventual inheritance ("the inheritance of his fatherhood," 136,27-28; τέκνα θεοῦ γενέσθαι,
1:12). Finally, Koschorke judges that the reference to the
"fullness" to be enjoyed (137,4) resembles the πλήρωμα in which
all believers participate (1:16).[138] Thus, Koschorke concludes,
"Den bislang bekannten Belegen gnostischer Exegese von Joh 1
ist nun, wie unser Beitrag zu zeigen versuchte, EpPt hinzuzu-
fügen."[139] He suggests that the *Ep. Pet. Phil.* provides a
paraphrase of the Johannine prologue, and apparently a re-
mythologized paraphrase at that.

Our evaluation of Koschorke's thesis should begin by noting that Koschorke is correct in recognizing that the *Ep. Pet.
Phil.* is written with a considerable awareness of other Christian and Gnostic literature. Indeed, as we are suggesting, our
tractate does mean to provide a Christian Gnostic interpretation of various traditional materials. Hence Koschorke's thesis is by no means rendered impossible or even unlikely by the
character of the document. Furthermore, the *Ep. Pet. Phil.*
136,16-137,4 has a general purpose similar to that of John 1;
both passages proclaim that the heavenly Savior has come down
to this world and has put on a body, for the sake of the salvation and fullness of his people.

When we look at the particular parallels highlighted by
Koschorke, however, we note that they are not altogether convincing. As he also notes,[140] the parallel concerning the

ⲉⲝⲟⲩⲥⲓⲁ which is given is the closest and most impressive similarity. But as for the other parallels, the evidence is not
persuasive. The account of the *Ep. Pet. Phil.* does not emphasize the Johannine concern for the λόγος becoming σάρξ; in
fact, 136,21-22 seems to suggest that the divine Savior was not
really σάρξ at all! Some of the other parallels are trivial or
even farfetched. For example, the λόγος of John is hardly a
close and meaningful parallel to the ⲁⲓⲱⲁⲭⲉ (136,22-23) of the
Ep. Pet. Phil. The most important parallels between these two
passages seem to be precisely in those areas where numerous
Gnostic sources agree. The fall of the seed, the descent of
the Savior, his encounter with a body, the lack of recognition
of the powers--such themes as these are treated in various
Gnostic sources, and often the parallels with the *Ep. Pet.
Phil.* are more significant in these sources. Furthermore, the
theme of the obedience of ⲡⲉⲧⲉ ⲡⲱⲓ is also nicely paralleled
in Gnostic documents, as we soon shall notice.

Hence, most of the similarities between the *Ep. Pet. Phil.*
136,16-137,4 and John 1 seem to reflect terms and themes shared
with other versions of the Gnostic account of the descent of
the heavenly redeemer. In this way the Gnostic background of
the Johannine λόγος hymn is underscored, to be sure, but the
suggested dependence of the *Ep. Pet. Phil.* upon the Gospel of
John is called into question. In spite of its current context
within a set of revelatory answers delivered by the resurrected
Christ, we may even wonder whether 136,16-137,4 could reflect
a non-Christian Gnostic redeemer myth, a myth with certain affinities to the λόγος hymn adopted and adapted by John.[141]

It remains to be discovered what is meant by ⲡⲉⲧⲉ ⲡⲱⲓ
(136,23), a phrase paralleled in the third revelatory answer at
137,5-6. This rather ambiguous phrase apparently functions as
the antecedent for the masculine singular pronouns that are
used in the succeeding lines, which provide an account of the
salvation of ⲡⲉⲧⲉ ⲡⲱⲓ. Several interpretations have been given.
Bethge proposes that perhaps Adam the Primal Man is meant; "Was
Jesus dann den Aposteln sagt, ist im Grunde nur eine Wieder-
holung dessen, was in der Urzeit bereits Adam mitgeteilt
wurde."[142] Koschorke maintains that "das menschliche Gefäss

des Soter ('der Meinige') als Prototyp aller erlösungsfähigen
Menschen ('die Meinigen') erscheint," that is to say, the human
Jesus, "der erste in der Reihe derer, denen der Soter ἔδωκεν...
ἐξουσίαν τέκνα θεοῦ γενέσθαι."[143] In both his translation and
his commentary Ménard refers to "la race" in this connection,
"(la race) qui est mienne";[144] this suggestion may also be compared with the apparent concern of Jesus for the "seed"
(ⲥⲡⲉⲣⲙⲁ), the pneumatic light trapped in the world of darkness.

The *Ap. John* illustrates some of the same ambiguity concerning the one who responds to the heavenly call. At II 24,32-
25,16 Seth and the ⲥⲡⲉⲣⲙⲁ are the object of the saving activities of the Spirit, ⲭⲉⲕⲁⲁⲥ ⲍⲟⲧⲁⲛ ⲉϥϣⲁⲛⲉⲓ ⲉ2ⲣⲁⲓ̈ ⲛ̄ϭⲓ ⲡⲉⲡⲛⲁ̄ ⲉⲃⲟⲗ
2ⲓⲧⲛ̄ ⲛⲁⲓⲱⲛ ⲉⲧⲟⲩⲁⲁⲃ ⲉϥⲛⲁϭⲉ2ⲱϥ ⲉⲣⲁⲧϥ ⲁⲩⲱ ⲛ̄ϥⲧⲁ̄6ⲁϥ 2ⲙ̄ ⲡϣⲧⲁ ⲭⲉⲕⲁⲁⲥ
ⲉⲣⲉⲡⲡⲗⲏⲣⲱⲙⲁ ⲧⲏⲣϥ ⲛⲁϣⲱⲡⲉ ⲉϥⲟⲩⲁⲁⲃ ⲁⲩⲱ ⲛ̄ⲁⲧϣⲧⲁ, "so that, when the
Spirit comes down through the holy aeons, he may raise him up
and heal him of the deficiency, so that the entire fullness may
become holy and without deficiency" (25,11-16). At a later
point in the tractate, as the risen Christ is describing his
descent from the light, he recounts how he issued the call to
awaken. Christ proclaims, ⲡⲉⲧⲥⲱⲧⲙ̄ ⲧⲱⲟⲩⲛ ⲉⲃⲟⲗ 2ⲙ̄ ⲫⲓⲛⲏⲃ ⲉⲧ2ⲟⲣϣ,
"you (sing.) who hear, arise from heavy sleep!" (31,5-6). The
one thus called responds, and this "primal sleeper" hearkens
(ⲥⲱⲧⲙ̄, 31,15) and follows his root, Christ, into light and
life, ⲭⲉⲕⲁⲁⲥ ⲛ̄ⲛⲉⲡⲙⲟⲩ ϭⲛ̄6ⲁⲙ ⲉⲣⲟϥ ⲭⲛ̄ ⲛ̄ⲧ̄ⲓⲛⲁⲩ, "so that death might
not have power over him from now on" (31,24-25).

The point of these references, as Koschorke realizes, is
the symbolic or prototypical character of the one who responds
to the call of the heavenly redeemer. The heavenly redeemer, a
stranger to this world of darkness, comes to the light-seed en-
snared within the cosmos. Being from the light, he comes to
save the light, and to return it to the fullness of the Father.
Hence, depending upon whether it is considered collectively or
individually, the ⲙⲉⲣⲟⲥ or ⲥⲡⲉⲣⲙⲁ of light can be ⲡⲉⲧⲉ ⲡⲱⲓ̈ or
ⲛⲉⲧⲉ ⲛⲟⲩⲉⲓ.

In other Gnostic sources, too, such phrases become descriptions of the people of the light. In the *2 Apoc. Jas.*, for example, the Savior talks to his brother James the Just about
those who belong to the light, as opposed to those who are

strangers. He proclaims to James, who himself has an exalted
role, ⲛ̄ⲧⲟⲕ ⲅⲁⲣ ⲁⲛ ⲡⲉ ⲡⲓⲣⲉϥⲥⲱⲧⲉ ⲙ̄ⲛ̄ⲛ ⲟⲩⲃⲟⲏⲑⲟⲥ ⲛ̄ⲧⲉ ⳉⲉⲛϣⲙ̄ⲙⲟ˙ ⲛ̄ⲧⲕ̄
ⲟⲩⲣⲉϥⲧⲟⲟⲧⲉ ⲉⳉⲟⲩⲛ ⲙ̄ⲛ̄ ⲟⲩⲣⲉϥⲥⲱⲧⲉ ⲛ̄ⲧⲉ ⲛⲉⲧⲉ ⲛⲟⲩⲉⲓ˙ ϯⲛⲟⲩ ⲁⲉ ⲛ̄ⲧⲉ ⲛⲉⲧⲉ
ⲛⲟⲩⲕ, "For you are not the redeemer or a helper of strangers;
you are an illuminator and a redeemer of those who are mine,
and now of those who are yours" (V 55,15-20). Likewise, in the
Treat. Seth Christ speaks in very similar terms: "I came to
those who are mine (ⲛⲉⲧⲉ ⲛⲟⲩⲉⲓ ⲛⲉ) and united them with me" (VII
59,9-11). ⲛⲉⲧⲉ ⲡⲱⲓ̈ and ⲛⲉⲧⲉ ⲛⲟⲩⲉ̄ⲓ are thus two ways of referring to the light trapped below, awaiting salvation and restoration through the ⲫⲱⲥⲧⲏⲣ.

The light has fallen into ⲟⲩϣⲱⲱⲧ, but is to be restored to
ⲟⲩⲡⲗⲏⲣⲱⲙⲁ: this is the message of the *Ep. Pet. Phil.* 136,16-
137,4. In fact, the first two revelatory answers, which as we
have seen are structurally related, come together at the conclusion of the second answer to provide a soteriological cli-
max. Unfortunately, 137,1-2 cannot be reconstructed with any
confidence.[145] The sense of the passage, however, is clear.
The fallen light, dimmed in the deficiency of this world and
estranged from the heavenly realm, returns to the fullness. As
Christ is the ⲡⲗⲏⲣⲱⲙⲁ, so also the light becomes ⲡⲗⲏⲣⲱⲙⲁ, since
Christ and the light are essentially the same. Hence the destiny of Christ and the Gnostic coincide: both attain to the
ⲡⲗⲏⲣⲱⲙⲁ of light.[146]

The Third and Fourth Revelatory Answers (137,4-13)

The last two of the set of four revelatory answers are
very brief, and also very similar to each other in structure
and function. If the first two answers provide insights into
basic Gnostic soteriology--the fall and restoration of the
light--, the last two answers provide specific answers to the
questions of the daily struggles of Gnostic believers. What
about their imprisonment here below? What about their struggle
with the powers of the world?

The third revelatory answer of the resurrected Christ
(137,4-9) speaks most clearly to the first (and possibly also
the third) of the direct questions raised by the apostles.[147]

The third answer opens, like the fourth, with a slightly different formula for the section subtitle (ⲉⲧⲃⲉ ⲡⲏ ⲁⲉ ⲭⲉ, 137,4-
5.10) than that of the first two answers. This third answer
purports to speak to the problem of the detention, the incar-
ceration in this dwelling place (134,24). Although the answer
provided is very brief, it does give a reason for the detention
and suggest a solution. The reason given is one that suggests
hostility, the conflict between the forces of light and the
powers of darkness. The megalomaniacal demigods of the world,
in their jealousy and wickedness, imprison the heavenly light
within a cosmos of death. In spite of their ignorance, they
attempt to browbeat, coerce, curse, and even rape the beings
under their control, those who have fallen from the light. Because you are children of the light, strangers to this dark
world but at home in the light, ⲭⲉ ⲛ̄ⲧⲱⲧⲛ̄ ⲛⲉⲧⲉ ⲛⲟⲩⲉⲓ (137,5-6),
Christ says, therefore you are opposed by the powers of this
mortal world. And just as these powers persecuted Christ, so
also do they persecute those belonging to Christ.[148]

        According to the *Ep. Pet. Phil.*, the way out of this pre-
dicament involves stripping away the corruptible part of our
being, the mortal bodies (ⲍⲉⲛⲥⲱⲙⲁ ⲉⲩⲙⲟⲟⲩⲧ, 136,12-13). This
motif is well known in Gnostic documents. In the *Dial. Sav.*
the problem is described with great clarity; as the Lord tells
Matthew, you cannot see the glorious place of life and light
ⲉⲫⲟ[ⲥⲟⲛ ⲉⲕ]ⲫⲟⲣⲓ ⲛ̄ⲧⲥⲁⲣⲝ, "as long as you wear the flesh" (III
132,11-12). In the *Gos. Thom.* Jesus compares his disciples to
children who are placed in a field belonging to others. When
these owners return to claim their field, the children ⲥⲉⲕⲁⲕ
ⲁⲍⲏⲩ ⲙ̄ⲡⲟⲩⲙⲧⲟ ⲉⲃⲟⲗ ⲉⲧⲣⲟⲩⲕⲁⲁⲥ ⲉⲃⲟⲗ ⲛⲁⲩ ⲛ̄ⲥⲉϯ ⲧⲟⲩⲥⲱϣⲉ ⲛⲁⲩ, "strip
themselves before them in order to release it to them and to
give back their field to them" (II 37,4-6). Though the meta-
phor is mixed, the message is apparent: the children of the
light are to let go of this world, take off the bodies that are
clothing them, and be released from mortal existence to immortal life.[149] Similarly in the *2 Apoc. Jas.* Christ speaks to
James about his entry into the body and his release from the
body: ⲛ̄ⲧⲟⲕ ⲅⲁⲣ ⲍⲱⲥ ⲉⲛⲧⲕ̄ ⲟⲩϣⲟⲣⲡ̄ ⲉⲁⲕϯ ⲍ̄ⲧⲱⲱⲕ· ⲛ̄ⲧⲟⲕ ⲟⲛ ⲡⲉ ⲡϣⲟⲣⲡ̄
ⲉⲧⲛⲁⲕⲁⲁⲕϥ̄ [ⲁ]ⲍⲏⲟⲩ· ⲁⲩⲱ ⲉⲕⲉϣⲱⲡⲉ ⲛ̄ⲑⲉ ⲉⲛⲉⲕϣⲟⲟⲡ ⲙ̄ⲙⲟⲥ ⲍⲁⲑⲏ

ємпатекклак а2ноγ, "For even as you are the first to have
clothed yourself, so also are you the first who will strip himself, and you shall become as you were before you stripped
yourself" (V 56,7-14). Perhaps here a new, transformed sort of
glorious clothing, fitting for an exalted being of light, may
be alluded to, though elsewhere in the tractate (46,14-19;
58,20-23) the imperishable Christ can be described as naked.

In similar fashion the stripping of the mortal flesh and
the reclothing with the spiritual garment can be indicated in
other Gnostic sources. In the *Ap. Jas.*, for example, the ascending Jesus states that he will strip himself so that he may
clothe himself anew (I 14,35-36).[150] In the "Hymn of the
Pearl" the king's son takes off the filthy garment (τὸ ῥυπαρὸν
ἔνδυμα) that he has been using as a disguise in the worldly
land of Egypt (*Acts of Thomas* 111), and puts on his glorious
image, his royal robe (τὴν στολήν μου τὴν βασιλικήν), back at
his father's house (112-13).

Though the *Ep. Pet. Phil.* here makes no mention of any
heavenly garment to be worn, the emphasis remains essentially
the same: strip yourselves of what is perishable, and shine
like the light that you are! In the words attributed to the
Naassenes by Hippolytus, the house of God is the place ὅπου ὁ
ἀγαθὸς θεὸς κατοικεῖ μόνος, εἰς ὃν οὐκ εἰσελεύσεται, φησίν,
ἀκάθαρτος οὐδεις, οὐ ψυχικός, οὐ σαρκικός, ἀλλὰ τηρεῖται
πνευματικοῖς μόνοις, ὅπου δεῖ γενομένους βαλεῖν τὰ ἐνδύματα
καὶ πάντας γενέσθαι νυμφίους ἀπηρσενωμένους διὰ τοῦ παρθενικοῦ
πνεύματος (*Ref.* 5.8.44).[151]

The concept of souls wearing clothing was a common image
during late Hellenism.[152] During its descent the heavenly soul
was thought to put on the qualities and passions of the seven
cosmic spheres, and upon ascending it was believed to remove
these garments again, so that it might live in purity and
divinity in heaven. Such an image is exceedingly ancient, and
already can be seen in an early form in the Sumerian and Ak-
kadian myths of the descent of Inanna (Ishtar) into the underworld.[153] In order to see her older sister Ereshkigal, the
queen of the underworld, Inanna must pass through seven gates
on her descent, and take off clothes and jewels at each gate,

so that she arrives naked before the throne of Ereshkigal.
Upon returning to the earth, however, her clothes are given
to her once again at the appropriate gates, and she appears
safe and sound in the realm of the living. In a similar fashion, in a different mythological context and at a much later
time, Gnostics can also portray the light and the heavenly redeemer being progressively clothed with the various somatic and
psychic garments during the descent to earth, and progressively
unclothed again during the ascent. Thus in *Poimandres* 24-26
the narrator Nous-Poimandres describes how, after the fleshly
body has been abandoned, with its senses and passions, the person ascends through the seven cosmic circles, and hands back
the various capacities and inclinations to the appropriate
circle. Thus stripped (γυμνωθείς), the person arrives in the
presence of the Father, praises God, and becomes God (θεωθῆναι).

The naked soul is also discussed, though in a much more
negative fashion, in the NT, where the possibility of a final
condition without a body or clothing is denied or viewed with
horror. Indeed, as in Judaism, so also in the NT, it is the
unfaithful who arise without bodies or clothing; and in 2 Corinthians Paul emphasizes that there is a heavenly dwelling for
us, so that we might put it on and οὐ γυμνοὶ εὑρεθησόμεθα
(5:2-3).[154]

The *Gos. Phil.* enters into this debate concerning naked-
ness, physical bodies, and spiritual bodies, where the fear of
some people at the prospect of rising naked is discussed. The
Gos. Phil. maintains that in actuality those who wear the ⲥⲁⲣⲝ
are naked, and those who strip themselves (ⲕⲁⲕⲟⲩ ⲉ₂ⲏⲩ, II 56,
31-32) are not naked; 1 Cor 15:50 is even brought in as evidence in the discussion (56,32-34). After additional comments
about resurrection in the flesh, this section of the *Gos. Phil.*
closes with the statement that "in this world those who put on
clothes are better than the clothes; in the kingdom of heaven
the clothes are better than those who have put them on" (57,
19-22)--that is, the spiritual person wears inferior fleshly
clothing in this world, but superior clothing of heavenly glory
in the next.

The *Ep. Pet. Phil.* has Jesus promise that when the corruptible is taken off, then the believer will become a ⲫⲱⲥⲧⲏⲣ.
Presumably the full realization of this enlightened state will
come at death, when the material body will be discarded, and
the believer will finally leave this dwelling place (134,23-26).
Yet the *Ep. Pet. Phil.* here emphasizes that the apostles are to
become illuminators ⳿ⲛ ⲧⲙⲏⲧⲉ ⲛ̄ⲍⲉⲛⲣⲱⲙⲉ ⲉⲩⲙⲟⲟⲩⲧ (137,9). Hence
already the believers can realize salvation, already they can
anticipate the freedom of living in the light and not in slavery to the flesh.[155] Such hope for the present life is also
proclaimed in the *Hyp. Arch.*, which promises that all true
Gnostics, all those who know the Way, have life: ⲟⲩⲟⲛ ⲁⲉ ⲛⲓⲙ
ⲛ̄ⲧⲁⲍⲥⲟⲩⲱⲛ ⲧⲉⲓ̈ⲍⲟⲇⲟⲥ ⲛⲁⲉⲓ ⲥⲉⲱⲟⲟⲡ ⲛ̄ⲁⲑⲁⲛⲁⲧⲟⲥ ⲍⲛ̄ ⲧⲙⲏⲧⲉ ⲛ̄ⲣ̄ⲣⲱⲙⲉ
ⲉⲱⲁⲩⲙⲟⲩ, "and all those who have known this Way are deathless
in the midst of dying people" (II 96,25-27).

Thus, like Christ, the Gnostic Christians can also become
ⲍⲉⲛⲫⲱⲥⲧⲏⲣ. Just as Christ is a fullness and an illuminator,
so also the Gnostics become fullnesses and illuminators.
Christ's fate is their fate, his lot their lot. Among the
Gnostics the realization of salvation can involve a mystical
identification with Christ, so that the author of the *Gos. Phil.*
can proclaim that one is mystically united with the divine:
ⲁⲕⲛⲁ[ⲩ] ⲁⲡⲡⲛ̅ⲁ̅ ⲁⲕⲱⲱⲡⲉ ⲙ̄ⲡⲛ̄ⲁ̄ ⲁⲕⲛⲁ[ⲩ ⲁ]ⲡⲭ̅ⲥ̅ ⲁⲕⲱⲱⲡⲉ ⲛ̄ⲭ̅ⲥ̅ ⲁⲕⲛⲁⲩ ⲁⲡ[ⲉⲓⲱⲧ
ⲕ]ⲛⲁⲱⲱⲡⲉ ⲛ̄ⲉⲓⲱⲧ, "You saw the Spirit, you became spirit; you saw
Christ, you became Christ; you saw the [Father, you] will become the Father" (II 61,29-32).[156]

The fourth revelatory answer of the risen Christ (137,10-
13) functions as the answer to the fifth direct question of the
apostles. While the question is worded in such a way as to
emphasize the active hostility of the powers, the subtitle of
the answer assumes the active participation of the apostles;
in either case the issue being discussed is the struggle between the Gnostics and the powers of the cosmos.[157] The brief
answer given seems to relate especially to the ⲉⲧⲃⲉ ⲟⲩ of the
question at 135,2. The reason for the ongoing warfare between
the people of the light and the powers of this world, Christ
says, is that the powers do not have rest, and they oppose the
salvation of the people of the light. ⲛ̄ⲧⲟⲛ frequently

translates ἀνάπαυσις, and these two terms function in a technical manner within Gnostic documents.[158] These terms designate
the salvific state of the enlightened person, the state of being filled with knowledge, of being whole. As 137,11-12 hints,
already the believers "have rest." But ultimately, we are suggesting, the final rest or repose for the author of the *Ep.
Pet. Phil.* comes with the new world, the total liberation.

In the *Gos. Thom.*, on the other hand, the focus is clearly
on the repose which is attainable now. The disciples ask Jesus
a question, and place the phrases ⲧⲁⲛⲁⲡⲁⲩⲥⲓⲥ ⲛ̄ⲛⲉⲧⲙⲟⲟⲩⲧ (II 42,
8-9) and ⲡⲕⲟⲥⲙⲟⲥ ⲃ̄ⲃ̄ⲣ̄ⲣⲉ (42,10) in balanced parallelism: "When
will the rest for the dead happen, and when will the new world
come?" Jesus responds to this apocalyptic question by destroy-
ing any preoccupation with the future: ⲧⲏ ⲉⲧⲉⲧⲛ̄ϭⲱϣⲧ ⲉⲃⲟⲗ ϩⲏⲧⲥ̄
ⲁⲥⲉⲓ ⲁⲗⲗⲁ ⲛ̄ⲧⲱⲧⲛ̄ ⲧⲉⲧⲛ̄ⲥⲟⲟⲩⲛ ⲁⲛ ⲙ̄ⲙⲟⲥ, "What you look forward to
has come, but you do not know it" (42,11-12). According to the
Gos. Thom., then, the ⲙ̄ⲧⲟⲛ or ἀνάπαυσις is now; as the *Gos.
Truth* also proclaims, the Gnostic is the one who has rest, for
"since he knows, he does the will of him who called him; he
wants to please him; he receives rest (ⲙ̄ⲧⲁⲛ)" (I 22,9-12).

Yet some Gnostic sources maintain that ultimate rest lies
in the fullness of the heavenly light, the final oneness with
the Father. Hence the *Ap. John* states that the soul which has
left the flesh, and upon which the spirit of life (ⲡⲛ̄ⲁ̄ ⲙ̄ⲡⲱⲛϩ)
and the power (ⲧϭⲟⲙ) have come, will be saved, ⲁⲩⲱ ϣⲁⲩϫⲓⲧⲥ̄
ⲉϩⲣⲁⲓ̈ ⲉⲧⲁⲛⲁⲡⲁⲩⲥⲓⲥ ⲛ̄ⲁⲓⲱⲛ, "and it is taken up to the repose of
the aeons" (II 26,21-32).[159]

This, then, is the perfect rest, beyond all the difficul-
ties and sufferings described in the *Ep. Pet. Phil.* And this
perfect rest, anticipated as it is in the present, is precisely
what the cosmic powers do not have. They are not of the light,
and in spite of their bravado they are weak and ignorant.
Strangers to the light, they oppose the creatures of the light,
and want to keep them imprisoned below.

An Additional Question and Answer, and the Conclusion
(137,13-138,10)

The author of the *Ep. Pet. Phil.* does not conclude the
revelatory section of the tractate with the selection of prefixed questions and four revelatory answers. Rather, the author provides an indication of a seam in the tractate by paus-
ing to reset the stage appropriately with a quotation formula
which harks back to the setting for the first group of questions
and answers. This appended question (137,13-17) builds upon
the previous question and answer, where the cosmic battle is
described. The specific request in this additional question
has to do, once again, with the struggle with the cosmic powers:
ⲁϣ ⲧⲉ ⲑⲉ? In this question and answer, however, the Greek loan
word ⲁⲣⲭⲱⲛ is utilized, a technical term used only here in the
tractate. The fearful nature of this struggle is suggested by
the apostles in their concluding clause: ⲛⲓⲁⲣⲭⲱⲛ ⲥⲉⲛ̄ⲧⲡⲉ ⲙ̄ⲙⲟⲕ.
The same fear is expressed by the disciple Judas in the *Dial.
Sav.*, where he says, ⲉⲓⲥ ϩⲏⲏⲧⲉ ⲉⲓⲥ ⲛ̄ⲁⲣⲭⲱⲛ ϣⲟⲟⲡ ϩⲛ̄ ⲧⲡⲉ ⲙ̄ⲙⲁⲛ
ⲛ̄ⲧⲟⲟⲩ ϭⲉ ⲡⲉ ⲉⲧⲛⲁⲣ̄ϫⲟⲉⲓⲥ ⲉϫⲱⲛ, "Behold, the archons are above us,
so surely they will lord it over us" (III 138,11-14). In this
latter instance, however, Jesus quickly points out that, on the
contrary, the disciples and the Gnostics will lord it over
these archons.

The revelatory answer (137,17-138,3) is introduced by
means of a statement referring to the mode of revelation; the
quotation formula refers to the ⲥⲙⲏ which calls out from the
appearance. Whether ⲡⲏ ⲉⲧⲉ ⲛⲉϥⲟⲩⲟⲛϩ̄ (137,19) is best translated as "him who was appearing" or "that which was appearing"
is difficult to say. To be sure, the appearance is that of the
resurrected Christ, but Christ is appearing as a light. Hence
this phrase seems patterned after the opening formula at 135,
3-4. The answer itself opens with a preliminary statement in
two parts. The first of the two parts (137,20-22) provides an
introduction to the answer which follows, and concludes with a
statement of substantiation. The second part (137,22-23) reiterates the introduction provided by the first part, but
strengthens the impact by means of a verb with a third future
form. Such a repetition has encouraged Bethge to suggest the

possibility of dittography. The statement of substantiation,
he posits, "dürfte eine sekundäre Glosse sein, die eine Ditto-
graphie verursacht hat."[160] Such a suggestion is not unreason-
able, and deserves some consideration. Yet the significant
place of the statement of substantiation, and the intensifica-
tion provided by the reiteration with the verb in the third
future, should caution us against dismissing the supposed in-
trusions in too facile a manner. The preliminary statement
thus concludes with an exceedingly strong declaration, almost
a demand: "you should, you must fight against them in this way."

The brief statement of substantiation reflects the true
character of the struggle between the people of the light and
the cosmic powers: ⲛⲓⲁⲣⲭⲱⲛ ⲉⲩϯ ⲙ̄ⲛ ⲡⲓⲣⲱⲙⲉ ⲉⲧⲥⲁ₂ⲟⲩⲛ (137,21-22).
The archons oppose the light, the spirit within, the ἔσω ἄνθρω-
πος πνευματικός;[161] their war is a spiritual war, and so the
tactics of the believers must make use of the spiritual weapons
at their disposal. According to Irenaeus, some of the Valentinian Gnostics around Marcus emphasize τὴν γνῶσιν (εἶναι)
ἀπολύτρωσιν τοῦ ἔνδον ἀνθρώπου. Such redemption is not somatic,
for the σῶμα is φθαρτόν; it is not psychic, for the ψυχή is
also from the ὑστέρημα. No, this redemption is spiritual
(πνευματική); λυτροῦσθαι γὰρ διὰ γνώσεως[162] τὸν ἔσω ἄνθρωπον
τὸν πνευματικόν, καὶ ἀρκεῖσθαι αὐτοὺς τῇ τῶν ὅλων ἐπιγνώσει·
καὶ ταύτην εἶναι λύτρωσιν ἀληθῆ (*Adv. Haer.* 1.21.4). The
battle described in the *Ep. Pet. Phil.* is reminiscent of the
spiritual warfare depicted by the Paulinist in Eph 6:10-20,
where it is emphasized that since the believers are not fighting πρὸς αἷμα καὶ σάρκα but rather πρὸς τὰς ἀρχάς, πρὸς τὰς
ἐξουσίας, πρὸς τοὺς κοσμοκράτορας τοῦ σκότους τούτου, πρὸς τὰ
πνευματικὰ τῆς πονηρίας ἐν τοῖς ἐπουρανίοις (6:12), therefore
their weaponry ought to be correspondingly spiritual.[163]

The spiritual weaponry and strategy recommended by Christ
in the *Ep. Pet. Phil.* seems to reflect the life of the Gnostic
Christians who are behind our tractate. The believers are to
combat the archons (137,23-25) through the gathering and the
preaching also mentioned at the very opening of the tractate
(132,19-133,1).[164] This emphasis in the *Ep. Pet. Phil.* illustrates the concern of this author and group for both the

ecclesiastical meetings and the missiological programs. A
rhythm of life, a plan of action, is present in the *Ep. Pet.
Phil.*; the apostles, and the community, ought to neglect
neither the worship of the group nor the mission in the world.
In the gatherings the voice of Christ is heard, and in the
mission the light of Christ is disseminated. In addition, God
the Father will provide help (ʙοнθι); he provides power with
which the people of the light can gird themselves (137,25-27),[165]
he is responsive to prayer (137,27-28),[166] and thus he helps
continually just as he helped by sending Christ (137,28-30).[167]
As a result, the apostles have nothing to fear[168] in the struggle with the archons, for they will certainly prevail over them.
The revelatory answer closes with an additional reference to
the continuity between the teachings of the historical Jesus
and those of the resurrected Christ (138,2-3). Thus reassured
and mandated, the disciples may go forth, and the revelatory
appearance may come to an end.

As τοτε was used to introduce both the additional question
(137,13) and the additional answer (137,17), so also τοτε is
used for both parts of the account of the meeting's conclusion
(138,3.7). The ascension of the risen Christ (138,3-7) concludes the revelatory appearance, and emphasizes the special
character of the appearance. Lightning and thunder accompany
this ascension, for there has been a theophany.[169] This ascension should not be confused, however, with the ascension as depicted in Luke-Acts. In the *Ep. Pet. Phil.* the portrayal depicts a glorious appearance of the light and voice of Christ
from heaven, while in Luke-Acts the author wishes to have the
ascension function in a particular way within his scenario of
redemptive history. Hence in Acts the emphasis is placed upon
the ascension as an event quite separate from the resurrection.
The resurrection and ascension accounts in Acts agree, however,
in emphasizing the corporeality of both of these events, and
the ascension account pictures Christ almost being levitated.[170]
Luke is concerned about continuity, the continuity from the
earthly Jesus to the earthly church, and he shapes his resurrection and ascension accounts to speak to these concerns. In
the *Ep. Pet. Phil.*, on the other hand, the revelatory appearance

of the risen Christ is a theophany, and the withdrawal of the
light and voice is depicted as a return to heaven, though it is
true that the language of 138,5-7 approaches that of Acts.[171]
The author of the *Ep. Pet. Phil.* is not fighting the theological battles of Luke, and operates with a different scenario.
For the author of our tractate the glorious Christ speaks au-
thoritatively not only to the apostles but also in the church
of the author's day.

After the return of the glorious Christ to heaven, the
apostles themselves give thanks and return to Jerusalem (138,
7-10). Here the scene comes to a natural conclusion, and does
so in a manner reminiscent of Luke 24:52-53 and Acts 1:12. As
in Luke-Acts, the apostles in the *Ep. Pet. Phil.* return to
Jerusalem,[172] and offer worship to the Lord.[173]

Scene on the Road to Jerusalem (138,10-139,9)

An additional scene is inserted into the narrative at
138,10. The seams of the insertion are apparent in the clause
(138,10-11) linking this scene to the preceding scene, and in
the conclusion to this scene (139,4-6), where the account of
the return to Jerusalem is reiterated.[174] The scene on the
Jerusalem road focuses upon a theme which is crucial for the
Ep. Pet. Phil. in general, and which dominates the concluding
pages of the tractate: suffering, both the suffering of the
apostles and the suffering of Christ. Such a preoccupation
with suffering may derive in part from the traditions reflected
in our document. Lucan materials, with which the author of the
Ep. Pet. Phil. was generally familiar, certainly illustrate a
great concern for the sufferings of the early church, the per-
secutions which characterized the beginnings of the history of
Christianity.[175] Likewise, the traditional credo of the *Ep.
Pet. Phil.* (139,15-21), with formulae familiar from early
Christian literature, echoes the concern of the early church
for the proclamation and interpretation of the passion and
death of Christ.

Yet the *Ep. Pet. Phil.* also indicates that the community
which produced this tractate is a Gnostic Christian group ex-
periencing hostility and persecution. Their prayer to Christ

(134,8-9), the questions asked of the risen Christ (134,23-
135,2; 137,15-17) or raised by the group (138,15-16), and the
supportive words of the resurrected Christ (137,20-138,3;
138,22-139,4; 140,17-23) and the apostle Peter (139,15-140,1)
all indicate that the Gnostic Christian community of the *Ep.
Pet. Phil.* was intimately involved with the problem of suffering and persecution. The struggle of the believer for survival
and victory in a hostile world was very real to this community,
and very much a part of the self-understanding of the group.
This concern may reflect the hostile political environment
during portions of the first three centuries C.E.; Christians
were forced to cope practically and theologically with the
problem of persecution. Gnostic Christians, too, experienced
suffering and death at the hands of the persecutors,[176] although such opponents of heresy as Ignatius and Irenaeus could
level at the Gnostics the blanket charge that they were docetists with regard to Christ's passion and opponents of martyr-
dom.[177] These Gnostic Christians could also assert that they
suffered at the hands of others who claimed to be Christians,
probably from an oppressive Great Church, which may come ⲉⲡⲣⲁⲛ
ⲛ̄ⲧⲉ ⲟⲩⲣⲉϥⲙⲟⲟⲩⲧ, "in the name of a dead man,"[178] and impose its
will upon the Gnostic believers.

Furthermore, many Gnostics were acutely aware of the hostility of the cosmic environment. Numerous powers and archons,
heavenly authorities, angels of darkness and death, and the
countless minions of the world rulers make mortal existence a
constant struggle against imprisonment and death. In the words
of the *Ep. Pet. Phil.*, ⲥⲉⲕⲱⲧⲉ ⲛ̄ⲥⲱⲛ ⲉ₂ⲟⲧⲃ̄ⲛ (134,8-9)! But these
cosmic rulers also have their earthly accomplices; as the author of the *Apoc. Pet.* puts it, the ignorant opponents of the
Gnostics are belligerent fools, ϫⲉ ⲉⲩⲁ₂ⲉ ⲣⲁⲧⲟⲩ ⲍ̄ⲛ ⲟⲩϭⲟⲙ ⲛ̄ⲧⲉ
ⲛⲓⲁⲣⲭⲱⲛ, "because they stand through (the) power of the archons"
(VII 74,28-30). In a similar fashion, in the *1 Apoc. Jas.*
Jesus warns his brother James to flee from Jerusalem, since
this city always treats the children of light with bitterness,
and ⲟⲩⲙⲁ ⲛ̄ϣⲱⲡⲉ ⲡⲉ ⲛ̄ⲛⲟⲩⲏⲡⲉ ⲛ̄ⲛⲁⲣⲭⲱⲛ, "it is a dwelling place of a
large number of archons" (V 25,18-19). Presumably these archons
designate not simply heavenly powers, but also human powers

within the churches or synagogues of Jerusalem.[179] Thus the
struggle against the hostility of the archons may involve
politics and ecclesiology as well as cosmology; the archons are
not only the cosmic bureaucrats, the τελῶναι or heavenly tax-
collectors, but also the political and religious officials.[180]

The scene on the Jerusalem road, then, opens with an introductory question (138,10-16). After a statement referring
back to the appearance of Christ as the light (138,10-13), a
quotation formula is used to introduce the question per se.
Part of this quotation formula has been altered by the scribe
or a later reader.[181] At 138,14 the last word in the line
originally had been written as a third person masculine singular (active) circumstantial, ϥϫⲱ, but subsequently the form
was changed to a third person common plural (passive) circumstantial, ⲉⲩϫⲱ. Apparently it had been noted that the main
clause includes no speaker, and thus a passive circumstantial
construction is more appropriate. The question raised seems to
be a rhetorical question in the form of a *qal wa-homer* (*a mino-
ri ad maius*); the argument seems to proceed from Christ's participation in suffering to the even more certain suffering in
store for his followers. This question appears quite abruptly,
since it is the first specific indication of the passion of
Christ, a theme to be treated extensively in the ensuing lines.

As in the first section of the NT Acts, and also throughout the narrative framework of the *Ep. Pet. Phil.*, Peter functions as the leader and spokesman of the apostles. Hence in
response to the query that has been raised, Peter as a Gnostic
Christian speaks to the matter of the suffering of Christ and
of believers. After Peter's insightful remarks the voice of
the resurrected Christ again comes forth to amplify upon the
matter of the suffering of the believers.

Peter's speech (138,17-20) contrasts the suffering of
Christ with that of his followers. To be sure, the suffering
of Christ is assumed in both the introductory question and the
answer of Peter, although the precise nature of that suffering
is not to be addressed until Peter's longer speech is presented (139,9-140,1). Christ suffered, Peter maintains,
ⲉⲧⲃⲏⲏⲧⲛ̅, "on account of us" or "for our sakes." The Coptic

preposition ⲉⲧⲃⲉ can translate a variety of Greek prepositions,
including διά, περί, and ὑπέρ, although, as Gerard Luttikhuizen notes, in the Sahidic NT ϩⲁ usually is used for ὑπέρ and
ⲉⲧⲃⲉ for διά or περί.[182] ⲉⲧⲃⲏⲏⲧⲛ̄ reproduces a common and ancient soteriological theme: the passion of Christ has taken
place *pro nobis*, for us and for our benefit. Thus in the NT
we read that Christ suffered διά τά παραπτώματα ἡμῶν (Rom 4:25;
Sahidic: ⲉⲧⲃⲉ ⲛⲉⲛⲛⲟⲃⲉ), περί ἡμῶν (1 Thess 5:10; Sahidic:
ⲉⲧⲃⲏⲏⲧⲛ̄).[183]

The followers of Christ, on the other hand, suffer on
account of themselves. Not exempt from suffering, we must
suffer, Peter declares, ⲉⲧⲃⲉ ⲧⲉⲛⲙⲛ̄ⲧⲕⲟⲩⲓ, "on account of our
smallness." "Smallness" can be used in a number of technical
ways in Gnostic documents. In one way of thinking of smallness, it is a state to be cherished and praised, the state of
childlike simplicity and innocence. Just as Jesus can praise
children in the NT gospels (Mark 9:33-37 par. Matt 18:1-5,
Luke 9:46-48; Mark 10:13-16 par. Matt 19:13-15, Luke 18:15-17),
so also in the *Gos. Thom.* he can consider little children in an
exemplary fashion. The disciples are like children (ϩⲛ̄ϣⲏⲣⲉ
ϣⲏⲙ, *logion* 21; II 37,1), those entering the Kingdom are like
little babies at the breast (ϩⲛ̄ⲕⲟⲩⲉⲓ ⲉⲩⲭⲓ ⲉⲣⲱⲧⲉ, *logion* 22;
37,20, also 37,21-22), and a little child of seven days
(ⲟⲩⲕⲟⲩⲉⲓ ⲛ̄ϣⲏⲣⲉ ϣⲏⲙ ⲉϥϩⲛ̄ ⲥⲁϣϥ̄ ⲛ̄ϩⲟⲟⲩ, *logion* 4; 33,7-8) knows of
life; ⲡⲉⲧⲛⲁϣⲱⲡⲉ ϩⲛ̄ ⲧⲏⲩⲧⲛ̄ ⲉϥⲟ ⲛ̄ⲕⲟⲩⲉⲓ ϥⲛⲁⲥⲟⲩⲱⲛ ⲧⲙⲛ̄ⲧⲉⲣⲟ, "whoever
of you becomes a child will know the Kingdom" (*logion* 46;
41,10-12). Here and in numerous other Gnostic, Manichaean,
and Mandaean sources smallness is valued highly as being characteristic of the true Gnostics, or even of the Savior himself.[184]

In the *Ep. Pet. Phil.*, however, such a positive evaluation
is not made.[185] Here smallness is considered as characteristic
not of innocent childhood but rather of mortal existence. If
the life above is one of fullness, greatness, and glory, the
life below is one of deficiency, smallness, and humility. The
Treat. Res. makes this contrast very clear in a portion of the
Valentinian quotation inserted into its text: ⲟⲩϫⲱⲱⲣⲉ ⲡⲉⲥⲩⲥⲧⲏⲙⲁ
ⲙ̄ⲡⲡⲗⲏⲣⲱⲙⲁ ⲟⲩⲕⲟⲩⲉⲓ ⲡⲉ ⲡⲉⲛⲧⲁϩⲃⲱⲗ ⲁⲃⲁⲗ ⲁϥϣⲱⲡⲉ ⲛ̄ⲕⲟⲥⲙⲟⲥ, "Strong is

the system of the fullness, small is what broke away and became
(the) world" (I 46,34-38). In other words, the Pleroma or
fullness is potent, but the deficiency or smallness is impotent, weak, mortal. As the *Gos. Phil.* maintains, this mortal
world is not directly derived from the immortal Sophia above,
but rather from Echmoth, the Sophia of death, ⲧⲕⲟⲩⲉⲓ ⲛ̄ⲥⲟⲫⲓⲁ,
"the little Sophia" (II 60,15). For this world is little, full
of ignorance and death, a place reflecting the character of the
pathetic rulers of this place, ⲉⲍⲉⲛⲕⲟⲩⲉⲓ ⲛⲉ ⲗⲩⲱ ⲛ̄ⲁⲧⲥⲃⲱ, "for
they are small and ignorant."[186] Hence, Peter states to the
apostles, because we are entangled and imprisoned in this realm
of darkness, deficiency, and smallness, we must suffer, and
endure the hostility of the powers, until we finally attain to
fullness and light.[187]

Following Peter's speech the voice of Christ breaks forth
to expand upon the matter of the suffering of the believers
(138,21-139,4).[188] The voice comes unsolicited, although as
usual it comes when the apostles are gathered together, and it
speaks to the question just raised by the apostles. The other
experiences of revelation occur when the apostles are gathered
for prayer or worship; they call to Christ in prayer (133,17-
134,9; 137,13-17; 140,1-7) and they offer liturgical utterances
(140,13-15). In this instance, at a more informal gathering of
the apostles, the revelatory voice comes forth to indicate the
necessity of suffering. The voice emphasizes the continuity
between this revelation and previous revelatory utterances.
Previously, when Christ was embodied, it is suggested, he had
already spoken many times of the necessity of suffering. Indeed, as we scan the NT gospels, we note that various statements regarding suffering are attributed to Jesus. In the *Ep.
Pet. Phil.* reference is made to suffering of a specific sort,
and the reference seems to reflect particular NT passages. In
the so-called "Little Apocalypse" in Mark 13, along with the
parallel passages (Mark 13:9 par. Matt 10:17-18, Luke 21:12), a
statement occurs which closely parallels 138,24-27.[189] Of the
three forms of this statement, all relate nicely to the passage
in our tractate, but the versions in Matthew and Luke are
closer than that in Mark to the *Ep. Pet. Phil.* A form of ⲉⲓⲛⲉ

occurs in 138,25, and it is most likely a passive form; ⲉⲓⲛⲉ could conceivably reflect either the ἀχθήσεσθε of Matt 10:18[190] or the ἀπαγομένους[191] of Luke 21:12, since ⲉⲓⲛⲉ is attested as a Coptic translation for both ἄγειν or ἀπάγειν.[192]

The conclusion to the speech presented by the voice is, unfortunately, damaged beyond repair, but the general contents can be surmised. After having emphasized the necessity of suffering, Christ gives a warning concerning the fate or character of the one who attempts to avoid suffering. Such a person's lot will not be promising, for that person refuses to heed and follow the Savior, and participate in the struggle for salvation.[193]

Following the apparent conclusion of the comments by the revelatory voice in 139,4, the scene draws to a close with a summary statement reminiscent of the materials presented in the NT Acts. Here (139,4-9) and possibly at a later occasion (140,7-13) summary statements are given which possess a character and function quite similar to those in the Lucan Acts (2:42-47; 4:32-37; 5:12-16, 42).[194] Here, as in Acts, the summary statement seems very general in character, and provides generalizations of material very much like that in Acts. Picking up the theme of 138,9-10, before the intruding scene, the author reiterates that "they went up to Jerusalem" (139,5-6). They were filled with joy (Luke 24:52: ⲟⲩⲛⲟϭ ⲛ̄ⲣⲁϣⲉ), and returned to the city of Jerusalem (Luke 24:52; Acts 1:12). In Jerusalem they went to the temple (Luke 24:53; Acts 2:46; 3: 1-26; 5:20-21, 42), and taught about salvation in Christ's name (Luke 24:47; Acts 2:38; 3:6, 16; 4:10, 17-18, 30; 5:28, 40-41; 8:12),[195] while they also healed many (Acts 3:1-10; 5:12-16). Thus the summary statement at 139,4-9 includes a number of themes also found in the early chapters of the NT Acts, unites these themes into a general statement, and perhaps uses this statement "to divide and to connect."[196] While providing an indication of the typical activities of the apostles, the narrative summary separates the speeches and yet unites the story. It maintains the narrative framework within which the vital speeches and revelations are given.

Account of the Speech of Peter (139,9-140,1)

Following the summary statement, with little stage-setting,
Peter's speech is presented as a paradigm of the proclamation
of a devout Gnostic Christian. As the apostle par excellence,
and the guarantor of the Gnostic Christian heritage, Peter is
able to preach a fine Gnostic sermon which presents and interprets traditional kerygmatic formulae.

It is said that Peter speaks to ⲛⲉϥⲙⲁⲑⲏⲧⲏⲥ (139,10). This
term is striking for a couple of reasons. First of all, this
Greek loan word is utilized only here in the *Ep. Pet. Phil.*;
elsewhere the Greek loan word ⲁⲡⲟⲥⲧⲟⲗⲟⲥ is used. As we have
noted previously, the verb ⲡⲉϫⲁϥ is also to be found only at
139,10.15 in our tractate, and adds to the grammatical peculiarity of this section of the tractate. Secondly, the word
ⲛⲉϥⲙⲁⲑⲏⲧⲏⲥ is also of interest because of the ambiguity of its
prefixed possessive adjective: whose disciples does Peter address? It is possible that these followers are thought to be
Peter's disciples, students in the entourage of the master. It
may even be that the position of Peter as the apostolic leader
is so exalted that the other apostles are here considered as
his disciples.[197] On the other hand, it is also feasible that
these disciples are Christ's disciples and Peter's fellow
disciples.[198] It could be the case that the prefix ⲛⲉϥ- once
had "Christ" as a less ambiguous antecedent in a source, and
that the abrupt presentation of the speech in our tractate
created the present ambiguity.

Klaus Koschorke has devoted a considerable amount of attention to the speech of Peter in the *Ep. Pet. Phil.*[199] As the
title of his article indicates, he judges that the speech of
Peter in our tracate is a Gnostic version of the Pentecost
sermon of Peter. Koschorke rightly notes the similarities between our tractate and the NT Acts, and hence concludes that
the speech of Peter is a model of how Gnostic Christians ought
to participate in the spiritual struggle with the archons
(137,24-25):

> Die Archonten werden durch die "*Verkündigung in der
> Welt*" bekämpft, wozu die Apostel durch die "ver-
> heissene" Gabe des Pfingstgeistes (bzw. der "Kraft

meines Vaters") befähigt sein werden (137,22ff).
Das Modell solcher den Aposteln aufgetragenen Ver-
kündigung scheint die Pfingstpredigt des Pt. zu
sein.[200]

It is very true that spiritual power is a dominant theme in the
Ep. Pet. Phil.. This spiritual power is probably intimated in
the salvific promise (132,21-22; 137,25); it is requested in
the prayer to the Son (134,8) and the prayer for the "spirit of
understanding" (140,3-7); it is available for the strengthening
of the apostles (137,26-27), who are mandated with a blessing
of power (140,19-21) by a Christ who is eternally present
(134,17-18; 140,22-23). Thus Peter, too, delivers his exemplary sermon when ⲁϥⲙⲟⲩⲍ ⲉⲃⲟⲗ ⲍ̄ⲛ ⲟⲩⲡⲛ̄ⲁ̄ ⲉϥⲟⲩⲁⲁⲃ,[201] just as in
the NT Acts Peter can speak when πλησθεὶς πνεύματος ἁγίου (4:8;
Sahidic: ⲁϥⲙⲟⲩⲍ ⲉⲃⲟⲗ ⲍ̄ⲛ̄ ⲡⲉⲡⲛ̄ⲁ̄ ⲉⲧⲟⲩⲁⲁⲃ).[202]

But it is not completely accurate to speak of the speech
of Peter in the *Ep. Pet. Phil.* as a Pentecost sermon in the
Lucan sense. It is an exemplary, spirit-filled sermon, to be
sure, but it functions in our tractate in a different fashion
from the Pentecost sermon of Acts 2. It occurs before the general apostolic group is filled with holy spirit (140,9); indeed, the fact that here Peter is already spirit-filled[203]
illustrates that the "Pentecost," the outpouring of holy spirit,
in the *Ep. Pet. Phil.* is interpreted in a different manner from
the Lucan Pentecost. Spiritual power, holy spirit, a spirit of
understanding, is available to the followers of Christ when they
request and appropriate spiritual power. In our tractate the
"Pentecost" event is portrayed less as the one great impartation
of the Spirit on the day designated for the Feast of Weeks, as
in Acts 2, than as the possession of spiritual power and dis-
cernment whenever the followers of Christ have need of it.

The sermon of Peter in the *Ep. Pet. Phil.* is an example of
a Gnostic Christian sermon preached by one who has spiritual
power and insight. Just as Peter can deliver several exemplary
speeches in the NT Acts,[204] speeches which Luke often presents
as sermons which show "how the gospel is preached and ought to be
preached,"[205] so also in the *Ep. Pet. Phil.* Peter preaches a
sermon which functions as a paradigm for the proclamation of

Gnostic Christian teachings. After a few introductory remarks
(139,11-13), Peter proceeds to present the sermon per se, a
sermon with three parts: the citation of a traditional credo
(139,15-21), the interpretation of that credo (139,21-28), and
a concluding exhortation (139,28-140,1). The introductory remarks again establish the continuity between the preaching of
the Gnostic Christian Peter and the revelation of the earthly
Jesus. When Jesus was embodied, when he descended to the
cosmos, he showed the truth to his followers. This revelatory
life of the heavenly Christ who came down--and suffered--is the
basis for the sermon Peter is about to preach. Peter closes
his introductory remarks with an appeal to the apostles for
their attention.[206] This appeal utilizes the vocative (ⲚⲀⲤⲚⲎⲨ),
which also introduces the second and third parts of the sermon
(139,21.28), and which is similar to the brotherly terms of
address in the speeches of Acts (ἄνδρες ἀδελφοί, 1:16; 2:29;
15:7; ἀδελφοί, 3:17; 6:3). With this appeal for attention the
body of the sermon may begin.

After the sermon has been formally introduced with an indication of its spirit-filled character and with a quotation
formula, Peter cites the traditional credo upon which his sermon focuses. As at 133,27, Jesus is referred to as an illuminator (ⲠⲈⲚⲪⲰⲤⲦⲎⲢ), the radiant light which descended and was
crucified. The individual items in the Christological credo
are all familiar from early Christian literature: "he [wore] a
crown of thorns" (Matt 27:29; John 19:2; also Mark 15:17; *Gos.
Pet.* 3.8; particularly John 19:5: φορῶν[207] τὸν ἀκάνθινον στέφα-
νον); "he put [on] a purple robe"[208] (Mark 15:17, 20; *Gos. Pet.*
3.7; also Matt 27:28; perhaps Heb 9:19; *Barn.* 7.8-8.1; especially John 19:2, also 5: φορῶν...τὸ πορφυροῦν ἱμάτιον); "he was
[crucified] upon a cross"[209] (Acts 5:30 and 10:39: κρεμάσαντες
ἐπὶ ξύλου);[210] "he was buried in a tomb" (Mark 15:46; Matt 27:
60; Luke 23:53; John 19:41-42; Acts 13:29; also 1 Cor 15:4); "he
rose[211] from the dead" (Mark 9:9; Matt 17:9; John 2:22; 20:9;
21:14; Acts 3:15; 4:10; 10:41; 13:30, 34; 17:3, 31; 1 Cor 15:4,
12, 20).[212] Such items as these were combined very early in
Christian circles to form kerygmatic formulae testifying to the
passion of Christ. Already in the NT we can see such credos in

1 Cor 15:3-5, a pre-Pauline formulation which Paul has received
from the church tradition and passes on to his readers, and in
several passages in Acts (for example 2:22-24; 3:13-15; 5:30-31;
10:36-42), where Luke has Peter and the apostles bear witness
to the passion and resurrection of Christ. The credo in the
Ep. Pet. Phil. also affirms the passion and resurrection of
Christ, and is a formulation which reflects the common affirmation of the Great Church and these Gnostic Christians.

    The structure of this credo deserves special mention.
According to Luttikhuizen, the credo "is rather unskilfully
interpolated with the sentence" which includes the formulae on
the crown of thorns and the purple robe.[213] "This interpola-
tion," Luttikhuizen continues, "focuses the attention on the
passion of Jesus."[214] While we do not deny the emphasis upon
the passion of Jesus, it does seem that Luttikhuizen's interpretation may betray a misunderstanding of the structure of the
credo. In our interpretation the citation of the traditional
kerygmatic formulae opens with a twofold formula which introduces the credo and may show the hand of a Gnostic Christian
editor. Jesus is termed ⲡⲉⲛⲫⲱⲥⲧⲏⲣ; and his descent, already
mentioned in the introductory remarks at 139,13, is mentioned
once again. Such a reference to the descent of the Savior in
the content of his suffering is not unusual, since his descent
and incarnation are key elements in his suffering, particularly
in Gnostic Christological systems. Furthermore, the initial
reference to his crucifixion (139,16) seems to be of an introductory sort, intended to provide, in a word, a comprehensive
reference to the passion of Christ. Following this introductory formula five terse formulae are listed as witnesses to
specific moments in the passion and resurrection of Christ.
These five formulae follow in a regular and logical order; the
first two of these five formulae are listed in the same order
as John 19, an order which diverges from that of Mark, Matthew,
and the *Gos. Pet.* The punctuation mark at 139,17 comes as
something of a surprise, and could lead one to postulate that
the statement concerning the crown of thorns may have been
added as an additional formula for the credo. On the other
hand, such a conclusion on the basis of an ambiguous point of
punctuation is probably too subtle.

Opening with the vocative ⲛⲁⲥⲛⲏⲩ, the second part of the
sermon provides a Gnostic Christian interpretation of the credo
that has just been affirmed. The various formulae in this
credo are not considered individually; rather, Jesus' suffering
is addressed in a more general manner, as a life of suffering
while he was embodied. Thus Peter begins by contrasting Jesus'
sufferings and his followers'; this contrast is emphasized
syntactically by means of a fine chiasm.[215] Peter maintains
that "Jesus is a stranger to this suffering" (139,21-22). As
the cosmic powers are strangers to the Father (136,2-3), so
also Jesus is a stranger to suffering.

Elsewhere in Gnostic literature the Gnostic redeemer or believer can also be depicted as a stranger, a foreigner, an alien
in this world.[216] Such a person's plight is essentially that of
the prince in the "Hymn of the Pearl"; he found himself in
worldly Egypt, μόνος δὲ ὢν ἐξενιζόμην τὸ σχῆμα καὶ τοῖς ἐμοῖς
ἀλλότριος ἐφαινόμην. In order to cope in this worldly environment, in order to obtain the pearl, he dressed up in a disguise:
ἐνεδυσάμην δὲ αὐτῶν τὰ φορήματα, ἵνα μὴ ξενίζωμαι (109). Thus also
in the *Treat. Seth*, as we have already seen, the heavenly Christ
presents himself as a stranger to the lower realms (VII 52,8-10).

In the *Ep. Pet. Phil.* Jesus is also presented as a stranger,
a stranger to suffering. Jesus has come down from above, and in
no way was he previously involved with suffering. Indeed, suffering is as foreign to the essence of Jesus as darkness is
foreign to light and as deficiency is foreign to fullness. We
humans, on the other hand, endure suffering for good reason; we
have been born, have fallen into a corruptible world, and are
entangled in the web of evil that has come into being on account
of "the transgression of the mother" (139,23), the fall of the
mother as portrayed by the revelatory voice of the risen Christ
earlier in the tractate (135,8-136,15).[217] We humans have been
cast into deficiency, mortality, and corruptibility, and have
been detained in this cosmic dungeon--hence for us suffering is
inevitable as long as we are bound with the fetters of this
world.

Yet the *Ep. Pet. Phil.* also wishes to proclaim that Jesus
did suffer for humans. Just as he came down into a body for the

sake of the heavenly seed (136,17-18), and suffered for us
(138,18), so also has he accomplished everything "in a likeness
to us" (139,25). Although this phrase "in a likeness to us" is
somewhat obscure and difficult to understand, it is clear that
the tractate means to highlight the similarity between the suffering of Christ and human sufferings. It may even be that
this phrase intends to denote a similarity which approaches a
virtual identity between the experiences of Christ and human
experiences, so that ⲕⲁⲧⲁ ⲟⲩⲉⲓⲛⲉ resembles ⲕⲁⲧⲁ ⲑⲉ in meaning.[218]
We can assume that a Greek *Vorlage* underlies ⲕⲁⲧⲁ ⲟⲩⲉⲓⲛⲉ, and
the original Greek could very well have been καθ' ὁμοίωμα or
καθ' ὁμοίωσιν.[219] A similar expression occurs in Ignatius'
Trall. where the author affirms that God the Father raised
Christ from the dead just as (κατὰ τὸ ὁμοίωμα) he also will
raise believers (9.2).[220] καθ' ὁμοίωσιν, on the other hand, is
used in the Greek of Gen 1:26, where God creates man according
to the image and likeness of God, that is, similar to God in
important ways. Not surprisingly, this passage is cited frequently in early Christian literature,[221] and the phrase ⲕⲁⲧⲁ
ⲛ̄ⲛⲉⲓⲛⲉ is to be found, in various forms, in such Gnostic documents as the *Ap. John* (II 15,3; also 12,34; 15,10; 19,31; 22,35),
where the creation and formation of a world meant to be similar
to a heavenly prototype is under discussion--though, as the *Ep.
Pet. Phil.* notes, this creation is actually a dissimilarity, a
misrepresentation (ⲟⲩⲙ̄ⲛ̄ⲧⲁⲧⲉⲓⲛⲉ, 136,14), because the creators
are blind and impotent.[222] Elsewhere in the *Ap. John* ⲕⲁⲧⲁ ⲛⲓⲛⲉ
can be used in a different context; the angels who cavorted
with the daughters of men (Gen 6:1-4) changed themselves to
resemble (ⲕⲁⲧⲁ ⲛⲓⲛⲉ, 29,27) the husbands of those women, and
produced offspring from the darkness, like (ⲕⲁⲧⲁ ⲛⲉⲓⲛⲉ, 30,8-9)
their spirit of darkness.

The use of the phrase ⲕⲁⲧⲁ ⲟⲩⲉⲓⲛⲉ in the *Ep. Pet. Phil.*,
then, like similar phrases found in other documents, emphasizes
the similarity between Christ's experiences in the world and
those of his followers. As Peter proclaims to the disciples,
Christ did everything like us. He came into the world embodied,
like us. He allowed himself to descend and endure the suffering
of incarnation, to live among mortals--even though he was

actually not a mortal person. He, the stranger to suffering, suffered like us--and he did this for us, for "the seed that had fallen away" (136,18). We are fallen, imprisoned, suffering; and for this reason (ⲉⲧⲃⲉ ⲡⲁⲓ̈, 139,24) our illuminator Jesus came down to his own to lead us to fullness, life, and light. Hence he can be termed ⲡⲓⲁⲣⲭⲏⲅⲟⲥ ⲛ̅ⲧⲉ ⲡⲉⲛⲱⲛ̅ⲍ̅ (139,27-28) and ⲡⲁⲣⲭⲏⲅⲟⲥ ⲛ̅[ⲧⲉ ⲡⲉ]ⲛⲙ̅ⲧⲟ[ⲛ] (140,4). Like the Peter of the NT Acts, who can proclaim Christ as ὁ ἀρχηγὸς τῆς ζωῆς (3:15),[223] the Gnostic Christian Peter of the *Ep. Pet. Phil*. also preaches that Jesus is "the author of our life." For Jesus is the leader of the restoration of the light, and it is those who hearken to him who will receive their inheritance (136,27-28), and be restored from deficiency to fullness (137,2-4) and life (139, 28). Jesus, the fullness and the illuminator, "the Son of the immeasurable glory of the Father" (139,26),[224] was not implicated in the fall of the mother; but because he descended to this world and voluntarily suffered, his people also can become fullness and illuminators like him.

Thus the *Ep. Pet. Phil*. proclaims a heavenly Jesus whose sufferings are still taken seriously. On the one hand, Jesus is the heavenly light, the fullness, the illuminator, the "Son of immortality" (134,4-5) who descends to earth in disguise (136,19), goes unrecognized (136,20-21), and is mistaken for a mortal person (136,21-22)--indeed, he is a stranger to suffering. On the other hand, Jesus comes in the body, lives like a human being, and endures his passion and death--indeed, he suffers for his people. The *Ep. Pet. Phil*. presents a paradoxical portrait of a Jesus who is both invulnerable and vulnerable, both immortal and dying, a Jesus whose body is both a mortal disguise and a body of death. Like the *Gos. Truth*,[225] the *Ep. Pet. Phil*. maintains a kerygmatic tension in its Christology. Here there is no thought of the laughing Jesus whose body is illusory and who suffers and dies only in appearance;[226] but yet Jesus' divinity is uncompromised, and Jesus is proclaimed as the immortal light and heavenly fullness. The Christological tension is allowed to remain, and the result is a proclamation with power and mystery, which still manages to keep its feet on the ground. For the Gnostic Christians of the *Ep. Pet. Phil*., like

Christ, have their true home and identity in the light above,
yet their place and task is on the earth, as "illuminators in
the midst of mortal people" (137,8-9).

The third and final part of the sermon of Peter is a concluding exhortation, which unfortunately is poorly preserved.
Also beginning with the vocative, this exhortation functions as
a call to response and action. The exhortation includes en-
couragement to pay no heed to "these lawless ones" (139,29-30).
The word ἄνομος is used frequently in early Christian literature, and may be applied to unjust judges, Gentiles without the
law, wicked people, and even the lawless one of the last days.[227]
The plural form is used without a noun in Acts 2:23 to describe
those who killed Jesus, in *Mart. Pol.* 16.1 to depict those responsible for the execution of Polycarp, in Mark 15:28 and Luke
22:37 to cite Isa 53:12. In the *Ep. Pet. Phil.* it is difficult
to ascertain precisely who the "lawless ones" are. Presumably
they could include the archons as well as the hostile collabor-
ators of the archons on the earth, the opponents afflicting the
Gnostic Christians. Thus the concluding exhortation seems to
be a call to continue the struggle in which Jesus also partici-
pated, the struggle against darkness and death and toward light
and life. Hence, Peter may exhort, let us not bow to the will
and pleasure of the wicked ones, but rather follow the light![228]

Account of the Final Meetings of the Apostles (140,1-27)

Following the sermon of Peter, the *Ep. Pet. Phil.* provides
accounts of two final meetings of the apostles, after which
they are sent forth on their mission. The first of these meetings focuses upon the reception of the spirit (140,1-13), the
second upon the final commission (140,13-23). Thus are the
apostles qualified for their task, the preaching of the gospel
with power.

The account of the first of these two meetings opens with
a familiar theme, the gathering of the apostles. As we have
already seen, this theme occurs frequently in the tractate: in
Peter's letter concerning the Lord's command (132,19; 133,3.7),
in the account of Peter gathering the other apostles

(133,12-13.18) in a customary gathering place (133,15-16), in
the advice of the resurrected Christ on strategy against the
archons (137,24), possibly in the informal meeting on the Jerusalem road (138,11-139,4), implicitly in the sermon of Peter to
the disciples (139,9-140,1), as well as in the accounts of the
final meetings of the apostles (140,2.13-14). More than mere
indications of seams or doublets[229]--though seams and doublets
may be observed in our tractate--the gatherings and dispersings
function for the author of the tractate as a model for the life
of Gnostic Christians. Like the apostles, these Gnostic Christians also gather for worship and retreat, so that they might
obtain revelatory guidance from the Lord and power for living.
It is important to note the liturgical items which are mentioned in connection with the apostolic gatherings, and which
seem to reflect the worship of the Gnostic Christian group behind the *Ep. Pet. Phil.*: the kneeling posture (133,19-20), the
two initial prayers (133,21-134,1; 134,3-9) and later prayer of
Peter (140,3-7), the sermon of Peter, and the liturgical "Amen"
(140,15). Like the apostles, those Gnostic Christians also
disperse to teach and preach the gospel, to function as lights
in the darkness, to fight against the cosmic powers with spiritual power and mighty deeds. They too must go forth "in the
power of Jesus, in peace" (140,27).

    Peter offers a prayer for ογπ︤π︦λ︥ ν̄τε ογєπιϲτнмн (140,5-6).[230]
The first of the two meetings thus seems to be our author's
"Pentecost" account, an account which resembles the Lucan account in some important ways but also shows crucial differences.
As in the Lucan account, here Peter functions in a central role,
Christ is termed the ἀρχηγός, and the empowering πνεῦμα, a
πνεῦμα ἅγιον, enables the apostles to do marvelous things and
to preach. Here, however, in contrast to the Lucan Pentecost,
the spirit is specified as a πνεῦμα ἐπιστήμης, so that knowledge, understanding, and insight are of particular concern.
Furthermore, the little "Pentecost" in the *Ep. Pet. Phil.* seems
to be accompanied by an appearance of the resurrected Christ
(140,8), like the "Pentecost" of John 20:19-23, where the disciples
are happy, ἰδόντες τὸν κύριον (20:20), who greets them with a
greeting of peace, commissions them, and imparts πνεῦμα ἅγιον

to them (20:22). Once again, the "Pentecost" of our tractate
is to be seen in the context of the previous account of apostolic preaching and healing in the summary statement of 139,
4-9, where it may be implied that the apostles already have
spiritual power. In addition, Peter too has previously been
described as filled with holy spirit (139,14) before the de-
livery of the sermon. Thus the *Ep. Pet. Phil.* provides another
account of the acquisition of the spirit, the reception of
spiritual power. Just as the Lucan and Johannine accounts show
the peculiar interests of their authors, so also the present
account illustrates the special concerns of this author: a
knowledge of salvation, the power to do mighty things, and the
preaching of the gospel.

The second and final meeting of the apostles is begun with
the liturgical "Amen." It is said that the apostles gathered
together, greeted (ⲁⲩⲡⲁⲥⲡⲁⲍⲉ) each other, and utilized this
acclamation; hence this acclamation probably refers to the use
of "Amen" in Christian worship, where the "Amen" could function
as an acclamation of response to prayer and thanksgiving, and
as an element within a prayer or doxology. Usually "Amen"
comes at the conclusion of such prayers or doxologies, though
in Rev 7:12 it occurs at both the beginning and the end, and
serves as a response to the doxological statement of 7:10.
ἀμήν is, of course, merely a transliteration of the Hebrew אָמֵן,
"it is sure," and its use among Christians is derived from its
use within Judaism. The meaning of this Hebrew utterance is
retained within the Greek-speaking world, so that ἀμήν can be
utilized before the sayings of Jesus as a witness to their
reliability. In fact, the "Amen" can even be hypostasized, so
that in Rev 3:14 Christ seems to be called ὁ ἀμήν, and in some
Gnostic documents the heavenly powers can be termed "the
Amens."[231]

In the *Ep. Pet. Phil.* the apostles say "Amen," and in
answer to this liturgical statement of verification the resurrected Christ appears to them once again to give them a final
blessing and commission. The greeting, a blessing of peace, is
extended[232] not only to the apostles as they are about to go
forth, but also to "everyone who believes in my name"

(140,18-19). Hence the believing readers of the *Ep. Pet. Phil.*
are explicitly included in the blessing. The apostles go forth
with the blessing of Jesus, and especially the blessing of
power (140,21). They are not to fear; as Jesus has already
promised at 134,17-18, he will be with them for ever. Thus, as
in the NT gospels and Acts,[233] the resurrected Christ of the
Ep. Pet. Phil. sends the apostles forth with his blessing.

Consequently the apostles part to preach (140,23-27). It
is said that they went out ⲉ₂ⲣⲁ̈ⲓ ⲉⲡⲓ⟨ⲧⲟⲟⲩ ⲛ̄ⳝⲁ̅ⲭⲉ, literally
"into four words," here translated "with four messages" (140,
25). It is extremely tempting to emend the text here,[234] since
the text as transmitted is somewhat obscure, to say the least.
Within this context we might rather expect a reference to the
four directions, perhaps ⲡⲓ⟨ⲧⲟⲟⲩ ⲛ̄ⲥⲁ.[235] After all, such references to a Christian mission to the four directions, that is,
to the whole world, are very common in early Christian literature. We need only think of the *Acts of Thomas* 28, where it is
said that the gospel is being proclaimed εἰς τὰ τέσσαρα κλίματα
τῆς οἰκουμένης; or the *Epistula Apostolorum* 30, where the
apostles are commissioned by the risen Christ to go and preach
to the East, West, North, and South; or the gospel which the
heretics "in quattuor tomos secantes librum quattuor angulorum
et cardinum mundi appellarunt," mentioned by Bishop Maruta of
Maiperkat in his *De sancta synodo Nicaena*;[236] or the *Pistis
Sophia*, which closes with the apostles going out by threes to
preach the gospel in the four directions, in the whole world.
Yet it may still be possible to interpret the present text of
the *Ep. Pet. Phil.* in an understandable manner.[237] For, as
Irenaeus proposes, the concept of four directions may be related to that of four gospels; since there are τέσσαρα κλίματα
τοῦ κόσμου ἐν ᾧ ἐσμὲν εἰσί, and the church is all over the
earth, and the gospel is the στύλος of the church, therefore it
is concluded that τέσσαρας ἔχειν αὐτὴν στύλους, that is, the
fourfold gospel (*Adv. Haer.* 3.11.8). While this is certainly a
curious bit of argumentation for four gospels, such an argument
may provide added meaning for the text transmitted in the *Ep.
Pet. Phil.* The gospel is to be preached in the whole world,
to be sure; but that task may be depicted as one involving four

messages--perhaps the four gospels--for the four regions of
the world.

Finally, the apostles depart from their gathering in order
to proclaim the gospel. The tractate thus closes like the
Soph. Jes. Chr., the *Gos. Mary*, and the *Pistis Sophia*, on a
positive note of challenge: the departure of the apostles to
preach.[238] They, like the Gnostic Christians of the *Ep. Pet.
Phil.*, have a task in the world. And they, like the Gnostic
Christians, have the spiritual power and peace of Jesus with
them.

CHAPTER IV

[1]The title of a tractate in the Nag Hammadi library may be indicated by means of an *incipit*, a subscription, a superscription, or several combinations of these indicators. Sometimes multiple titles are given. At other times tractates have been transcribed or transmitted without titles, and the modern title has been supplied by means of some relevant phrase or the general contents of the tractate, while in a few instances an untitled tractate was found to be a Coptic translation of a previously known document. It may be suggested, in general, that a title implied in an *incipit* could be earlier than a title added in a subscribed or superscribed fashion. On the question of titles see Robinson, "The Coptic Gnostic Library Today," 383-401; idem, "*Logoi Sophon*: on the *Gattung* of Q," esp. pp. 91-92 in *The Future of Our Religious Past* (ed. J. Robinson; New York: Harper & Row, 1971); Johannes Munck, "Evangelium Veritatis and Greek Usage as to Book Titles," *ST* 17 (1963) 133-38; Krause and Labib, *Die drei Versionen*, 28-29; idem, *Gnostische und hermetische Schriften*, 16-21.

[2]For a discussion of this genre of literature within early Christianity, see William G. Doty, *Letters in Primitive Christianity* (Guides to Biblical Scholarship, NT Series; Philadelphia: Fortress, 1973).

[3]On the question of the interpretation of ⲣⲁϣⲉ at III 70,2 (ⲭⲁⲓⲣⲉ[ⲧⲉ] at V 1,3), see Paulinus Bellet, "The Colophon of the *Gospel of the Egyptians*: Concessus and Macarius of Nag Hammadi," *Nag Hammadi and Gnosis*, 56-59, esp. n. 16.

[4]Optatus of Milevis, *De schismate Donatistarum* 1.5: "Cum in epistula Petri apostoli legerimus, 'Nolite per opinionem judicare fratres vestros,'" "Since in the Letter of Peter the Apostle we have read, 'Refrain from judging your brothers through prejudice.'" See Puech, "Les nouveaux écrits," 117 n. 4; Hennecke-Schneemelcher, 2.91; also compare this passage with Jas 2:1 and 4:11.

[5]The *Epistula Petri* and *Contestatio* have been analyzed as elements within the so-called *Kerygmata Petrou*. See especially Georg Strecker, *Das Judenchristentum in den Pseudoklementinen* (Berlin: Akademie Verlag, 1958); "The Kerygmata Petrou," Hennecke-Schneemelcher, 2.102-27; "On the Problem of Jewish Christianity," in Walter Bauer, *Orthodoxy and Heresy in Earliest Christianity* (Philadelphia: Fortress, 1971) 241-85. After the closing of the *Epistula*, the *Contestatio* opens as follows: Ἀναγνοὺς οὖν ὁ Ἰάκωβος τὴν ἐπιστολὴν μετεκαλέσατο τοὺς πρεσβυτέρους καὶ αὐτοῖς ἀναγνοὺς, he spoke to the assembled group about the kerygmatic materials of Peter; this transition may be compared with 133,8-11 in our tractate.

[6]See Doty, *Letters in Primitive Christianity*, 65-81;
Edgar J. Goodspeed, *A History of Early Christian Literature*
(rev. and enlarged by R. M. Grant; Chicago: University of
Chicago, 1966) 7-29. Grant (p. 29) mistakenly refers to our
tractate as "a letter of Peter and Philip." For a similarly
mistaken reference, see Roland K. Harrison (*Archaeology of the
New Testament* [New York: Association, 1964] 84) where he mentions "the *Epistle of Philip to Peter*."

[7]See the discussion above, pp. 113-18; additional discussion and analysis in Kurt Rudolph, "Der gnostische 'Dialog'
als literarisches Genus," pp. 85-107 in *Probleme der koptischen
Literatur* (Wissenschaftliche Beiträge, K2; Halle-Wittenberg:
Martin-Luther-Universität, 1968); also Robinson, "*Logoi Sophon*,"
96-100.

[8]χ: P. Merton 86; χα: P. Oxy. 120; χαι: P. Oxy. 62; χαιρ:
P. Oxy. 61 (additional data on file in the Nag Hammadi Archive,
Institute for Antiquity and Christianity). On the itacism, see
above, p. 69.

[9]See Bellet, "The Colophon," 57-59 n. 16; also Jack T.
Sanders, "The Transition from Opening Epistolary Thanksgiving
to Body in the Letters of the Pauline Corpus," *JBL* 81 (1962)
348-57.

[10]Letters lacking closing elements are known, of course,
and can be observed even in the NT. The letter of James has a
typical epistolary opening, but no conclusion; James, however,
is less a true letter than a paraenetical tractate with an
epistolary veneer. Of the two private or semi-private letters
in Acts (15:23-29; 23:26-30), the former utilizes the final
greeting ἔρρωσθε, while the latter does not include a final
greeting in P[74], B, A, et al. (but ἔρρωσο is used in א and
other manuscripts, and ἔρρωσθε is found in H, P, and a few
other sources).

[11]Peter and Philip both figure importantly in Gnostic
literature. Peter is particularly prominent, and can function
as an anti-Gnostic sexist, a subordinate disciple, or--as in
the *Ep. Pet. Phil.*--an enlightened Gnostic teacher. See
Hennecke-Schneemelcher, 1.271-78; 2.45-50, 57-58; Perkins,
"Peter in Gnostic Revelation."

[12]Not only is such an endearing description appropriate
for an epistolary opening (Acts 15:23; Rom 1:7; 2 Cor 1:1; Col
1:1-2; 2 Tim 1:2; Phlm 1; 3 John 1); Philip also can be described elsewhere in such a manner (see *Pistis Sophia* 44).
On ἀδελφός, "spiritual brother," a very common term within
Christianity, see Hans F. von Soden, "ἀδελφός κ.τ.λ.," *TDNT*,
1.145-46.

[13]See Karl H. Rengstorf, "ἀπόστολος," *TDNT*, 1.420-24;
Kirsopp Lake, "The Twelve and the Apostles," pp. 37-59 (esp. 51)
in *The Beginnings of Christianity*. Part I: *The Acts of the
Apostles*, vol. 5 (ed. F. J. Foakes Jackson and K. Lake; London:
Macmillan, 1920-33).

[14] See Eusebius, *Historia Ecclesiastica* 3.31.3; Clement, *Stromateis* III.6 §52.4-5; in general, H. H. Platz, "Philip," *IDB*, 3.785, where additional sources are cited.

[15] On "God" as a title of Jesus, see (with Bethge) John 20:28; Ign. *Rom.* 3.3; *Smyrn.* 1.1; also note the occurrence of this title in the apocryphal Acts of the Apostles, passim.

[16] Note the parallel at 137,23-25. On teaching and preaching closely linked together, note, with Edmund W. Fisher ("The Letter of Peter to Philip and Its Relationship to New Testament Apocrypha" [seminar paper, Claremont Graduate School, 1967] 16-18), that the couplet "teach and preach" is also found frequently in the *Epistula Apostolorum* (for example, chaps. 19, 23, 30, 31, and 46). On the use of ἐπαγγελία in Luke-Acts and elsewhere, see Hans Conzelmann, *The Theology of St. Luke* (New York: Harper & Row, 1960) 220-21; also Julius Schniewind and Gerhard Friedrich, "ἐπαγγέλλω κ.τ.λ.," *TDNT*, 2.581-82.

[17] E. Haenchen, *The Acts of the Apostles* (Philadelphia: Westminster, 1971) 90-112.

[18] Ibid., 103.

[19] Ibid., 99.

[20] On pre-Pauline Hellenistic Christianity, and the Hellenists in Acts, see Haenchen, *The Acts of the Apostles*, 259-69; Hans Conzelmann, *History of Primitive Christianity* (Nashville: Abingdon, 1973) 56-59, 68-77; Henry J. Cadbury, "The Hellenists," pp. 59-74 in *The Beginnings of Christianity*, vol. 5; Walter Schmithals, *Paul and James* (SBT 46; London: SCM, 1965) 16-37; Charles H. Scobie, "The Origins and Development of Samaritan Christianity," *NTS* 19 (1972-73) 390-414; Marcel Simon, *St. Stephen and the Hellenists in the Primitive Church* (London: Longmans, Green, 1958).

[21] We might speculate that the rivalry between Peter and Philip in the *Ep. Pet. Phil.* could reflect the concern of certain Gnostic Christians for the status of these two apostles. Then, by the willing submission of Philip to Peter, the author of our tractate could mean to suggest that the Gnostic Christian advocates of Philip likewise should acknowledge the supreme authority of Peter, and join his advocates in following Peter as the chief apostle. Also see Ménard (7-8) on "l'impression d'un rapprochement entre le groupe de Pierre et celui de Philippe," and "l'Unité originelle."

[22] Bethge, col. 162. See also Ménard (5-6), where he cautiously presents a slightly different "hypothèse de travail": "Notre opuscule appartiendrait à des Actes apocryphes des Apôtres dont ne nous aurait été conservé au début qu'un fragment de Lettre suivi d'un traité dogmatique. On pourrait alors donner comme titre à l'ensemble: Fragment apocryphe des Actes des Apôtres...."

[23]Bethge, col. 162. Note may also be taken of the paper of François Bovon, "Gnostic Traditions in Certain Unpublished Fragments of the Apocryphal Acts of Philip?" presented at the International Conference on Gnosticism, Yale University, 29 March 1978. Unfortunately, a comparative study of the *Acts of Philip*, and the possible gnosticizing motifs to be found there, lies beyond the scope of our analysis.

[24]In the *Ep. Pet. Phil.*, ⲧⲟⲧⲉ is nearly always a signal for a new beginning of some sort: a new paragraph, a new action, a new scene. In addition to this passage, see also 133,17-18; 134,9.18; 135,3; 137,13.17; 138,3.7.21; 140,7.15.23. The only exception is the use of ⲧⲟⲧⲉ at 137,7-8, where ⲧⲟⲧⲉ is utilized emphatically to introduce the apodosis of the sentence.

[25]Luke 24:49; Acts 1:4, and esp. 1:6 (Οἱ μὲν οὖν συνελθόν-τες; Sahidic: ⲛ̄ⲧⲟⲟⲩ ϭⲉ ⲁⲩⲥⲱⲟⲩⲍ).

[26]On the Mount of Olives as a customary gathering place for Christ and the disciples, see the references in BAG, s.v. "ἐλαία," "ἐλαιών;" note esp. Luke 22:39 (κατὰ τὸ ἔθος!), perhaps also John 18:2.

[27]Sahidic: ⲉⲃⲟⲗ ⲍ̄ⲙ̄ ⲡⲧⲟⲟⲩ ⲉϣⲁⲩⲙⲟⲩⲧⲉ ⲉⲣⲟϥ ϫⲉ ⲡⲧⲟⲟⲩ ⲛ̄ⲛ̄ϫⲟⲉⲓⲧ; Bohairic uses merely ϫⲉ ⲫⲁⲛⲓⲭⲱⲓⲧ, like our text. In the Greek NT the name is usually given with a form of ὄρος; but in three instances a form of ἐλαιών is used without a titular ὄρος, and all three occurrences are in Luke-Acts (Luke 19:29; 21:37; Acts 1:12).

[28]See, for example, the *Gospel of Bartholomew* 4.1-12; *Acts of John* 97 and following.

[29]See, for instance, the Ethiopic *Apoc. Pet.* 1; 15-17; the Greek *Apocalypse of Paul* 51.

[30]For a brief phenomenological survey of the sacred mountain, see Mircea Eliade, *Patterns in Comparative Religion* (New York: New American Library, 1963) 99-102.

[31]See Werner Foerster, "ὄρος," *TDNT*, 5.483-87.

[32]Passing reference should also be made to the preservation of revelatory materials upon mountains. See the *Gos. Eg.* III 68,1-5 and IV 80,15-19; *Allogenes* XI 68,20-23.

[33]Cp., for example, *Gos. Mary* BG 8,12, where Christ is termed ⲡⲙⲁⲕⲁⲣⲓⲟⲥ.

[34]At 136,13 ⲥⲱⲙⲁ is utilized with the plural indefinite article, but the construction is quite different.

[35]See BAG, s.v. "σῶμα" 1b; Eduard Schweizer, "σῶμα κ.τ.λ.," *TDNT*, 7.1060-62.

[36]See Heinrich Schlier, "γόνυ," *TDNT*, 1.738-40; Heinrich Greeven, "προσκυνέω," *TDNT*, 6.758-66.

[37]It may also be the case that the description is merely
traditional, and that the verb has outlived the custom. We
judge, however, that the description of genuflection could
easily function as one of several liturgical elements reflecting the communal worship of the Christian Gnostic group of the
Ep. Pet. Phil.

[38]Such descriptive clauses, which are Coptic translations
of Greek participial or relative clauses, have been analyzed
as characteristic of hymns. See Eduard Norden, *Agnostos Theos*
(Leipzig: Teubner, 1913) esp. 166-76, 201-39, also 240-76.

[39]On the petition of the first prayer, cp. the *Dial. Sav.*
III 121,5-7: ϲⲱⲧⲙ̄ ⲉⲣⲟⲛ ⲡⲉⲓⲱⲧ ⲕⲁⲧⲁ ⲑⲉ ⲛ̄ⲧⲁⲕⲥⲱⲧⲙ̄ ⲉⲡⲉⲕⲙⲟⲛⲟⲅⲉⲛⲏⲥ
ⲛ̄ϣⲏⲣⲉ, "Hear us, Father, just as you have heard your only
begotten Son."

[40]A lucid translation and precise understanding of the
ⲉⲡⲓⲇⲏ clause (134,8-9) is difficult to achieve. Either the
third plural subject of ⲕⲱⲧⲉ is indefinite here, perhaps because of its original use in another context, or a passive
construction is intended.

[41]Also note, with Bethge, Jas 1:17, where God is described
as ὁ πατὴρ τῶν φώτων.

[42]See the brief summation in Hans Conzelmann, "φῶς κ.τ.λ.,"
TDNT, 9.327-43.

[43]*Epistula Apostolorum* 19, trans. from the Ethiopic by
Hugo Duensing ("Epistula Apostolorum," Hennecke-Schneemelcher,
1.203).

[44]ⲁⲫⲑⲁⲣⲥⲓⲁ and ⲁⲫⲑⲁⲣⲧⲟⲥ are used in the Codex III version
of the *Gos. Eg.* but not the Codex IV version. The latter prefers a form of the Coptic ⲁⲧⲭⲱϩⲙ̄ rather than a Greek loan word.
See Böhlig and Wisse, *The Gospel of the Egyptians*, 11-17.

[45]ⲁⲗⲟⲩ is attested as translating παῖς, particularly in
Bohairic; see Crum, 5a.

[46]Also cp. Acts 3:13, 26; *1 Clem.* 59.2-4; *Mart. Pol.*
14.1-3; 20.2; *Diogn.* 8.9-11; 9.1.

[47]Cp. Walther Zimmerli and Joachim Jeremias, "παῖς θεοῦ,"
TDNT, 5.654-717, esp. 700-12; also Richard F. Zehnle, *Peter's
Pentecost Discourse* (SBLMS 15; Nashville: Abingdon, 1971) 48-49.

[48]On the use of ⲙⲁⲧⲉ to translate εὐδοκεῖν, see Crum,
189b-90a.

[49]On the transfiguration accounts, and 2 Pet 1:17 in
particular, see above, p. 107.

[50]Phil 2:15 encourages believers to shine as φωστῆρες ἐν
κόσμῳ; cp. 137,8-9 in our tractate.

[51]See, for example, the use of φωϲτηⲣ in the *Apoc. Adam*; at V 85,28-31 the term is used in conjunction with the enigmatic words Yesseus, Mazareus, Yessedekeus. On Mani as apostle and φωϲτηⲣ, see the *Kephalaia*, passim, esp. in the formulae near the openings of the chapters. Also see the *Acts of Philip* 21, where reference is made to τὸν φωστῆρα τῆς ζωῆς 'Ιησοῦν. In general, on φωστήρ as applied to holy men and Christ, see G. W. H. Lampe, *A Patristic Greek Lexicon* (Oxford: Clarendon, 1961) s.v. "φωστήρ." Literally, of course, φωστήρ refers to the heavenly bodies, e.g. the sun, the moon, or the stars.

[52]See BDF, §162,6.

[53]For examples of such phrases, see Son of Light (*Treat. Seth* VII 51,2) and Son of Compassion (*Acts of Thomas* 10).

[54]For the use of ⲣⲉϥϲⲱⲧⲉ, λυτρωτής, and related words in the OT and in Coptic literature, see BAG, s.v. "λυτρωτής κ.τ.λ.," O. Procksch and F. Büchsel, "λύω κ.τ.λ.," *TDNT*, 4.328-56; Crum, 362b. In the OT, λυτρωτής (ʾ֭ĕ֭λ) is used of God in Ps 18:15 (19:14) and 77:35 (78:35), and in both instances λυτρωτής is used in conjunction with βοηθός.

[55]See Luke 24:49 and Acts 1:4, where the resurrected Christ has similar instructions to give. The witness of several of the early Christian sources is that Peter was the first (or among the first) to whom the risen Christ appeared. See 1 Cor 15:5; Luke 24:34; John 20:1-10 (first into empty tomb; cp. Luke 24:12); also Mark 16:7; 9:2-8 and parallels; 1 Pet 1:3; 2 Pet 1:16-19; John 21:1-23; Matt 16:17-19. Also see Oscar Cullmann, *Peter* (Philadelphia: Westminster, 1962) 57-66, esp. n. 93.

[56]The meaning of σῶμα in Paul is still the subject of considerable debate. Note the discussions in Rudolf Bultmann, *Theology of the New Testament* (New York: Scribner's, 1951) 1.192-203; Schweizer, "σῶμα κ.τ.λ.," *TDNT*, 7.1060-62; Hans Conzelmann, *1 Corinthians* (Hermeneia; Philadelphia: Fortress, 1975) 281-83.

[57]That Paul reflects Jewish and Hellenistic concepts regarding the resurrection is undoubted. To be sure, within Judaism there are a variety of ways of understanding eternal life: something approaching immortality of the soul (Essenes, Therapeutae), or a resurrection of spirits or souls (*1 Enoch* 102-04), or some variety of resurrection of the body (Pharisees); transformation of the body into a glorious body of splendor (*2 Apoc. Bar.* 51), or re-creation of the body (2 Maccabees 7); exaltation to shining, starlike glory (Daniel 12), and ascension to the glory of heaven (*As. Mos.* 10, *2 Apoc. Bar.* 51); and so forth. See George W. E. Nickelsburg, Jr., *Resurrection, Immortality, and Eternal Life in Intertestamental Judaism* (HTS 26; Cambridge: Harvard University, 1972); Kirsopp Lake, *The Historical Evidence for the Resurrection of Jesus Christ* (New York: Putnam's, 1907) esp. 13-43. It is difficult to ascertain whether Paul has a single, definite position

concerning the resurrection. Here in 1 Corinthians 15 he emphasizes the spiritual and glorious bodies, but in Rom 8:11 he
states that God ζωοποιήσει καὶ τὰ θνητὰ σώματα. Here he seems
to speak of transformation, but elsewhere he can speak of καινή
κτίσις (Gal 6:15). Here Paul has a rather unified view of
human existence, but in 2 Corinthians 5 and 12 he suggests some
contrast between the inner person over against the earthly,
somatic cloak.

[58]See Bultmann, *The History of the Synoptic Tradition*
(New York: Harper & Row, 1963) 259-61; Charles E. Carlston,
"Transfiguration and Resurrection," *JBL* 80 (1961) 233-40; Hans
Dieter Betz, "Jesus as Divine Man," p. 120 in *Jesus and the
Historian: Written in Honor of Ernest Cadman Colwell* (ed. F.
Thomas Trotter; Philadelphia: Westminster, 1968); reconsidered
by Robert H. Stein, "Is the Transfiguration (Mark 9:2-8) a
Misplaced Resurrection-Account?" *JBL* 95 (1976) 79-96.

[59]Mark 9:9; Matt 17:9; Luke 9:36. The witnesses to the
transfiguration are told to keep silence εἰ μὴ ὅταν ὁ υἱὸς τοῦ
ἀνθρώπου ἐκ νεκρῶν ἀναστῇ.

[60]See Bultmann, *The History of the Synoptic Tradition*, 259.

[61]Note also the Ethiopic *Apoc. Pet.*; the *Acts of Peter* 20;
esp. the *Treat. Res.* I 48,3-19.

[62]Also see Acts 7:54-60, where Stephen beholds the δόξα
θεοῦ; 10:9-16, where Peter has a vision and hears a φωνή; note
also the accounts of Jesus walking on the water (Mark 6:45-52;
Matt 14:22-23; John 6:16-21).

[63]See Eliade, *Patterns in Comparative Religion*, "Subject
Index," s.v. "lightning" and "thunder"; Helmer Ringgren, *Religions of the Ancient Near East* (Philadelphia: Westminster,
1973) esp. 61-62, 132-34, 155-56. From the tablets discovered
at Ras Shamra see the Baal cycle 2.5.6-9, where Baal is said
to speak forth with a voice (*ql*) from the clouds. In the OT
see Ps 18:13-14, where God's thundering in heaven and the
uttering of his voice (φωνή, קּוֹל), as well as his arrows and
his lightnings, are used in poetic parallelism; also Ps 77:18;
104:7; Exod 19:16; 20:18. In the NT, see esp. John 12:28-29;
also Rev 6:1; 10:3-4; 14:2; 19:6. On thunder, lightning, and
light in the writings of Jewish apocalyptic, see the sources
cited by Otto Betz, "φωνή κ.τ.λ.," *TDNT*, 9.285-86; Conzelmann,
"φῶς κ.τ.λ.," *TDNT*, 9.323-27. Also, in the Greek magical
papyri, cp. the so-called "Mithras Liturgy," passim, esp. lines
692 and following; and Papyrus 46 of the British Museum (= *PGM*
5), lines 150-51 (ἐγώ εἰμι ὁ ἀστράπτων καὶ βροντῶν).

[64]In general, see Otto Betz, "φωνή κ.τ.λ.," *TDNT*, 9.299-
301; Conzelmann, "φῶς κ.τ.λ.," *TDNT*, 9.327-43.

[65]According to the version of the *Ap. John* in BG 8502,
this appearance takes place on a mountain, a desert(ed) place
(ⲡⲧⲟⲟⲩ ⲟⲩⲙⲁ ⲛ̄ϫⲁⲉⲓⲉ, 20,5); this passage must be restored at
II 1,19.

[66]*Trim. Prot.* seems to have been secondarily Christianized, and the few references to Christ (XIII 37,[31]; 38,22; 39,7; 49,8) are probably Christian interpolations. See Gesine Schenke of the Berlin Arbeitskreis, "'Die dreigestaltige Protennoia': Eine gnostische Offenbarungsrede im koptischer Sprache aus dem Fund von Nag Hammadi," *TLZ* 99 (1974) 733-34.

[67]Also note the *Acts of John*, a document permeated with the glory, light, and voice of the exalted Christ; the *Gos. Pet.*, a gospel with certain gnosticizing affinities, 9-14 (35-60); *Poimandres*, with its vision and revelation of light and λόγος.

[68]For a brief discussion (with additional bibliography) on aretalogies, see Bultmann, *The Gospel of John* (Philadelphia: Westminster, 1971) 225-26 n. 3; Raymond E. Brown, *The Gospel According to John* (AB; Garden City: Doubleday, 1966), "Appendix IV: *Egō Eimi*--'I am,'" 1.533-38; George MacRae, "The *Ego*-Proclamation in Gnostic Sources," pp. 122-34 in *The Trial of Jesus* (SBT 13, 2nd series; ed. Ernst Bammel; Naperville: Allenson, 1970).

[69]Conzelmann, *The Theology of St. Luke*, 203. Also note p. 204, where Conzelmann observes that for Luke the post-ascension appearances from heaven "are of a different kind, for they establish no relationship with the Lord in the special sense that the Resurrection appearances do."

[70]Here Western texts (D and Marcion) have φάντασμα rather than πνεῦμα.

[71]Cp. also Matt 28:2-4.

[72]See Bultmann, *Theology of the New Testament*, 2.10-14; idem, *The Gospel of John*, esp. 24 and following; also Ernst Käsemann, *The Testament of Jesus* (Philadelphia: Fortress, 1968), including his own interpretation of John and docetism on p. 26. It is thus appropriate that countless Gnostics, from the commentator Heracleon and on, found in John a kindred spirit.

[73]For example, Peter now plays a primary role as the first examiner, along with Thomas as well as Andrew, who looks to see whether Jesus' feet leave footprints (Ethiopic) or touch the ground (Coptic); cp. the *Acts of John* 93.

[74]A further exploration of the traditions relating to the appearances of the resurrected Christ exceeds the bounds of this study. On the matter of divine appearances in human likeness, a phenomenon attested in both Greek (e.g. Hermes and Zeus appearing in human guise, Ovid, *Metamorphoses* 8.611-724; cp. Acts 14:8-20) and Jewish sources (e.g. Yahweh appearing to Abraham via the visit of the three men, Gen 18:1-8), as well as the matter of the empty tomb traditions, see the summary article, with a citation of some of the most recent secondary literature, by John E. Alsup, "Theophany in the NT," IDBSup, 898-900; also Jörg Jeremias, "Theophany in the OT," IDBSup, 896-98.

[75]Cp. *Apoc. Adam* V 64,5-6; *Pistis Sophia* 6.

[76]Cp. the questions given, with laughter, by the Savior, near the opening of the *Soph. Jes. Chr.*, esp. the last question: ⲉⲧⲉⲧⲛ̄ⲱⲓⲛⲉ ⲛ̄ⲥⲁ ⲟⲩ, "for what are you seeking?" (III 92,3); also the opening of the *Ap. John*, where the risen Christ asks John about his doubts and his fears, provides reassurance, and continues with a self-predication and promise: [ⲁⲛ]ⲟ̣ⲕ ⲡⲉⲧϣⲟⲡ ⲛ̄ⲙ̄ⲙⲏ[ⲧⲛ ⲛⲟⲩ]ⲟⲉⲓϣ ⲛⲓⲙ, "I am the one who is with you for all time" (BG 21,18-19).

[77]On ⲏ̄ (ⲏ̂) used to link questions in a series, cp. the citations below from *Zost.*, *Testim. Truth*, and the *Excerpta ex Theodoto*; also *Great Pow.* VI 36,27-37,2; *Pistis Sophia* 6.

[78]The direct questions should not (in opposition to the translations of Wisse and Bethge) be considered as five individual questions which may be separated with sets of quotation marks for each; the introductory ⲭⲉ in 134,23 functions for the whole series.

[79]It is particularly easy to see how ⲡⲉⲕⲡⲗⲏⲣⲱⲙⲁ could be a desirable reading, since the Savior identifies himself with the fullness at 136,16. Yet, as the answer suggests, the restoration of the fullness of others is the purpose of the work of the Savior. On the emendation, see above, pp. 36-37 n. to 134,22.

[80]Acts 4:29, 31; esp. the *Acts of Philip* 97, where Philip is asked, by the marvelous leopard, ἵνα δώσῃς μοι ἐξουσίαν κτήσασθαι παρρησίαν. See Heinrich Schlier, "παρρησία κ.τ.λ.," *TDNT*, 5.882-86.

[81]For similar lists of questions, see Hippolytus, *Ref.* 5.7.8; 7.26.2; also see Bethge, col. 165 n. 4. In addition to such questions, we might also note the prominence of the motifs of asking and seeking at the opening of such tractates as the *Treat. Res.*, the *Gos. Thom.*, the *Hyp. Arch.*, *Thom. Cont.*, *Eugnostos*, and the *Soph. Jes. Chr.*

[82]Rudolph, "Der gnostische 'Dialog,'" 85.

[83]A lengthy discussion of the genre of the Gnostic dialogue exceeds the limits of this volume. A few additional remarks, however, should be added here. It is important that we distinguish between dialogues, "questions and answers," and revelatory discourses, though in Gnostic literature such distinctions frequently are difficult. Indeed, the general consensus today is that the Gnostic dialogue is not a true dialogue at all in the classical sense. Thus Wilhelm Schneemelcher ("Types of Apocryphal Gospels," Hennecke-Schneemelcher, 1.82) observes that this literature includes "practically no genuine dialogues, the questions merely giving occasion to the revelation discourses of the Redeemer"; see also Rudolph, "Der gnostische 'Dialog,'" 86. According to Heinrich Dörrie and Hermann Dörries ("Erotapokriseis," *RAC*, 6.368), a distinction

can be made between the dialogue and the "question and answer":
"Deutlicher ist die Abgrenzung zwischen den E. u. dem Dialog;
denn wenn auch sie in förmliche Gespräche übergehen können, der
Schüler sich mit einer Antwort nicht zufrieden gibt, neue
Fragen daran knüpft, so begehrt er doch Auskunft oder Weisung:
die Antwort soll dem Frager sichere Wahrheit übermitteln,
während der Dialog, sofern es sich nicht lediglich um ein
Streitgespräch handelt, unter aller Mitwirken unerkannte Wahrheit finden möchte." Rudolph (p. 88 n. 12), on the other hand,
judges that this distinction "zu sehr am idealen frühplato-
nischen Dialog orientiert ist." Rather, Rudolph (p. 89) proposes a "Mischung von Dialog und (orakelhaftem) 'Frage-Antwort-
Schema' oder der Problemataform ('Probleme und Lösungen'),"
especially in Gnostic literature. For, Rudolph insists, the
Gnostic "dialogue" consistently retains the dramatic framework
of a dialogue, but also stresses the "Lehrer-Schüler-Verhältnis"
and the authority of the teacher, as in the "question and
answer" literature. To be sure, the Gnostic dialogues do highlight the revelatory character of the authoritative disclosures,
and thus resemble "die Offenbarungsliteratur." This revelatory
emphasis is also noted by Douglas M. Parrott, who takes a different approach to the question of genre in his dissertation,
"A Missionary Wisdom *Gattung*: Identification, *Sitz im Leben*,
History and Connections with the New Testament" (Ph.D. dissertation, Graduate Theological Union, 1970). Parrott (p. 1)
offers the following brief descriptive definition of the *Gattung* he is exploring: "A person, or persons, with usually some
special preparation and/or character, receives a revelation
from a divine being. This revelation is characterized by the
fact that it encompasses great spans of time (past, present
and future) and vast historical or cosmological events, that
it is presented without visions, dreams, or any modes of expression that could be considered deliberately cryptic or enigmatic, and that it often contains dialogue as well as discourse.
Those who receive the revelation are expected to convey it to a
larger number." He judges this *Gattung* to be "a previously unrecognized *Gattung*," with features of wisdom and apocalyptic
literature, and he traces its development out of "the seething
ferment of the Judaism of the Maccabean period" (p. 111). According to Parrott, the *Ep. Pet. Phil.* is one example of this
missionary wisdom genre of literature.

[84]See especially Martin Krause, "Das literarische Verhältnis des Eugnostosbriefes zur Sophia Jesu Christi," pp. 215-23
in *Mullus: Festschrift für Theodor Klauser* (Jahrbuch für Antike
und Christentum, Ergänzungsband 1; ed. Alfred Stuiber and Alfred Hermann; Münster: Aschendorffsche Verlagsbuchhandlung,
1964); more briefly, his introduction to these two tractates in
Foerster, 2.24-27; also Douglas M. Parrott's introduction in
The Nag Hammadi Library, 206-07.

[85]But note the references to the Son of Man (III 81,13.
21-22; 85,11-12.<13>), the Savior (III 82,2-3.7; 84,[2].8;
85,14), and the Church or Assembly (ⲉⲕⲕⲗⲏⲥⲓⲁ; III 81,5; 86,16-
17.22-23; 87,4-5).

[86]On the alternate interpretation of the name and title, "Macarius the Cognizant One," see Bellet, "The Colophon," 54-56.

[87]138,2-3.22-23; 139,11-12; perhaps also 133,15-17.

[88]*Adv. Haer.* 1.30.14; 1.3.2. In the former account, on the Ophites, a distinction is made between the heavenly Christ who, with Sophia, descends upon Jesus at baptism and ascends again just before the crucifixion; and Jesus, who functions as the vessel or vehicle upon which Christ rides, but who is not forgotten in death. See above, pp. 133-34, with n. 143.

[89]*Pistis Sophia* 1; *Books of Jeu* 44.

[90]See Acts 1:3-12; Haenchen, *The Acts of the Apostles*, esp. 140-42. For further discussion on this phenomenon of periodization, see *Epistula Iacobi Apocrypha* (ed. Michel Malinine et al.; Zürich: Rascher, 1968) xii and 40; also James M. Robinson, "Ascension," *IDB*, 1.246-47.

[91]138,3-7 does function as something of an ascension account, complete with apocalyptic accompaniments; yet for the author of the *Ep. Pet. Phil.* this departure by no means precludes the possibility of additional appearances of Jesus (see 138,21-139,4; 140,15-23).

[92]ⲉⲧⲃⲉ ⲡⲏ ⲁⲉ ⲭⲉ (137,4-5); in the second case (137,10) the ⲉⲧⲃⲉ is elided.

[93]ⲙⲉⲛ, used only here in the tractate, seems to function with the later occurrences of ⲁⲉ (esp. 136,16; also 137,5.10) to bind this section together.

[94]1 Cor 7:1, 25; 8:1, 4; 12:1. The use of περί or *de* in titles of Greek and Latin works in general is well known.

[95]Cp. the short answer given in the *Dial. Sav.*: ⲧⲉⲧⲛ̅ϣⲟⲟⲡ ⲍ̅ⲙ ⲡⲙⲁ ⲉⲧⲉ ⲡϣⲱⲱⲧ ⲛ̅ⲙⲁⲩ, "you are in the place where the deficiency is" (III 139,17-18).

[96]Note the *Ap. John* II 9,25 (ⲧⲥⲟⲫⲓⲁ); 10,21 (ⲧⲉϥⲙⲁⲁⲩ); 13,32 (ⲧⲙⲁⲁⲩ); *Soph. Jes. Chr.* III 114,14-15 (ⲧⲥⲟⲫⲓⲁ ⲧⲙⲁⲁⲩ ⲛ̅ⲡⲧⲏⲣϥ); 104,17-18 par. *Eugnostos* V 9,4-5; *Eugnostos* III 82,21 (ⲡⲁⲛⲙⲏⲧⲱⲣ ⲥⲟⲫⲓⲁ); Irenaeus, *Adv. Haer.* 1.29.4; Hippolytus, *Ref.* 6.34.8; and so on. For further references, see *The Nag Hammadi Library*, "Index of Proper Names," s.v. "Mother," "Sophia," and related terms; Foerster, "Index of Gnostic Concepts," s.v. "Mother" and "Sophia, wisdom." It must be kept in mind, however, that the term "Mother" can be applied to any number of female deities (see, for example, in *Thund.* and *Trim. Prot.*), and that Sophia can be considered an inhabitant of the Pleroma as well as the fallen mother outside the Pleroma. For additional discussion and bibliography, see Ulrich Wilckens, "σοφία κ.τ.λ.," *TDNT*, 7.509-14; G. C. Stead, "The Valentinian Myth of Sophia," *JTS* 20 n.s. (1969) 75-104.

[97]Greatness or majesty (ⲘⲚ̄ⲧⲚⲟϬ, μέγεθος, and similar terms) is a common epithet used to describe the Father. See the *Ap. John* II 4,1-2 (ⲘⲈⲅⲈⲐⲟⲤ); 6,15 (ⲘⲚ̄ⲧⲚⲟϬ); Irenaeus, *Adv. Haer.* 1.2.1-2; it can also be hypostacized, as in the *Dial. Sav.* and the *Paraph. Shem.* See W. Grundmann, "μεγαλωσύνη" and "μέγεθος," *TDNT*, 4.544.

[98]In spite of the punctuation mark in 135,14, it seems clear that the phrase beginning with ⲈⲬ̄Ⲙ (135,13-14) belongs most naturally with what follows. The phrase provides the circumstances for the creative desire of the mother, and relates well to similar descriptions in other versions of the myth.

[99]Irenaeus, *Adv. Haer.* 1.2.2: version A in Stead; on this nomenclature see p. 77 n. 2 of his article.

[100]Hippolytus, *Ref.* 6.30.7: version B in Stead.

[101]Cp. also *Val. Exp.* XI 34,23-38. According to Irenaeus, the Barbelognostics claimed that Sophia, also known as Holy Spirit and Prunikos, found herself without a consort. Noting that all the other aeons had their own consorts, she began to look about for a consort, and even examined the realm below; but she made her great leap "sine bona voluntate patris" (1.29.4).

[102]BG 46,10-11; the other versions have different readings. On Sophia producing a ⳝⲟⲩⳅⲉ or ἔκτρωμα, see Foerster, "Index of Gnostic Concepts," s.v. "Abortion."

[103]Genesis 3; 1 Tim 2:14; *Barn.* 12.5.

[104]Note, for example, Sophia Zoe (Zoe=Eve) and Zoe daughter of Sophia in *Orig. World*; Zoe the daughter of Pistis Sophia in the *Hyp. Arch.*; Zoe as the Epinoia of light, and Sophia who is called Zoe, ⲧⲘⲁⲁⲩ Ⲛ̄ⲚⲉⲧⲟⲚⳅ, "the mother of the living" (II 23,24), in the *Ap. John*. See George MacRae, "The Jewish Background of the Gnostic Sophia Myth," *NovT* 12 (1970) 86-101.

[105]Irenaeus, *Adv. Haer.* 1.2.2.

[106]*Excerpta ex Theodoto* 23.2.

[107]She transgressed by attempting to approach the unapproachable, or by acting without the approval of the Father, or by trying to create without a consort. Also note *Val. Exp.* XI 36,28-31, on the will of the Father and the significance of the syzygy.

[108]We should note that a single Sophia is assumed by our tractate, and not two Sophias, as is the case in many of the more developed traditions. It is theoretically possible, of course, that the abbreviated character of the Sophia myth in the *Ep. Pet. Phil.* accounts for the deceptively simple presentation of the myth, with the omission of details. Yet the

clear indication of only one Sophia is important, and suggests that the *Ep. Pet. Phil.* may reflect a relatively simple and early version of the myth.

[109] Note, for instance, the *Hyp. Arch.* II 90,29; 92,27; 94,17; in each of these three cases ⲁⲩⲑⲁⲗⲏⲥ is used together with a noun.

[110] *Adv. Haer.* 1.29.4. Note also the use in Latin of *Authadiae* for the Greek Αὐθαδείᾳ.

[111] Hence he can be called, in addition to Yaldabaoth, Sakla(s), "Fool," and Samael, "Blind God"; see *Ap. John* II 11, 16-18.

[112] Cp. Isa 45:5-6, 46:9. Additional examples and discussion of such Gnostic statements can be found in MacRae, "The *Ego*-Proclamation," 123-29.

[113] *Orig. World* II 100,10-16. Yaldabaoth proved to be ignorant, but he did know what he could call himself from that voice (ⲥⲙⲏ) of Pistis Sophia. In general the author of *Orig. World* claims that "the gods and the angels and the people complete what came into existence by means of the word" (ⲉ̇ⲓ̇ⲧⲛ̄ ⲡⲱⲁⲭⲉ; 100,17-19). On the mother calling out the name of the archon, see also the *Ap. John* II 10,19.

[114] See the *Hyp. Arch.* II 86,27-87,4; *Orig. World* II 102, 35-103,32.

[115] Cp. *Orig. World* II 109,22-25, where a description is given of the consequences of the cosmic fall following one after another, until death reigns; ⲟⲩⲱϩ ⲛ̄ⲥⲁ- is used for "follow."

[116] On ⲙⲉⲣⲟⲥ, cp. especially *Trim. Prot.* XIII 40,13 and 41,21; also *Hyp. Arch.* II 87,12.21; 94,14.32.

[117] Also see the *Ap. John* II 10,19-21; 13,22-23. In Irenaeus, *Adv. Haer.* 1.29.4, the verb *abstulisse*, "steal," is used.

[118] On the substantival use of ϣⲱⲱⲧ in the Codex III version of the *Ap. John*, see Krause and Labib, *Die drei Versionen*, "Indices: Koptische Worter," s.v. "ϣⲱⲱⲧ." In some instances II uses ϣⲧⲁ where III uses ϣⲱⲱⲧ.

[119] On seeking to go from the place of the left, the ninety-nine, the ὑστέρημα, to the place of the right, the completed one hundred, the ἕν, see Irenaeus, *Adv. Haer.* 1.16.2; *Gos. Truth* I 31,35-32,34; additional references in Lampe, *A Patristic Greek Lexicon*, s.v. "ὑστέρημα"; and Ulrich Wilckens, "ὕστερος κ.τ.λ.," *TDNT*, 8.598-601.

[120] See, for example, the *Apoc. Adam* V 76,8; 85,29; *Excerpta ex Theodoto* 1.2; 26.3; 38.3; 41.1-2; 42.2.

[121]See Irenaeus, *Adv. Haer*. 1.5.6, on Ptolemaeus; these Gnostic believers claim to have τὸν πνευματικὸν ἄνθρωπον ἀπὸ τῆς μητρὸς τῆς 'Αχαμώθ. Also see the *Excerpta ex Theodoto* 53.1-5; 2.1-2; Hippolytus, *Ref*. 6.34.6; and Wilhelm Bousset, *Kyrios Christos* (trans. John E. Steely; Nashville: Abingdon, 1970) 259-60.

[122]On the joy and service of the powers, as well as the haughtiness of Yaldabaoth, see *Orig. World* II 102,11-23.35-103,15; the myriads and hosts of angels, powers, gods, and lords give glory, praise, and service to Yaldabaoth.

[123]"The Preexistent One" and "the Preexistent Father" are common names for the high God; note, for example, the *1 Apoc. Jas*. V 33,22, "the Preexistent Father." See *The Nag Hammadi Library*, "Index of Proper Names," s.v. "Father," "Preexistent One."

[124]Cp. the *Ap. John* II 10,1-19 on the imperfect and different character of Yaltabaoth in comparison with his heavenly mother.

[125]κωϩ, and thus also ρϥⲕωϩ, connotes both envy and imitation (Crum, 132b); the translation of ρϥⲕωϩ as "rival" seems to capture both of these levels of meaning. Also cp. Exod 20:5; *Ap. John* II 13,8-9.

[126]Irenaeus, *Adv. Haer*. 1.17.2; ἐκφυγούσης αὐτὸν τῆς ἀληθείας, ἐπηκολουθηκέναι τὸ ψεῦδος, and so his work is sure to fall apart one day.

[127]*Ap. John* II 14,13-15,13.

[128]*Orig. World* II 107,18-108,14.

[129]*Hyp. Arch*. II 87,11-33.

[130]On the opposite substitution, where one's body and entire existence are transformed in a most glorious way, see the *Gos. Thom. logion* 22 (II 37,20-35). The same sorts of formulae and constructions, however, are utilized in both passages; note esp. 37,34-35, which includes the phrase ογϩ ⲓⲕωⲛ ⲉⲡⲙⲁ ⲛ̄ογϩ ⲓⲕωⲛ. See also 1 Cor 15:49.

[131]On the misrepresentation of the image, see the *Hyp. Arch*. II 87,15-20, where it is shown how the powerless rulers are unable to grasp the likeness (ⲡⲓⲛⲉ) which had appeared in the waters, for such psychic beings from below cannot grasp the spiritual from above. In fact, as the *Hyp. Arch*., the *Ap. John*, and other documents claim, the rulers cannot even make their human model arise; he grovels in the dust until finally he is given some of his mother's spiritual power.

[132]On the absolute use of ⲁⲛⲟⲕ ⲡⲉ (ἐγώ εἰμι) without a predicate, see Brown, *The Gospel According to John*, 1.533-38, also 254-56.

[133]On the use of the term πλήρωμα in the NT, early Christian literature, and Gnostic sources, see Gerhard Delling, "πλήρης κ.τ.λ.," *TDNT*, 6.298-305; also Eduard Lohse, *Colossians and Philemon* (Hermeneia; Philadelphia: Fortress, 1971) 57-58, 99-101.

[134]*Excerpta ex Theodoto* 32.1-2; Irenaeus, *Adv. Haer.* 1.14.2; *Gos. Truth* I 41,14-19.

[135]An interesting parallel to this aretalogical statement in the *Ep. Pet. Phil.* is a similar self-predication in the *Gos. Thom. logion* 77: ⲁⲛⲟⲕ ⲡⲉ ⲡⲟⲩⲟⲉⲓⲛ ⲡⲁⲉⲓ ⲉⲧ₂ⲓⲭⲱⲟⲩ ⲧⲏⲣⲟⲩ ⲁⲛⲟⲕ ⲡⲉ ⲡⲧⲏⲣϥ ⲛⲧⲁⲡⲧⲏⲣϥ ⲉⲓ ⲉⲃⲟⲗ ⲛ₂ⲏⲧ· ⲁⲩⲱ ⲛⲧⲁⲡⲧⲏⲣϥ ⲡⲱ₂ ϣⲁⲣⲟⲉⲓ, "I am the light which is over them all. I am the All; from me the All has come forth, and to me the All has attained" (II 46,23-26). While the first portion of this self-predication resembles John 8:12, the second portion is quite similar to our tractate, except that "All" here replaces "fullness." Yet the theological message remains basically the same; in both cases Jesus is the heavenly redeemer, possessing all the fullness of the divine Unity. Also note the *Ap. John* II 30,15-16.

[136]On the descent of Christ through the heavens, his resemblance to the forms of the angels of the various heavens, and the lack of recognition on the part of the angels, see the long account in the *Ascension of Isaiah* 10. In general, the descent of Christ to earth may be compared with the descent into Hades; see J. N. D. Kelly, *Early Christian Creeds* (New York: David McKay, 1972) 378-83; J. M. Robinson, "Descent into Hades," *IDB*, 1.826-28 (with bibliography).

[137]Koschorke, "Eine gnostische Paraphrase," 384.

[138]Ibid., 385: the chart of parallels between the *Ep. Pet. Phil.* 136,16-137,4 and John 1.

[139]Ibid., 388.

[140]"Hier ist die Abhängigkeit von Joh 1 am deutlichsten. 'Und ich gab ihm Vollmacht (ἐξουσία), in das Erbe seiner Vaterschaft einzugehen' entspricht fast wörtlich Joh 1,12b" (p. 387). In John 1:12, the Sahidic NT reads as follows: ⲛⲉⲛⲧⲁⲩⲭⲓⲧϥ̄ ⲁⲉ ⲁϥ† ⲛⲁⲩ ⲛ̄ⲧⲉ₂ⲟⲩⲥⲓⲁ ⲉⲧⲣⲉⲩϣⲱⲡⲉ ⲛ̄ϣⲏⲣⲉ ⲛ̄ⲧⲉ ⲡⲛⲟⲩⲧⲉ.

[141]Still helpful in this regard is Rudolf Bultmann's essay, "Die Bedeutung der neuerschlossenen mandäischen und manichäischen Quellen für das Verständnis des Johannesevangeliums," *ZNW* 24 (1925) 100-46 (reprinted in *Exegetica* [Tübingen: Mohr (Siebeck), 1967] 55-104); more briefly, cp. his article "Johannesevangelium," *RGG*³, 3.846-47. In the former article, Bultmann catalogues twenty-eight parallels between the Gospel of John and the Gnostic literature under his examination. For our study of the *Ep. Pet. Phil.*, the following of his statements about the redeemer are especially appropriate: "2. Er ist vom Vater in die Welt gesandt" (cp.

136,17; 137,28-30); "3. Er ist in die Welt gekommen" (cp. 136, 19-20; 139,12-13.15-16); "5. Der Vater hat ihn mit Vollmacht ausgerüstet" (cp. 134,26-135,1; esp. 136,26-28); "6. Er hat das Leben und spendet Leben" (cp. 134,3-4; 139,27-28); "7. Er führt aus der Finsternis ins Licht" (cp. esp. 133,26-134,1; possibly 136,28-137,2; also 137,8-9); "11. In Offenbarungsreden spricht er von seiner Person (ἐγώ εἰμι)" (cp. 134,17-18; 136,16; 140, 22-23); "12. Er kennt die Seinen, und sie kennen ihm" (cp. 136,22-25; 137,5-6); "14. Den Mächten dieser Welt erscheint der Gesandte als ein Fremder; sie kennen seine Herkunft nicht, denn er ist anderen Ursprungs als sie" (cp. esp. 136,20-22; also 135,28-136,3; perhaps 139,21-22); "16. Der Gesandte ist in der Welt preisgegeben und gehasst" (cp. 138,15-16; 139,15-21; also 134,8-9; 135,2; 137,10-13.15-17.20-23; 138,18-139,4.22-23); "17. Wie er gekommen ist, wird er fortgehen, wie er herab-gekommen ist, wird er emporsteigen" (cp. 136,16-137,4); "21. Als Erlöser führt der Gesandte die Erlösten mit sich" (cp. 136,28-137,4; also 139,27-28; 140,4); "25. Er befreit die Ge-fangenen" (cp. 136,26-137,9.28-30; 140,17-23). Such similari-ties provide further support for the conclusion suggested above, that the Gospel of John and the *Ep. Pet. Phil.* reflect motifs found in various versions of the Gnostic redeemer myth.

[142]Bethge, col. 164.

[143]Koschorke, "Eine gnostische Paraphrase," 389. See also p. 386, where Koschorke depicts пєтє пωї as "der Mensch..., in dem der Soter Wohnung nimmt"; also note, with Koschorke, an "'*innerer*,' pneumatischer 'Mensch'" at 137,22. On Jesus, as the *vas mundum* of Christ, being saved by Christ, see the so-called Ophites of Irenaeus, *Adv. Haer.* 1.30.12-14; especially *Trim. Prot.* XIII 50,12-20, including the reference to the sal-vation of пасперма ετε пωї пе (50,18).

[144]Ménard, 21, 44.

[145]See above, p. 39, n. to 137,1. To the suggested restorations cited there, we may add the translation used by Koschorke ("Eine gnostische Paraphrase," 385, 387): "Und ich trug [ihn hinauf in die Äonen]. Sie füll[ten] sich [mit......] durch Erlösung." He judges this restoration to be "ziemlich sicher," though we may not share his certainty.

[146]As Christ and the сперма descend and ascend in the *Ep. Pet. Phil.*, so also the Primal Woman can be described as des-cending and ascending in the *Ap. John.* Many of the same terms and concepts are used. Indeed, the same phenomenon is being depicted in a different mythological form: the coming of the light to the mortal realm below, and its return to the fullness above. In the *Ap. John* II 20,9-28 God sends a helper (оувонθос) to Adam, a Thought of Light (оуεπιnoιa ῆоуоєιn), that is out of him (таї оу євоλ ῆ₂нтч тє). This Thought, called Life (zωн), helps in the process of Adam's restoration to his fullness (пєчпλнρωма). The Thought of Life is hidden in Adam, and the rulers (ῆaρχωn) do not recognize her, but she aids in the rec-tification of the deficiency of the mother (пωта ῆтмаaу).

[147]Compare the direct questions and answers in the *Ep. Pet. Phil.*, particularly the second direct question, with a similar question and answer in the *Dial. Sav.* III 140,14-19: "Mariamme said, 'Tell me, Lord, why have I come to this place (ⲉⲧⲃⲉ ⲟⲩ ⲁⲉⲓⲉⲓ ⲉⲛⲉⲉⲓⲙⲁ)? To gain or to lose?' The Lord said, 'You are to disclose the greatness of the revealer (μηνυτῆς).'"

[148]Cp. John 15:18-21; 17:14-19. Numerous examples could be cited of the hostility and opposition between the redeemer and the beings of light on the one hand, and the archons and the powers of darkness on the other. Note, for example, the accounts of the struggle in such tractates as the *Ap. John*, the *Hyp. Arch.*, *Orig. World*, the *Treat. Seth*, and the *Apoc. Pet.*

[149]See Bertil Gärtner, *The Theology of the Gospel According to Thomas* (New York: Harper & Brothers, 1961) 184-86; esp. vivid is the citation from the *Manichaean Psalm-Book*. In the *Gos. Thom.* also note *logion* 37, and the discussion in Jonathan Z. Smith, "The Garments of Shame," *HR* 5 (1966) 217-38.

[150]Discussion and parallels in *Epistula Iacobi Apocrypha*, 72-79.

[151]Elsewhere in the *Ep. Pet. Phil.* (137,25-27), the apostles can also be urged to gird themselves with power. In connection with the passage in Hippolytus, we should note that the Gnostic ἱερὸς γάμος can function in an analogous manner to the heavenly garments; by being reunited with one's heavenly counterpart, one's "better half," one attains to spiritual glory and wholeness (cp. Irenaeus, *Adv. Haer.* 1.7.1). On the use of both heavenly garments and the heavenly bridal chamber, see the *Dial. Sav.* III 138,16-20; *Exeg. Soul* II 131,27-132,26; 133,10-15.31-134,15.

[152]On the naked and clothed souls, see Albrecht Oepke, "γυμνός," *TDNT*, 1.773-75; Franz Cumont, *The Oriental Religions in Roman Paganism* (New York: Dover, 1956) 125-26, 159, 269-70; idem, *Astrology and Religion Among the Greeks and Romans* (New York: Dover, 1960) 108; Hans Jonas, *The Gnostic Religion* (Boston: Beacon, 1963) 165-69; Bousset, *Kyrios Christos*, 267-68.

[153]Translations of the relevant mythological materials by Samuel Noah Kramer and E. A. Speiser can be found in *ANET*, 52-57, 106-09.

[154]See also Rev 3:18, 16:15, and the comments and references in R. H. Charles, *A Critical and Exegetical Commentary on the Revelation of St. John* (ICC; Edinburgh: T. & T. Clark, 1920) 1.98, 184-88, 2.194-99.

[155]Gnostic ethics may also reflect this experience of freedom from cosmic shackles, whether that ethics be more ascetic or more libertine. See Jonas, *The Gnostic Religion*, 270-77, 320-40; Wisse, "Die Sextus-Sprüche und das Problem der gnostischen Ethik." Cp. also the Hellenistic mystery cults,

in which initiation was thought to be an anticipation of the
bliss of death (so Plutarch, Fragment 178 of his *Moralia*, com-
paring τελευτᾶν and τελεῖσθαι; Apuleius, *Metamorphoses*, Bk. 11).
In the *Metamorphoses* and elsewhere, for example in the Mithraic
inscriptions under the Church of Santa Prisca in Rome, the one
initiated can be said to be *renatus*, *creatus*, and *recreatus*,
having already gone from death to new life. See Hans Dieter
Betz, "The Mithras Inscriptions of Santa Prisca and the New
Testament," *NovT* 10 (1968) 62-80, esp. 71-72.

[156]Also note *Pistis Sophia* 96, where Jesus declares identity with the truly enlightened: ⲁⲛⲟⲕ ⲡⲉ ⲛ̅ⲧⲟⲟⲩ· ⲁⲩⲱ ⲛ̅ⲧⲟⲟⲩ ⲡⲉ
ⲁⲛⲟⲕ, "I am they, and they are I" (on this famous formulation,
cp. E. R. Dodds, *Pagan and Christian in an Age of Anxiety* [New
York: Norton, 1970] esp. 72-74); Epiphanius, *Panarion* 26.9.9,
where the libertine Gnostic claims, ἐγὼ εἰμι ὁ Χριστός, ἐπειδὴ
ἄνωθεν καταβέβηκα διὰ τῶν ὀνομάτων τῶν τ̅ξ̅ε̅ ἀρχόντων. In the
quotation from the *Gos. Phil.* the use of the future tense may
suggest the same sort of eschatological reservation as we are
suggesting for the *Ep. Pet. Phil.*

[157]Cp. the emphasis upon struggling and suffering at
134,8-9; 137,13-138,3; esp. 138,10-140,1.

[158]Otto Bauernfeind, "ἀναπαύω κ.τ.λ.," *TDNT*, 1.350-51;
Gärtner, *The Theology of the Gospel According to Thomas*, 258-
67; Philipp Vielhauer, "ΑΝΑΠΑΥΣΙΣ: Zum gnostischen Hintergrund
des Thomasevangeliums," pp. 281-99 (esp. 299) in *Apophoreta:
Festschrift für Ernst Haenchen* (BZNW 30; ed. W. Eltester and
F. H. Kettler; Berlin: Töpelmann, 1964), on the use of ἀνάπαυσις
in the *Gos. Thom.* in comparison with other Gnostic sources.

[159]The texts of the *Ap. John* in Codices IV (41,20) and BG
8502 (68,12-13) have more typical forms of ⲛ̅ⲗⲓⲱⲛ with a double
ⲛ. Also see the *Dial. Sav.* III 141,3-12, with its discussion
on when and how rest will be attained, and whether suicide is
an appropriate means to achieve final rest.

[160]Bethge, col. 168 n. 25; in his German translation he
uses braces.

[161]Hippolytus, *Ref.* 7.27.6, on Basilides. Also cp. the
Interp. Know. XI 20,23-38; *Val. Exp.* XI 38,11-33.

[162]Here the Greek text reads Μωϋσέως, the Latin version
agnitionem. We read γνώσεως with Harvey.

[163]On the use of Eph 6:12 in Gnostic literature, cp. *Hyp.
Arch.* II 86,20-27; *Exeg. Soul* II 131,9-12; Elaine H. Pagels,
The Gnostic Paul (Philadelphia: Fortress, 1975) 119, 128-29.
More generally, cp. Isa 11:5, 59:17; Wis 5:17-21; 1 Thess 5:8.

[164]See above, p. 94. To the NT references mentioned
there we might add the following: on gathering together, Matt
18:20 (...ἐκεῖ εἰμι ἐν μέσῳ αὐτῶν; cp. 134,17-18; 140,22-23);
1 Cor 5:4; Heb 10:25; on teaching or preaching, Matt 28:19-20;
Luke 24:47-48; Acts 1:8 (programmatic for Acts).

^{165}Cp. Luke 12:35; 1 Pet 1:13; Pol. *Phil.* 2.1; and esp. Eph 6:14.

^{166}Cp. Luke 11:9-13 par. Matt 7:7-11; Matt 18:19; 21:22 par. Mark 11:24; John 14:13-14; 15:7; 16:23-24; 1 John 5:14-15; Phil 4:6; Jas 1:5-8.

^{167}Cp. the references in John to the Father sending Jesus; at 7:33 and 16:5, for example, the Father is referred to as τὸν πέμψαντά με. In both cases the Sahidic has ⲡⲉⲛⲧⲁϥⲧⲁⲩⲟⲓ, and thus utilizes the pronominal suffix, as is also the case at 137,30. On this phrase, see Ernst Haenchen, "Der Vater, der mich gesandt hat," *NTS* 9 (1963) 208-16; also Rudolf Bultmann, "Die Bedeutung der neuerschlossenen mandäischen und manichäischen Quellen," 105-06 (pp. 60-61); Jesse Sell, "A Note on a Striking Johannine Motif Found at CG VI:6,19," *NovT* 20 (1978) 232-40.

^{168}138,1 cannot be restored with certainty; see above, p. 41 n. to 138,1. Ménard's suggestion is as good as any, and the context would make such a reassuring comment ("Do not be afraid!") quite appropriate. On such reassuring comments in the NT gospels, see Mark 5:36 par. Luke 8:50; Mark 6:50 par. Matt 14:27 and John 6:20; Matt 10:31 par. Luke 12:7; Matt 17:7; 28:5, 10; and so on.

^{169}See above, pp. 105-13.

^{170}See Charles H. Talbert, *Literary Patterns, Theological Themes, and the Genre of Luke-Acts* (SBLMS 20; Missoula, MT: Society of Biblical Literature, 1974) 112-16; idem, *Luke and the Gnostics* (Nashville: Abingdon, 1966) 30-32.

^{171}In the Sahidic version of Acts 1:9, a cloud "received him" (ⲭⲓⲧϥ) and "he was taken up away from them" (ⲁⲩϥⲓ ⲙ̄ⲙⲟϥ ⲉϩⲣⲁⲓ ⲉⲃⲟⲗ ϩⲓⲧⲟⲟⲧⲟⲩ). The Sahidic of the account of Peter's vision is even closer to our passage; see 10:16, where "the object was taken up to heaven" (ⲁⲩϥⲓ ⲙ̄ⲡⲉⲥⲕⲉⲩⲟⲥ ⲉϩⲣⲁⲓ ⲉⲧⲡⲉ).

^{172}Acts 1-7 focuses upon Jerusalem, Luke's city of apostolic authority. On the special place of Jerusalem in Luke-Acts, see Conzelmann, *The Theology of St. Luke*, 73-94, 209-13; Haenchen, *The Acts of the Apostles*, 100-03, 143-44.

^{173}In Luke 24:53 the disciples are described as being in the temple εὐλογοῦντες τὸν θεόν (Sahidic: ⲉⲩⲥⲙⲟⲩ ⲉⲡⲛⲟⲩⲧⲉ). In 24:52 it is noted that the disciples return to Jerusalem μετὰ χαρᾶς μεγάλης; many texts (but not the Western texts!) also include a reference to them προσκυνήσαντες αὐτόν (Sahidic: ⲁⲩⲟⲩⲱϣⲧ̄ ϩⲱⲟⲩ ⲙ̄ⲙⲟϥ).

^{174}It could also be suggested that the first perfect ⲁⲩⲕⲟⲧⲟⲩ of 138,10 translates the inchoative aorist (see BDF, §§318, 331), and that the clause should be translated as follows: "they started to return to Jerusalem," or "they turned toward Jerusalem." In such a case 139,5-6 could be taken as

the natural conclusion to the scene: "they came to Jerusalem."
We judge, however, that the interpretation suggested above explains the data better than this latter suggestion. Not only
are seams apparent elsewhere in the tractate, but the two
clauses at 138,10-11 and 139,5-6 also use very similar constructions (ⲁⲩⲱ ⲁⲩⲕⲟⲧⲟⲩ ⲉⲍⲣⲁ̈ⲓ ⲉⲟⲧ̄ⲏ̄ⲙ̄...ⲁⲩⲱ ⲁⲅⲉⲓ ⲉⲍⲣⲁ̈ⲓ ⲉⲟⲧ̄ⲏ̄ⲙ̄,
ϰαὶ ὑπέστρεψαν εἰς ʾΙερουσαλήμ...ϰαὶ ἀνέβησαν εἰς ʾΙερουσαλήμ).
See also Menard, 5 and esp. 46.

[175]Conzelmann (*The Theology of St. Luke*) can rightly refer
to the *ecclesia pressa* in Acts; see his discussion on pp. 137-
49, 209-11, 233-34.

[176]See the *Ap. Jas.* I 4,37-6,21; *2 Apoc. Jas.* V 61,1-
63,33; *Apoc. Pet.* VII 72,4-9; 84,6-10, and passim; *Melch.* IX
6,24-28; 16,6-12; 26,2-9; discussion in Pagels, "Gnostic and
Orthodox Views of Christ's Passion: Paradigms for the Christian's Response to Persecution?" (paper presented at the International Conference on Gnosticism, Yale University, 28-31 March
1978) 11-15 (to be published in *The Rediscovery of Gnosticism*
[ed. Bentley Layton; Leiden: Brill]).

[177]Ign. *Trall.* 10.1; *Smyrn.* 2.1; 4.2; 5.1-3; Irenaeus,
Adv. Haer. 3.16.9-3.18.5; but cp. also *Adv. Haer.* 4.33.9 for
certain exceptions. See Pagels, "Gnostic and Orthodox Views of
Christ's Passion," 5-11.

[178]*Apoc. Pet.* VII 78,17. See James Brashler, "The Coptic
Apocalypse of Peter: A Genre Analysis and Interpretation"
(Ph.D. dissertation, Claremont Graduate School, 1977) 216-35;
Pagels, "Gnostic and Orthodox Views of Christ's Passion," 14-15.

[179]Also see E. Pagels, "'The Demiurge and His Archons'--
A Gnostic View of the Bishop and Presbyters?" *HTR* 69 (1976)
301-24.

[180]On the correspondence between the heavenly rulers and
the earthly rulers, cp. also the archons as the guardians of
the seventy nations (Dan 10:13, 20-21; 12:1; *1 Apoc. Jas.* V
26,13-27,12), and the powers as the ἄγγελοι of the churches
(Rev 2:1-3:22).

[181]On the alteration, see above, p. 41, n. to 138,14.

[182]Luttikhuizen, "The Letter of Peter to Philip and the
New Testament," *Nag Hammadi and Gnosis*, 100 n. 20. See also
the *Concordance du Nouveau Testament Sahidique* (CSCO; ed.
Michel Wilmet; Louvain: Secrétariat du CSCO, 1957) s.v. "ⲉⲧⲃⲉ-,"
"ⲉⲧⲃⲏⲏⲧ⸗," "ⲍⲁ-." As the *Concordance* indicates, ⲉⲧⲃⲉ- or
ⲉⲧⲃⲏⲏⲧ⸗ is used to translate ὑπέρ only three times in the Sahidic NT: John 1:30, 11:4; 2 Cor 12:8.

[183]See Luttikhuizen, "The Letter of Peter to Philip and
the New Testament," 100 n. 20; also Harald Riesenfeld, "ὑπέρ,"
TDNT, 8.508-12. For a parallel passage in the Nag Hammadi
library, see *Interp. Know.* XI 5,27-38.

[184]See Gärtner, *The Theology of the Gospel According to
Thomas*, 217-29; Albrecht Oepke, "παῖς κ.τ.λ.," *TDNT*, 5.639-52;
more generally cp. O. Michel, "μικρός," *TDNT*, 4.650-56. Note
also *Ap. John* II 2,1-2, where Christ appears as a youth; *Apoc.
Paul* V 18,3-19,20, where the little child appearing to Paul
seems to be Christ; *Apoc. Pet.* VII 80,8-21, where ⲛⲓⲕⲟⲩⲉⲓ is
the name of the Christian Gnostics. On this last passage in
the *Apoc. Pet.*, see Eduard Schweizer, "The 'Matthean' Church,"
NTS 20 (1973-74) 216; idem, "Zur Struktur der hinter dem
Matthäusevangelium stehenden Gemeinde," *ZNW* 65 (1974) 139.

[185]It may be possible to interpret ⲧⲉⲛⲙⲛ̄ⲧⲕⲟⲩⲓ in a more
positive fashion, as in the *Gos. Thom.* and other Gnostic documents. It could be argued that the followers of Christ must
suffer because they are little ones, children of the light and
true Gnostics. For this reason the struggle with the cosmic
powers goes on, the struggle between light and darkness; see
the discussion above, pp. 135-40, on 137,4-13. Such an interpretation, however, is not as convincing as the one we are
suggesting here.

[186]*Treat. Seth* VII 69,11-12; note the use of ⲙⲛ̄ⲧⲕⲟⲩⲉⲓ for
the archons' description of Adam at 54,4, and for the dwelling
place of Adam at 54,10. Also see *Tri. Trac.* I 115,3-11 (Jesus
takes on smallness when born in body and soul); similarly
Interp. Know. XI 10,27-30.

[187]For a Valentinian version of such a transformation, see
the *Excerpta ex Theodoto* 68.

[188]If the speech of Peter is interpreted as a secondary
Gnostic Christian addition, then the section could be described
as originally consisting of an apostolic question and the
answer of Jesus. In such a case, the section originally may
have had no overtly Gnostic elements.

[189]Also cp. Luke 12:11-12, as well as Matt 24:9-14 and
John 16:2. On the necessity of suffering see, with Luttikhuizen, Luke 24:26 and perhaps Acts 14:22, although his conclusion concerning the Emmaus road story ("The Letter of Peter
to Philip and the New Testament," 101) is not convincing. We
might add 1 Thess 3:3-4, 2 Thess 1:5-8, 1 Tim 3:12-13; also
Ap. Jas. I 4,37-6,21, esp. 6,15-17: ⲛⲉⲙⲛ̄ ⲗⲁⲩⲉ ⲛⲁⲟⲩⲭⲉⲉⲓ ⲛ̄ⲛⲉⲧⲡ̄
ⲍⲁϯⲉ ⲍⲏⲧ[ϥ̄] ⲛ̄ⲡⲙⲟⲩ, "none of those who fear death will be saved"
(see *Epistula Iacobi Apocrypha*, 52).

[190]The preference of Luttikhuizen, "The Letter of Peter to
Philip and the New Testament," 101 n. 21.

[191]The Koine texts, A, W, and other manuscripts prefer
ἀγομένους.

[192]The Lucan passage may be preferred as a tradition possibly reflected in our tractate, if a single specific tradition
is to be sought, on account of the numerous parallels between
the *Ep. Pet. Phil.* and Luke-Acts.

[193]On the person who refuses to suffer, see Mark 8:34-9:1 par. Matt 16:24-28 and Luke 9:23-27; Matt 10:33 par. Luke 12:9; Matt 10:37-39 par. Luke 14:25-27; Luke 17:33; John 12:25; 2 Tim 2:12; *Gos. Thom. logion* 55; *Ap. Jas.* I 6,1-21.

[194]On the summaries in Acts, see Haenchen, *The Acts of the Apostles*, 193-96; Henry J. Cadbury, "The Summaries in Acts," *The Beginnings of Christianity*, 5.392-402.

[195]4:18: † сⲃⲱ ⲍ̄ⲙ ⲡⲣⲁⲛ ⲛ̄ⲧⲥ̄; 5:28: † сⲃⲱ ⲉⲅⲣⲁⲓ ⲉⲭⲙ̄ ⲡⲉⲓⲣⲁⲛ.

[196]Cadbury, "The Summaries in Acts," 401.

[197]See Koschorke, "Eine gnostische Pfingstpredigt," 328. Additional support for the disciples as Peter's disciples may be provided by the so-called "shorter ending of Mark" (τοῖς περὶ τὸν Πέτρον) and Ign. *Smyrn.* 3.2; cp. Kurt Aland, "Bemerkungen zum Schluss des Markusevangeliums," *Neotestamentica et Semitica: Studies in Honour of Matthew Black* (ed. E. Ellis and M. Wilcox; Edinburgh: Clark, 1969) esp. 162-63, 179-80. We may also note, with Aland, Luke 8:45, 9:32; Acts 2:14, 5:29.

[198]See Bethge, col. 169 n. 40.

[199]Koschorke, "Die Polemik der Gnostiker gegen das kirchliche Christentum," 188-90 (published edition: 193-95); esp. "Eine gnostische Pfingstpredigt," 329-34.

[200]Koschorke, "Eine gnostische Pfingstpredigt," 329.

[201]The construction which utilizes ⲡⲛ̄ⲁ̄ ⲉϥⲟⲩⲁⲁⲃ with the indefinite article is also attested in the Sahidic NT (e.g. Acts 1:5, 7:55, 10:38), and may parallel the use of πνεῦμα ἅγιον without an article in the Greek Acts (see BAG, s.v. "πνεῦμα," 5cβ).

[202]Also see Acts 4:31; 7:55; 13:9, 52: the filling with the spirit for particular tasks. On the varied use of πνεῦμα in Acts, see Haenchen, *The Acts of the Apostles*, 187.

[203]It may also be that the reference in 139,8-9 to the healings performed by the apostles assumes their possession of spiritual power; note 140,9-11.

[204]Acts 2:14-36, 38-40; 3:12-26; 4:8-12; 5:29-32; 10:34-43; perhaps also 1:16-22; 4:19-20; 11:5-17; 15:7-11.

[205]Martin Dibelius, "The Speech in Acts and Ancient Historiography," p. 165 in *Studies in the Acts of the Apostles* (ed. Heinrich Greeven; London: SCM, 1956).

[206]Cp. Acts 2:22; also 135,15-16 in our tractate.

[207]p66 and a few other manuscripts read ἔχων rather than φορῶν.

208As noted above (p. 44, n. to 139,17), Bethge prefers
to emend this to read "[he] <was> clothed with a purple robe."
Such an emendation would bring this clause closer in form to
the following clauses, to be sure; but the active sense of the
text as given is also attested in John 19:5, and thus should
be allowed to remain.

209On Ménard's restoration, "they [nailed] him, see above,
p. 44, n. to 139,19. On nailing Jesus to a tree, see also the
Gos. Truth I 20,25; Treat. Seth VII 58,24-26.

210Both the Ep. Pet. Phil. and Acts provide evidence for
the application of Deut 21:22-23 to the Christian interpretation
of Jesus' crucifixion; also see Gal 3:31. Deut 21:22 LXX reads,
in part, as follows: κρεμάσητε αὐτὸν ἐπὶ ξύλου. On ειωε as the
Coptic for κρεμάννυμι, see Acts 5:30 and 10:39 in the Sahidic
NT, as well as Crum (88b).

211It is difficult to ascertain precisely how the verbal
form should be translated; see above, p. 44, n. to 139,20. If
this kerygmatic formula is derived from a tradition which, like
Luke-Acts, emphasizes the fact that God raised Jesus from the
dead (Acts 2:24, 32, etc.; Haenchen, The Acts of the Apostles,
92, 180), then it could be reasoned that, in spite of the ambiguity of the present passage, originally this formula was
meant to suggest that the active role in the resurrection was
played by God. For the present Gnostic Christian author, however, such a subordinationist Christology does not seem
appropriate.

212See BAG, s.v. "νεκρός."

213Luttikhuizen, "The Letter of Peter to Philip and the
New Testament," 101.

214Ibid., 101 n. 22.

215See above, p. 44, n. to 139,21.

216Heracleon, fragment 11, on John 2:12, in Origen, In
Joannem 10.11; Clement of Alexandria, Excerpta ex Theodoto
33.3; Stromateis III.4 §31.3; Gos. Truth I 31,1-4; Apoc. Adam V
69,17-18; Acts Pet. 12 Apost. VI 3,8-11; the tractate Allogenes,
and Seth as ἀλλογενής; also see Jonas, The Gnostic Religion,
49-51, on the "alien."

217On the peculiarity of the phrase "the transgression of
the mother," and the similarity between descriptions of mother
Sophia and mother Eve, see above, pp. 123, 174 (notes).

218See Koschorke, "Eine gnostische Pfingstpredigt," 329-30.
Koschorke also refers to the Paraph. Shem VII 3,11-15 for a
similar use of ειne with ⲧⲛ.

219According to Crum (80b), ειne as a noun can translate
either Greek word.

[220] Discussion and references in BAG, s.v. "ὁμοίωμα."

[221] BAG, s.v. "ὁμοίωσις."

[222] On the use of Gen 1:26 by the Gnostics, see also Irenaeus, *Adv. Haer.* 1.5.5 (on Ptolemaeus: καθ' ὁμοίωσιν is the psychic man, whose substance is termed πνεῦμα ζωῆς); 1.18.2 (on Marcus and others); 1.24.1 (on Saturnilus); 1.30.6 (apparently on the Ophites); Clement of Alexandria, *Excerpta ex Theodoto* 50.2-3 (cp. Irenaeus on Ptolemaeus); 54.2; Hippolytus, *Ref.* 6.14.5-6 (the *Megale Apophasis*).

[223] See also 5:31, in another speech by Peter and the apostles; also *2 Clem.* 20.5 (τὸν σωτῆρα καὶ ἀρχηγὸν τῆς ἀφθαρσίας); Heb 2:10, 12:2; discussion in Conzelmann, *The Theology of St. Luke*, 205-6; Zehnle, *Peter's Pentecost Discourse*, 47-48.

[224] As noted above (p. 44, n. to 139,26), the Coptic syntax of 139,26 will also allow the following translation: "the Son of the glory of the immeasurable Father." If this latter translation is accepted, in spite of its apparent awkwardness, then it could conceivably reflect the sort of negatively defined transcendence of God as is proclaimed in the *Ap. John* (II 3,10.[17]; 4,2.9-10). Also see John 1:14, Eph 1:17, 2 Pet 1:17.

[225] See *Gos. Truth* I 18,21-38; 20,15-21,2; 30,27-31,35. Also cp. the *Acts of John* 88-102, esp. the account of the round dance of Jesus and the mystery of the cross. In general, cp. Karl Wolfgang Tröger, "Doketistische Christologie in Nag-Hammadi-Texten: Ein Beitrag zum Doketismus in frühchristlicher Zeit," *Kairos* 19 (1977) 45-52, esp. 49-50. Tröger discusses four Gnostic approaches to the suffering and death of Christ, and focuses his attention upon the doctrine of the two natures of Christ. He includes *Zost.* (cp. VIII 48,27-29), *Teach. Silv.* (cp. VII 101,33-102,5), *1 Apoc. Jas.* (cp. V 31,14-22), and *Ep. Pet. Phil.* in his second group.

[226] For example, elsewhere the heavenly Jesus can be described as passing through mother Mary like water passes through a pipe (Epiphanius, *Panarion* 31.7.4); Jesus may only seem to be a human being (Irenaeus, *Adv. Haer.* 1.24.2), and may have a body which is not real but δοκήσει φαινόμενον (Epiphanius, *Panarion* 40.8.2); Jesus may claim, ⲛⲉⲓ̈ⲙⲟⲩ ⲡ₂ⲣⲁ̈ⲓ ₂ⲛ̄ ⲟⲩⲧⲁⲭⲣⲟ ⲁⲛ· ⲁⲗⲗⲁ ₂ⲛ̄ ⲡⲉⲧⲟⲩⲟⲛ₂̄, "I did not die in truth but in appearance" (*Treat. Seth* VII 55,18-19); also note the *Quran*, sura 4,157 (see Geoffrey Parrinder, *Jesus in the Qur'ān* [New York: Oxford University, 1977] 105-21; Tor Andrae, *Mohammed: The Man and His Faith* [New York: Harper & Row, 1960] 104, 112-13). A distinction may be made between those docetic traditions which assert that only the fleshly part of Jesus suffered (cp. *Apoc. Pet.* VII 81,3-24), and those which claim that another person (for example Simon of Cyrene) suffered in place of Jesus (cp. Basilides according to Irenaeus, *Adv. Haer.* 1.24.2; *Treat. Seth* VII 55,9-56,19; early Islamic interpretations of sura 4,157).

See also Tröger, "Doketistische Christologie in Nag-Hammadi-
Texten," esp. 47-51. In general, on docetism and the related
concept of divine ἀπάθεια in antiquity, see Wilhelm Michaelis,
"πάσχω κ.τ.λ.," *TDNT*, 5.904-39, esp. 906-07; Adolf von Harnack,
History of Dogma (New York: Russell & Russell, 1958) 1.258-60,
esp. the long n. 1; 2.276-87; and Jung Young Lee, *God Suffers
for Us: A Systematic Inquiry into a Concept of Divine Passibil-
ity* (The Hague: Martinus Nijhoff, 1974) 23-45.

[227] See BAG, s.v. "ἄνομος."

[228] Bethge (col. 168) suggests that the sense of the lacuna
may be as follows: "dem Fleisch, sondern nach dem Geist" (cp.
Rom 8:4). If we were to opt for Bethge's general suggestion
for reconstruction, we might also consider something like the
following as equally possible: "darkness, but in the light."

[229] Luttikhuizen ("The Letter of Peter to Philip and the
New Testament," 102) interprets 140,11-13 and 140,23-27 as
doublets. See also Ménard (p. 5) where he speaks of "indices
de fragments ou de morceaux réunis ultérieurement par le ré-
dacteur final."

[230] Cp. Acts 8:19, where Simon Magus requests τὴν ἐξουσίαν
ταύτην, to pass on πνεῦμα ἅγιον.

[231] In the *Ap. John* II 16,1, ⲀⲘⲎⲚ is credited with the
creation of the lips of Adam; *Pistis Sophia* can refer to the
three Amens and the seven Amens (1, 10, 86, 93, 96), like the
Books of Jeu (42, 44, 48, 50). On ἀμήν in the NT and early
Christian literature, see Heinrich Schlier, "ἀμήν," *TDNT*,
1.335-38; BAG, s.v. "ἀμήν." On ἀσπάζομαι understood as referring to the liturgical kiss of peace in Christian circles, see
Bethge, cols. 168, 169 n. 55; also Rom 16:16, 1 Cor 16:20,
2 Cor 13:12, 1 Thess 5:26, 1 Pet 5:14. Ménard (pp. 46-47) remains less certain whether ⲀⲤⲠⲀⲌⲈ here refers to a kiss or
simply a greeting.

[232] Cp. the standard Semitic greeting, םֶכָל םוֹלָשׁ. For parallels see John 20:19, 21, 26; Luke 24:36 (various manuscripts):
εἰρήνη ὑμῖν, ⲧⲢⲎⲚⲎ ⲚⲎⲧⲚ̄ (Sahidic).

[233] Matt 28:18-20, with the promise of Jesus' presence;
Luke 24:44-49, with the promise of δύναμις ἐξ ὕψους; John 20:
19-23, where Jesus sends the disciples as the Father sent him;
Acts 1:8, with the promise of power and the Holy Spirit; also
see Mark 16:15-18; *Soph. Jes. Chr.* III 119,1-8, with a similar
concluding commission.

[234] See above, p. 46, n. to 140,25.

[235] According to Crum (313a), ⲤⲀ can translate κλίμα.

[236] Cited and discussed by Puech in Hennecke-Schneemelcher,
1.231-32.

237The Coptic ϣⲁϫⲉ of the *Ep. Pet. Phil.* may very well
translate λόγος from the Greek *Vorlage* (cp. Crum, 613b). James
Brashler has suggested to me privately that we take this pre-
sumed λόγος in the sense of "section," "division," or "branch"
(cp. LSJ, s.v. "λόγος," VI 3d); according to this interpretation, the *Ep. Pet. Phil.* closes, like the *Pistis Sophia*, with
the apostles dividing themselves into four groups in order to
preach. Such a suggestion, however, although it remains a
possibility, probably pushes the meaning of λόγος too far,
since even the suggested translations "section," "division,"
and "branch" are given by the lexicon within the context of
spoken or written disclosures.

238The appropriate conclusion for the tractate casts more
doubt upon Bethge's theory about the tractate; see above,
p. 97.

CHAPTER V

CONCLUSION

The *Ep. Pet. Phil.* occupies most of the concluding nine
pages of Codex VIII of the Nag Hammadi library. Situated immediately after the long revelatory tractate *Zost.*, our tractate bears little literary or theological relationship to *Zost.*
Rather, the *Ep. Pet. Phil.* seems to have been included in Codex
VIII for a different reason: of the tractates the scribe was
commissioned to copy, this tractate was of an appropriate
length to fill the available pages of the codex. Like the
scribe, we recognize "The letter of Peter which he sent to
Philip" (132,10-11) as the tractate title, though the discrepancy between this title and the actual contents of the tractate
suggests that it has been secondarily applied as the tractate
title.

Like the other tractates within the Nag Hammadi library,
the *Ep. Pet. Phil.* is a Coptic translation of a Greek text.
The dialect represented by the Coptic of the tractate may be
termed Sahidic, although various dialectical peculiarities, and
particularly Bohairic forms, may be recognized. As we have
concluded, these dialectical variants do not support a Coptic
source theory for the *Ep. Pet. Phil.*, but rather indicate
either the dialectical disposition of the scribe or the dialectically "mixed" character of the Coptic language of that day.
In a similar fashion the grammatical peculiarities noted in our
tractate do not recommend a Coptic source theory either; where
particular sections of the *Ep. Pet. Phil.* show unique grammatical characteristics, these features usually may be taken to
reflect the Greek *Vorlage*.

Although we have described the *Ep. Pet. Phil.* as a unified
work, it must be acknowledged that various materials have been
brought together to form this tractate. These diverse elements
presumably were woven together in the Greek *Vorlage*. Indeed,
as we have observed, at times seams may be detected. Such appears to be the case at 133,12-13, where the attention turns
from Philip to the apostolic group; at 137,13-15, where the

189

quotation formula for the additional question resets the stage;
probably at 138,10-11, where a scene on the road intrudes into
the account of the return to Jerusalem, which is then mentioned
again at 139,4-6; and possibly at 140,11-15, where the theme of
dispersing and gathering is presented. Furthermore, certain
sections of the tractate may be distinguished by the grammatical peculiarities of the Greek *Vorlage*. Thus the additional
question and answer (137,13-138,3) makes use of the Greek loan
word ⲁⲣⲭⲱⲛ (137,16.17.21), whereas elsewhere terms such as ϭⲟⲙ[1]
and ⲉⲝⲟⲩⲥⲓⲁ are utilized to depict the cosmic rulers. Again,
the framework for the account of the sermon of Peter is unique
in its use of the Greek loan word ⲙⲁⲑⲏⲧⲏⲥ (139,10) rather than
the usual ⲁⲡⲟⲥⲧⲟⲗⲟⲥ, and the verb ⲡⲉⲭⲁϥ (139,10.15) rather than
the usual quotation formula with ⲭⲱ.[2]

In its present form the *Ep. Pet. Phil.* is clearly a
Christian Gnostic tractate. The major sections that have been
analyzed--the letter and the account of the gatherings and
departures of the apostles--indicate the Christian focus of
the tractate and its author. Taken as a whole, the tractate
is to be seen in the Petrine tradition: Peter is the leader,
the spokesman, and the preacher of the apostles.[3] The only
other apostle mentioned by name is Philip, who is submissive
to the authority of Peter and whose place in the tractate
seems intended to highlight the preeminent authority of Peter.
Further, with their leader, Peter, the apostles gather at
Olivet and are taught by the risen Savior; upon returning to
Jerusalem, they teach in the temple and perform healings; and
eventually they go forth to preach, filled with holy spirit.
In other words, not only the place of Peter but also the
scenario of the narrative would suggest that the *Ep. Pet. Phil.*
shares important features with part of the first--Petrine--
section of the NT Acts of the Apostles.

That the author of the *Ep. Pet. Phil.* makes use of Christian oral or written traditions cannot be doubted. In particular, numerous parallels between our tractate and the first half
of the NT Acts have been noted throughout this study. Such
parallels, we have seen, include scenes, themes, and terms
which are similar in these two documents. Even the genre of

literature they represent--a narrative on Peter and the
apostles within which are included revelatory, liturgical, and
edificatory materials--is similar, although in the case of the
Ep. Pet. Phil. the narrative has been prefixed with a letter of
Peter. Hence it may safely be surmised that the author of the
Ep. Pet. Phil. is aware of Lucan materials; but the precise
character of this awareness or the exact nature of the materials cannot be determined with confidence. For in addition to
the striking similarities between the two documents, certain
crucial differences call into question a direct dependence of
the *Ep. Pet. Phil.* on the NT Acts. For example, in spite of
the similarities between Peter's letter to Philip (132,12-
133,8) and Acts 8:4-25, the two accounts diverge precisely at
the point where Luke's theological hand is seen most clearly.
Again, in spite of the presence of an ascension account in both
our tractate (138,3-7) and Luke-Acts (Luke 24:50-51; especially
Acts 1:9-11), the accounts illustrate very different theological concerns in their portrayals of the significance and nature
of this ascension. Once again, although the *Ep. Pet. Phil.*
(140,1-13), like Acts (2:1-13), includes a "Pentecost" account,
our tractate seems not to recognize the unique Lucan concerns
regarding this event, and seems rather to resemble John 20:19-
23 in important ways. Furthermore, a number of the similarities in the use of technical terms (ⲡⲉⲕⲁⲗⲟⲩ ⲉⲧⲟⲩⲁⲁⲃ ⲓ̅ⲥ̅ ⲡⲉⲭ̅ⲥ̅,
ὁ ἅγιος παῖς σου ᾽Ιησοῦς; ⲁⲣⲭⲏⲅⲟⲥ, ἀρχηγός) occur in liturgical
passages, which are notoriously conservative in their retention
of such technical terms. Thus, we do best to conclude that the
author of the *Ep. Pet. Phil.* is not consciously using a specific Lucan text at all, but is familiar with themes and motifs
in the Lucan tradition.[4]

In addition to this acquaintance with Lucan materials, the
author of our tractate is also familiar with other Christian
traditions. We have seen that the Savior's second revelatory
answer (136,16-137,4) resembles in part the Johannine λόγος
hymn, though the similarities must not be overdrawn. Again,
the traditional kerygmatic formulae in the credo (139,15-21)
show certain affinities with John 19, and the little "Pentecost"
of the *Ep. Pet. Phil.* shares features with the Johannine

"Pentecost" account (20:19-23). Furthermore, the author of our tractate can mention previous revelatory utterances of the Savior (135,5-6; 138,2-3.22-24; 139,11-12), utterances frequently said to be given while Jesus was embodied. Presumably these revelations of the embodied Savior could refer to such teachings as are presented in the Christian gospels; and the "four messages" of 140,25 could have been understood as the four gospels. Hence, it is clear that our author is generally aware of early Christian materials, and desires to establish continuity with these earlier traditions. The author's understanding of the Christian message, it is maintained, is legitimate and authentic; indeed, Jesus said all these things before, but because of unbelief the message must now be proclaimed again (135,4-8)!

Within the narrative framework of the *Ep. Pet. Phil.* are included various materials, and the Gnostic emphases can be seen with greatest clarity in these materials. In particular this observation applies to the Gnostic "dialogue," the revelatory discourse of the Savior uttered in answer to the questions of the apostles. The first four revelatory answers (135,8-137,13) are at most marginally Christian, though they are taken over and legitimated as revelations of the risen Lord. The first answer, which provides an abbreviated version of the myth of the mother, illustrates no overtly Christian features at all. It reflects a rather simple version of the myth, and is similar to the Christian Sophia myth of the *Ap. John* and the Barbelognostics of Irenaeus in terminology (ⲧⲙⲁⲁⲩ, *mater*; ⲡⲁⲩⲑⲁⲁⲏⲥ, *Authadia*) and general presentation. This set of four revelatory answers furnishes a Gnostic perspective on the fall into deficiency and the attainment of fullness (the first two answers), and the imprisonment and the struggle of Gnostics in the world (the last two answers). To this set of answers has been appended an additional question and answer (137,13-138,3), which utilizes different terms and focuses upon the life and mission of the Gnostics. Gnostic in perspective like the other answers, this additional answer does show clear Christian concerns, and illustrates the emphases of the author and community of the *Ep. Pet. Phil.*: they are struggling Gnostic Christians, who gather for worship and disperse to preach the gospel in the world.

In addition to the questions and answers in the Gnostic
"dialogue," other materials used in our tractate similarly may
show Gnostic proclivities. The two prayers of the gathered
apostles (133,17-134,9) contain traditional terms and themes
commonly found in early Christian prayers, but also proclaim a
luminosity and glory which would make them especially appropriate and meaningful as the prayers of Gnostic Christians.
Again, the description of the resurrected Christ as a light and
a voice represents a primitive way of depicting the appearances
of the risen Lord, but among Gnostic Christians such theophanic
descriptions were particularly appreciated. Again, in the discussion of the sufferings of the Lord and the apostles, a motif
occurs which would be very meaningful to Gnostics: human
"smallness" (138,20). And again, the reception of "a spirit of
understanding" (140,5-6) and spiritual power (140,21.27) from
Christ would be especially important for Gnostic Christians.

In the brief sermon of Peter (139,9-140,1) Gnostic tendencies are even more clearly seen. To be sure, a traditional
Christian credo (139,15-21) constitutes the first part of the
sermon, and traditional terms are applied to Jesus (ⲡϫⲟⲉⲓⲥ ⲓ̄ⲥ̄,
139,25-26; ⲡϣⲏⲣⲉ, 139,26; ⲡⲓⲁⲣⲭⲏⲅⲟⲥ ⲛ̄ⲧⲉ ⲡⲉⲛⲱⲛϩ̄, 139,27-28). But
the traditional credo is interpreted according to the Gnostic
Christian theology of the author of the *Ep. Pet. Phil.* From
his incarnation on Jesus suffered, it is true, but he suffered
as one who is "a stranger to this suffering" (139,21-22). A
Christological tension thus remains as the sermon stresses both
the reality of Jesus' sufferings and the glory of his divinity.
In contrast to the suffering illuminator Jesus (139,15), the
sermon continues, the followers of Jesus suffer because of "the
transgression of the mother" (139,23). This phrase is reminiscent of references to the fall of mother Eve, and refers, for
the Gnostic Christian author, to the mother often named Sophia
in other versions of the myth. She is also called "the mother"
at 135,12, and her tragic fall is seen as the source of human
sufferings. Hence this reference to "the transgression of the
mother" may provide another important point of contact between
the figures of Eve and Sophia in Gnostic literature. In short,
the sermonette of Peter seems to function as the model of a

spirit-filled sermon delivered by an insightful Gnostic
Christian.

It is possible, then, to suggest a general outline for
the literary history of the *Ep. Pet. Phil*. Writing around the
end of the second century or into the third, the author of the
Greek *Vorlage* is a Christian Gnostic who is thoroughly familiar
with the Christian heritage, and who uses and interprets that
heritage in a Christian Gnostic fashion. A Gnostic "dialogue"
has been constructed, though it is less a true dialogue than a
revelatory discourse of Christ in answer to questions raised by
the apostles. Within this "dialogue" are included Gnostic
materials which are non-Christian or perhaps only marginally
Christian; these materials have been adopted, and baptized as
revelatory disclosures of the risen Christ. On the basis of
the Christian and Gnostic traditions with which the author is
familiar, and the concerns of this person and the Christian
Gnostic group, the author compiles a narrative document with a
revelatory focus. In addition, the letter itself is added at
the beginning of the narrative, in order to stress the authoritative place of Peter. Consequently, the *Ep. Pet. Phil*. can
receive its present title. Finally, the Greek tractate is
translated into Coptic, and finds its way into Codex VIII of
the Nag Hammadi library.

The *Ep. Pet. Phil*. is thus a tractate with Christian and
Gnostic features. It reflects the theology of a Christian
Gnostic community which legitimates itself and its message by
using and adapting apostolic--particularly Petrine--traditions
as its own. In fact, it claims to trace its roots and its
message ultimately back to the embodied Jesus himself. Now,
however, as the disembodied light and voice, the risen Savior
must speak again to his followers, and provide a renewed revelation and reaffirmation of Christian Gnostic truths. The
resultant tractate shows the author's concern for the apostles,
and this Christian Gnostic group, gathered for worship and dis-
missed for the proclamation of their gospel.

It remains for us to summarize certain key features of the
theology of this Christian Gnostic group. We shall briefly
consider the Christology, soteriology, and ecclesiology of this
group as reflected in the *Ep. Pet. Phil*.

To begin with, the Christology of this Christian Gnostic
group emphasizes Jesus as both the heavenly redeemer and the
suffering savior. Various titles are applied to Jesus, some
of which (for example ⲡⲉⲭⲥ̅, ⲡ(ⲉⲛ)ϫⲟⲉⲓⲥ, ⲡⲥⲱⲧⲏⲣ, ⲡⲉⲛⲛⲟⲩⲧⲉ,
ⲡⲙⲁⲕⲁⲣⲓⲟⲥ ⲛ̅ⲭⲥ̅, ⲡⲉⲕⲁⲗⲟⲩ ⲉⲧⲟⲩⲁⲁⲃ ⲓ̅ⲥ̅ ⲡⲉⲭⲥ̅, ⲡϣⲏⲣⲉ, ⲡⲉⲛⲣⲉϥⲥⲱⲧⲉ,
ⲡⲁⲣⲭⲏⲅⲟⲥ) are traditional, and common in their application.
Other titles, however, are among the Christological titles that
are preferred by Gnostic Christians, and these titles tend to
occur in sections of the tractate in which Gnostic coloration
is most striking. Thus Jesus is termed the ⲫⲱⲥⲧⲏⲣ both in the
first prayer offered by the gathered apostles (133,27) and in
the sermon of Peter (139,15).[5] This Petrine sermon also speaks
of Jesus as "a stranger" (139,21); and both the sermon and the
second apostolic prayer provide glorious amplifications of the
title ⲡϣⲏⲣⲉ (134,3-6; 139,26-27).

Furthermore, in the account of the descent of the Gnostic
illuminator, Jesus refers to himself as the ⲡⲗⲏⲣⲱⲙⲁ (139,16).[6]
According to the *Ep. Pet. Phil.*, the Savior, sent by the
Father, came down (136,16-17.19-20, in the second answer;
137,30, in the additional answer; 139,12-13.15-16, in the
Petrine sermon) from the fullness and glory of the divine
light, into the world of deficiency and darkness (133,26-134,1,
in the first prayer). A stranger here, Jesus traveled incognito, and was not recognized by the ignorant powers and inhabi-
tants of the world (136,20-21, in the second answer). Indeed,
Jesus was judged to be just another mortal person (136,21-22), for
when he came down into the world he dressed himself in a body
(136,16-17.19-20). He went about "in the body" (133,17; 138,3;
139,11), and from the moment of his incarnation he endured a
life of suffering (138,15-20, in the discussion on suffering;
139,15-21, in the Petrine sermon). In fact, his entire cosmic
experience could be considered uniformly as an experience of
suffering. In the Gnostic Christian interpretation of the traditional credo in the sermon of Peter, the specific moments
within the suffering of Jesus, from his incarnation until his
ultimate release from the body when "he rose from the dead"
(139,20-21), are not interpreted as particulars to be analyzed
individually, but rather are considered only within a general
assessment of Jesus' life of suffering.

Essentially Jesus' life of suffering is like that of his followers (139,24-25). Such a realization is important to the Gnostic Christians of the *Ep. Pet. Phil.*, for it is apparent that they see themselves as a suffering and struggling community. They suffer the deadly pains of being incarcerated within this cosmic prison and these mortal bodies (137,4-9; 138,19-20); they feel the murderous hostility of the powers, the authorities, the enslaving forces of heaven and earth (134,8-9; 137, 10-13); they struggle against those who would entrap their souls or spirits, those described as archons (137,13-138,3), "synagogues and governors" (138,25-26), "lawless ones" (139, 29-30). In various ways these Gnostic Christians are going through the same sort of suffering and persecution that Jesus experienced. In fact, Jesus proclaimed before, and here proclaims again, such suffering is inevitable and necessary, and must be faced with resolve (138,21-139,4). Jesus' suffering is like theirs, except that Jesus voluntarily took upon himself a mortal body, and suffered for them, the light-seed fallen into darkness (136,16-18; 138,18; 139,24-25); they, on the other hand, are caught in the cosmic web of the mother's fall, and suffer only what is their destiny (139,22-23).

The suffering savior is, paradoxically, the savior who is also "a stranger to suffering." He, the fullness and the illuminator, is both immortal and dying. And, having descended into the dark places of this dark world, the dying illuminator rises from the dead, to throw off the mortal cloak of his body[7] and attain to the pleroma of light. Hence, as a disembodied light and voice, the Savior can appear at will from his heavenly glory. Referring to that past time when he was embodied, the divine voice, free of fetters, continues to lead his people with his divine word and glorious light. For he will be with them, with power and light, for ever (134,17-18; 140,22-23).

Secondly, the soteriology of the *Ep. Pet. Phil.* stresses the importance of heeding the call of the Savior, and following his way. The call of the Savior goes forth to those who are his, and by hearkening to his call they can attain to a liberating peace and rest (136,22-28). The word of this heavenly illuminator is available to answer the most profound and

perplexing questions of a disoriented human condition, and to
point to the correct path. In addition to such insightful
answers, spiritual power and divine authority are also granted
to help in the struggle along this path (134,8; 136,26; 137,
25-30; 140,19-21.26-27).

The way to follow, then, is that of Jesus, a way of understanding, of suffering and dying to the corruptible world.
From his revelatory words may be gained an understanding of the
true meaning of existence, and from his life may be obtained a
pattern for the life of the Gnostic Christian. For Jesus is
the ⲁⲣⲭⲏⲅⲟⲥ, the author, founder, and originator of true life
and rest (139,27-28; 140,4); he leads his followers back from
deficiency to fullness (136,28-137,4), and his followers may
become mystically identified with him. For, like Jesus, they
too shall rise out of the darkness, strip off their bodily
vestments, and return to fullness and light. Their destiny is
the same as his: like Jesus, they shall finally live as children of the Father, they shall be full, as glorious illuminators. But even now, as they live in these bodies and suffer in
this world, they can experience a partial realization of this
salvation. As they free themselves from the slavery of this
world, and throw off the corruptible yoke, they can become
"illuminators in the midst of mortal people" (137,8-9). Even
now, while suffering and struggling, they have rest (137,11-12)
and peace (140,17-21.27).

Apart from the archetypical place of Christ as ⲁⲣⲭⲏⲅⲟⲥ,
and the traditional titles which are applied to him, the correspondence between the redeemer and the redeemed in the *Ep. Pet.
Phil.* is remarkable. They both have the same origin in the
light, a similar fall or descent to earth, and similar sufferings, though the author of our tractate does point out that
Jesus' sufferings are *pro nobis*. Again, both the redeemer and
the redeemed in the *Ep. Pet. Phil.* experience the same glorious
salvation, as fullness and illuminators. Thus, if we may speak
of the "two natures" of Christ ("fullness" and "mortal model")
in our tractate, we may also posit a dualistic anthropology,
with "two natures" for the believers ("the inner person" and
"that which is corruptible").

198   *Letter of Peter to Philip*

Finally, the ecclesiological perspective of the *Ep. Pet.
Phil.* reflects the self-understanding of this Christian Gnostic
group: they are the struggling followers of Christ, worshiping
together and preaching in the world. As we have seen, the
themes of gathering and dispersing play a central role in our
tractate, and seem to reflect the life of these Christian Gnostics. Like the apostles portrayed in the tractate, the Christian Gnostics gather for worship. It has been possible in this
study to identify various liturgical elements which are mentioned in connection with these gatherings, and which apparently reflect the worship of the group behind the *Ep. Pet. Phil.*:
the kneeling posture (133,19-20), the use of prayer (especially
the two liturgical prayers at 133,21-134,1 and 134,3-9), the
sermon of Peter, and the liturgical greeting (ⲀⲤⲠⲀⲌⲉ, 140,14)
and "Amen" (140,15). In their gatherings for worship the believers realize the enlightening presence and spiritual power
of the Savior; it is even possible that visions occur as the
light dawns and the voice of understanding is heard within the
group. Furthermore, the potent presence of holy spirit may
prompt wonderful deeds of power, perhaps healings (139,8-9;
140,10-11) and other mighty and miraculous things (140,6-7).[8]

It is in teaching and preaching that the spiritual power
of the Christian Gnostics comes to expression with most significance. In the programmatic statement describing their strategy
in the world, the Savior recommends that his followers not only
gather for worship but also "teach in the world the salvation
with a promise" (137,24-25). For this group is neither passive
nor escapist in the face of the world of darkness and death.
Rather, this is an activistic group, with a keen sense of mission in the world. As "illuminators in the midst of mortal people," they are to carry on the spiritual struggle against the
world rulers by means of their mission to the world. Like the
apostles, the Christian Gnostics are to go forth to preach, "in
the power of Jesus, in peace" (140,27).

[1] Ϭⲟⲙ almost certainly translates δύναμις. Cp. Crum, 815b; *Concordance du Nouveau Testament Sahidique*, s.v. "Ϭⲟⲙ" (Ϭⲟⲙ translates δύναμις one hundred twenty times, but other nouns only occasionally).

[2] ⲡⲉⲭⲁϥ could translate εἶπεν or even ἔφη, and ⲭⲱ surely translates forms of λέγω, including participial forms. Cp. Crum, 285ab, 754ab; *Concordance du Nouveau Testament Sahidique*, s.v. "ⲡⲉⲭⲉ-," "ⲭⲱ."

[3] It could very well be that Peter is thought to have his own disciples; see 139,10 and the discussion above, p. 150.

[4] It is tantalizing to suggest that the *Ep. Pet. Phil.* depends upon a Petrine source or sources similar to or identical with those used in the compilation of Luke-Acts. At the same time, however, it cannot be maintained that our tractate represents, in its present form, a Petrine source that was used and modified in Acts. Such a theory would have to account for the apparent general awareness of various Christian traditions, and place the simple but mature myth of the mother back into the first century C.E. Furthermore, this sort of theory would also have to recognize that in certain instances, for example in the summary statement at 139,4-9, the *Ep. Pet. Phil.* does resemble Acts at points where, as it is usually maintained, Luke's creative hand is seen with clarity. Naturally, the complex problems of the sources of Luke-Acts cannot be considered in this volume. In general, we here are concluding that the *Ep. Pet. Phil.* in its present form may be dated most safely and reasonably in the late second or early third century, when a vital Christian Gnosticism like that of our tractate could very well have existed.

[5] On the soteriological use of ⲫⲱⲥⲧⲏⲣ in the context of the third revelatory answer of the Savior (137,8), see above, p. 197.

[6] On the soteriological use of ⲡⲗⲏⲣⲱⲙⲁ in this second revelatory answer of the Savior (137,3-4), see above, p. 197.

[7] On the soteriological use of this stripping theme in the third revelatory answer (137,6-9), see above, p. 197.

[8] Whether the Christian Gnostics of the *Ep. Pet. Phil.* remained within the Great Church or gathered by themselves for worship cannot be said with certainty. On the one hand, these Christian Gnostics consciously build upon earlier traditions, and use a traditional Christian credo with value. On the other hand, the *Ep. Pet. Phil.* shows an awareness of the "unbelief" of the Great Church, interprets traditional materials in a

distinctively Christian Gnostic way, and reflects liturgical
elements with Christian Gnostic leanings. Hence, we would
prefer to think of these believers as forming their own con-
venticles. If they did remain within the context of the Great
Church, they probably functioned in a manner analogous to
ecclesiolae in ecclesia.

SELECTED BIBLIOGRAPHY

Aland, Kurt. "Bemerkungen zum Schluss des Markusevangeliums."
  *Neotestamentica et Semitica: Studies in Honour of Matthew
  Black.* Ed. E. Earle Ellis and Max Wilcox. Edinburgh:
  T. & T. Clark, 1969.

The Apostolic Fathers. Loeb Classical Library. 2 vols.
  Trans. Kirsopp Lake. Cambridge, MA: Harvard University,
  1913.

Bauer, Walter. *A Greek-English Lexicon of the New Testament
  and Other Early Christian Literature.* Trans. and adapted
  by William F. Arndt and F. Wilbur Gingrich. Chicago:
  University of Chicago, 1957.

Baumeister, Theofried. "Montanismus und Gnostizismus. Die
  Frage der Identität und Akkommodation des Christentums
  im 2. Jahrhundert." *Trierer Theologische Zeitschrift* 87
  (1978) 44-60.

Bellet, Paulinus. "The Colophon of the *Gospel of the Egyptians:*
  Concessus and Macarius of Nag Hammadi." *Nag Hammadi and
  Gnosis: Papers Read at the First International Congress of
  Coptology (Cairo, December 1976).* NHS 14. Ed. R. McL.
  Wilson. Leiden: E. J. Brill, 1978.

Bethge, Hans-Gebhard. "Der sogenannte 'Brief des Petrus an
  Philippus': Die zweite 'Schrift' aus Nag-Hammadi-Codex
  VIII, eingeleitet und übersetzt vom Berliner Arbeitskreis
  für koptisch-gnostische Schriften." *Theologische
  Literaturzeitung* 103 (1978) 161-70.

Blass, Friedrich, and Debrunner, Albert. *A Greek Grammar of
  the New Testament and Other Early Christian Literature.*
  Trans. and rev. Robert W. Funk. Chicago: University of
  Chicago, 1961.

Böhlig, Alexander, and Wisse, Frederik, in cooperation with
  Pahor Labib. *Nag Hammadi Codices III,2 and IV,2: The
  Gospel of the Egyptians (The Holy Book of the Great In-
  visible Spirit).* The Coptic Gnostic Library. NHS 4.
  Leiden: E. J. Brill, 1975.

Bousset, Wilhelm. *Kyrios Christos.* Trans. John E. Steely.
  Nashville: Abingdon, 1970.

Brashler, James. "The Coptic *Apocalypse of Peter:* A Genre
  Analysis and Interpretation." Ph.D. dissertation,
  Claremont Graduate School, 1977.

Brown, Raymond E. *The Gospel According to John.* The Anchor
  Bible 29-29A. Garden City, NY: Doubleday, 1966-70.

Brown, Raymond E; Donfried, Karl P.; and Reumann, John; eds.
    *Peter in the New Testament: A Collaborative Assessment by
    Protestant and Roman Catholic Scholars*. Minneapolis:
    Augsburg Publishing House, 1973.

Bultmann, Rudolf. "Die Bedeutung der neuerschlossenen
    mandäischen und manichäischen Quellen für das Verständnis
    des Johannesevangeliums." *Zeitschrift für die neutesta-
    mentliche Wissenschaft* 24 (1925) 100-46. Reprinted in
    Exegetica: Aufsätze zur Erforschung des Neuen Testaments.
    Ed. Erich Dinkler. Tübingen: J. C. B. Mohr (Paul Siebeck),
    1967.

_____. *The Gospel of John: A Commentary*. English transla-
    tion edited by G. R. Beasley-Murray. Philadelphia: West-
    minster, 1971.

_____. *The History of the Synoptic Tradition*. Trans. John
    Marsh. New York: Harper & Row, 1963.

_____. *Theology of the New Testament*. 2 vols. Trans. Ken-
    drick Grobel. New York: Charles Scribner's Sons, 1955.

Carlston, Charles E. "Transfiguration and Resurrection."
    Journal of Biblical Literature 80 (1961) 233-40.

Colpe, Carsten. "Heidnische, jüdische und christliche Über-
    lieferung in den Schriften aus Nag Hammadi VI." *Jahrbuch
    für Antike und Christentum* 20 (1977) 149-70.

Conzelmann, Hans. *1 Corinthians: A Commentary on the First
    Epistle to the Corinthians*. Hermeneia. Trans. James W.
    Leitch. Ed. George W. MacRae. Philadelphia: Fortress,
    1975.

_____. *The Theology of St. Luke*. Trans. Geoffrey Buswell.
    New York: Harper & Row, 1961.

Crum, Walter E. *A Coptic Dictionary*. Oxford: Clarendon, 1939.

Cullmann, Oscar. *Peter: Disciple, Apostle, Martyr; A Historical
    and Theological Study*. 2nd ed. The Library of History
    and Doctrine. Trans. Floyd V. Filson. Philadelphia:
    Westminster, 1962.

Cumont, Franz. *Astrology and Religion among the Greeks and
    Romans*. New York: Dover, 1960.

_____. *The Oriental Religions in Roman Paganism*. New York:
    Dover, 1956.

Dibelius, Martin. "The Speech in Acts and Ancient Historiog-
    raphy." *Studies in the Acts of the Apostles*. Ed. Heinrich
    Greeven. London: SCM, 1956.

Dörrie, Heinrich, and Dörries, Hermann. "Erotapokriseis."
    Reallexikon für Antike und Christentum. Vol. 6.
    Ed. Theodor Klauser. Stuttgart: Anton Hiersemann, 1950-.

Doresse, Jean. "Une bibliothèque gnostique copte." *La Nou-
    velle Clio* 1 (1949) 59-70.

_____. *The Secret Books of the Egyptian Gnostics: An
    Introduction to the Gnostic Coptic Manuscripts Discovered
    at Chenoboskion*. Trans. Philip Mairet. New York:
    Viking, 1960.

_____, and Mina, Togo. "Nouveaux textes gnostiques coptes
    découverts en Haute-Egypte: La bibliothèque de Chenobos-
    kion." *Vigiliae Christianae* 3 (1949) 129-41.

Doty, William G. *Letters in Primitive Christianity*. Guides
    to Biblical Scholarship, New Testament Series. Ed. Dan O.
    Via, Jr. Philadelphia: Fortress, 1973.

Epiphanius of Cyprus. *Panarion*. Die griechischen christlichen
    Schriftsteller der ersten drei Jahrhunderte 25, 31, 37.
    Ed. Karl Holl. Leipzig: J. C. Hinrichs, 1915-33.

The Excerpta ex Theodoto of Clement of Alexandria. SD 1.
    Ed. Robert Pierce Casey. London: Christophers, 1934.

The Facsimile Edition of the Nag Hammadi Codices: Codex VIII.
    Published under the auspices of the Department of Antiqui-
    ties of the Arab Republic of Egypt, in conjunction with
    the United Nations Educational, Scientific and Cultural
    Organization, with a "Preface" by James M. Robinson.
    Leiden: E. J. Brill, 1976.

Fisher, Edmund W. "The Letter of Peter to Philip and Its
    Relationship to New Testament Apocrypha." Seminar paper,
    Claremont Graduate School, 25 November 1967.

Foerster, Werner, ed. *Gnosis: A Selection of Gnostic Texts*.
    2 vols. English translation edited by R. McL. Wilson.
    Oxford: Clarendon, 1972.

Funk, Wolf-Peter. "Zur Syntax des koptischen Qualitativs."
    Zeitschrift für Ägyptische Sprache und Altertumskunde 104
    (1977) 25-39.

Gärtner, Bertil. *The Theology of the Gospel According to
    Thomas*. Trans. Eric J. Sharpe. New York: Harper &
    Brothers, 1961.

Gold, Victor R. "The Gnostic Library of Chenoboskion." *The
    Biblical Archaeologist* 15 (1952) 70-88.

Goodspeed, Edgar J. *A History of Early Christian Literature*.
    Rev. and enlarged by Robert M. Grant. Phoenix Books.
    Chicago: University of Chicago, 1966.

Guillaumont, A.; Puech, H.-Ch.; Quispel, G.; Till, W.; and
    Yassah 'Abd al Masīh; eds. *The Gospel According to
    Thomas*. Leiden: E. J. Brill, 1959.

Haenchen, Ernst. *The Acts of the Apostles: A Commentary*.
    English translation edited by R. McL. Wilson. Phila-
    delphia: Westminster, 1971.

_____. "Der Vater, der mich gesandt hat." *New Testament
    Studies* 9 (1963) 208-16.

Harrison, Roland K. *Archaeology of the New Testament*. New
    York: Association Press, 1964.

Hennecke, Edgar. *New Testament Apocrypha*. 2 vols. Ed. Wil-
    helm Schneemelcher. English translation edited by R. McL.
    Wilson. Philadelphia: Westminster, 1963.

Hippolytus. *Refutatio Omnium Haeresium*. Die griechischen
    christlichen Schriftsteller der ersten drei Jahrhunderte
    26. Ed. Paul Wendland. Leipzig: J. C. Hinrichs, 1916.

[Horner, G. W., ed.] *The Coptic Version of the New Testament
    in the Northern Dialect*. 4 vols. Oxford: Clarendon,
    1898-1905.

_____. *The Coptic Version of the New Testament in the
    Southern Dialect*. 7 vols. Oxford: Clarendon, 1911-24.

*The Interpreter's Dictionary of the Bible: An Illustrated
    Encyclopedia*. 4 vols. and a Supplementary Volume. Vols.
    1-4 edited by George Arthur Buttrick; Supplementary
    Volume edited by Keith Crim. Nashville: Abingdon, 1962,
    1976.

Irenaeus of Lyons. *Adversus Haereses*. 2 vols. Ed. W. Wigan
    Harvey. Cambridge: Typis Academicis, 1857; republished
    Ridgewood, NJ: Gregg Press, 1965.

Jackson, F. J. Foakes, and Lake, Kirsopp, eds. *The Beginnings
    of Christianity*. Part I: *The Acts of the Apostles*. 5 vols.
    London: Macmillan, 1920-33.

James, Montague Rhodes, ed. *The Apocryphal New Testament*.
    Oxford: Clarendon, 1924.

Jonas, Hans. *The Gnostic Religion: The Message of the Alien
    God and the Beginnings of Christianity*. 2nd ed. Boston:
    Beacon, 1963.

Kasser, Rodolphe. *Compléments au Dictionnaire Copte de Crum*.
    Bibliothèque d'Etudes Coptes, Tome 7. Cairo: Imprimerie
    de l'Institut Français d'Archéologie Orientale, 1964.

Koschorke, Klaus. "Eine gnostische Paraphrase des johanneischen
    Prologs: Zur Interpretation von 'Epistula Petri ad Philip-
    pum' (NHC VIII,2) 136,16-137,4." *Vigiliae Christianae* 33
    (1979) 383-92.

Koschorke, Klaus. "Eine gnostische Pfingstpredigt: Zur Aus-
    einandersetzung zwischen gnostischem und kirchlichem
    Christentum am Beispiel der 'Epistula Petri ad Philippum'
    (NHC VIII,2)." *Zeitschrift für Theologie und Kirche* 74
    (1977) 323-43.

_____. *Die Polemik der Gnostiker gegen das kirchliche
    Christentum: Unter besonderer Berücksichtigung der Nag-
    Hammadi-Traktate "Apokalypse des Petrus" (NHC VII,3) und
    "Testimonium Veritatis" (NHC IX,3)*. NHS 12. Leiden:
    E. J. Brill, 1978.

Krause, Martin. "Der koptische Handschriftenfund bei Nag
    Hammadi: Umfang und Inhalt." *Mitteilungen des Deutschen
    Archäologischen Instituts, Abteilung Kairo*, Band 18.
    Wiesbaden: Otto Harrassowitz, 1962.

_____. "Das literarische Verhältnis des Eugnostosbriefes
    zur Sophia Jesu Christi." *Mullus: Festschrift für Theodor
    Klauser*. JAC 1. Ed. Alfred Stuiber and Alfred Hermann.
    Münster: Aschendorff, 1964.

_____. "Die Petrusakten in Codex VI von Nag Hammadi." *Essays
    on the Nag Hammadi Texts in Honor of Alexander Böhlig*.
    NHS 3. Ed. Martin Krause. Leiden: E. J. Brill, 1972.

_____, and Labib, Pahor, eds. *Die drei Versionen des
    Apokryphon des Johannes im Koptischen Museum zu Alt-Kairo*.
    Abhandlungen des Deutschen Archäologischen Instituts
    Kairo, Koptische Reihe, Band 1. Wiesbaden: Otto Harras-
    sowitz, 1962.

_____, and Labib, Pahor, eds. *Gnostische und hermetische
    Schriften aus Codex II und Codex VI*. Abhandlungen des
    Deutschen Archäologischen Instituts Kairo, Koptische
    Reihe, Band 2. Glückstadt: J. J. Augustin, 1971.

Lake, Kirsopp. *The Historical Evidence for the Resurrection of
    Jesus Christ*. Crown Theological Library 21. New York:
    G. P. Putnam's Sons, 1907.

Lampe, G. W. H. *A Patristic Greek Lexicon*. Oxford: Clarendon,
    1961.

Layton, Bentley. "Coptic (Sahidic Dialect)." Typescript on
    file at the Institute for Antiquity and Christianity, to
    be published.

_____. "The Hypostasis of the Archons, or *The Reality of
    the Rulers*." *Harvard Theological Review* 67 (1974) 351-425.

Lefort, L.-Th.; Wilmet, Michel; and Draguet, René; eds. *Con-
    cordance du Nouveau Testament Sahidique*. CSCO 124, 173,
    183, 185, 196. Louvain: Secrétariat du Corpus SCO, 1950-
    60.

Lipsius, Richard Adelbert, and Bonnet, Max, eds. *Acta Aposto-lorum Apocrypha post Constantinum Tischendorf Denuo.* 2 vols. in 3. Leipzig: Hermann Mendelssohn, 1891-1903. Hildesheim: Georg Olms, 1959.

Luttikhuizen, Gerard P. "The Letter of Peter to Philip and the New Testament." *Nag Hammadi and Gnosis: Papers Read at the First International Congress of Coptology (Cairo, December 1976).* NHS 14. Ed. R. McL. Wilson. Leiden: E. J. Brill, 1978.

MacRae, George W. "The *Ego*-Proclamation in Gnostic Sources." *The Trial of Jesus: Cambridge Studies in Honour of C. F. D. Moule.* SBT 13, 2nd ser. Ed. Ernst Bammel. Naper-ville, IL: Alec R. Allenson, 1970.

_____. "The Jewish Background of the Gnostic Sophia Myth." *Novum Testamentum* 12 (1970) 86-101.

Malinine, Michel; Puech, Henri-Charles; Quispel, Gilles; Till, Walter; and Kasser, Rodolphe; eds. *Epistula Iacobi Apo-crypha.* Zürich: Rascher, 1968.

Ménard, Jacques-E. *La Lettre de Pierre à Philippe.* Biblio-thèque copte de Nag Hammadi, Section "Textes," Vol. 1. Quebec: Les presses de l'Université Laval, 1977.

_____. "La Lettre de Pierre à Philippe." *Gnosis: Fest-schrift für Hans Jonas.* Ed. Barbara Aland. Göttingen: Vandenhoeck & Ruprecht, 1978.

_____. "La Lettre de Pierre à Philippe: sa structure." *Nag Hammadi and Gnosis: Papers Read at the First Inter-national Congress of Coptology (Cairo, December 1976).* NHS 14. Ed. R. McL. Wilson. Leiden: E. J. Brill, 1978.

Munck, Johannes. "Evangelium Veritatis and Greek Usage as to Book Titles." *Studia Theologica* 17 (1963) 133-38.

The Nag Hammadi Library in English. Translated by members of the Coptic Gnostic Library Project of the Institute for Antiquity and Christianity, James M. Robinson, Director. San Francisco: Harper & Row; Leiden: E. J. Brill, 1977.

Nickelsburg, George W. E., Jr. *Resurrection, Immortality, and Eternal Life in Intertestamental Judaism.* HTS 26. Cam-bridge, MA: Harvard University, 1972.

Norden, Eduard. *Agnostos Theos: Untersuchungen zur Formen-geschichte religiöser Rede.* Leipzig: B. G. Teubner, 1913.

Pagels, Elaine H. "'The Demiurge and His Archons'--A Gnostic View of the Bishop and Presbyters?" *Harvard Theological Review* 69 (1976) 301-24.

Pagels, Elaine H. "Gnostic and Orthodox Views of Christ's
    Passion: Paradigms for the Christian's Response to Perse-
    cution?" Paper presented at the International Conference
    on Gnosticism, Yale University, 28-31 March 1978. Type-
    script, to be published in *The Rediscovery of Gnosticism*.
    Ed. Bentley Layton. Leiden: E. J. Brill.

Parrott, Douglas M. "A Missionary Wisdom *Gattung:* Identifica-
    tion, *Sitz im Leben*, History and Connections with the New
    Testament." Ph.D. dissertation, Graduate Theological
    Union, 1970.

Perkins, Pheme. "Peter in Gnostic Revelation." *Society of
    Biblical Literature: 1974 Seminar Papers*. 2 vols. Ed.
    George W. MacRae. Cambridge, MA: Society of Biblical
    Literature, 1974.

Pistis Sophia. The Coptic Gnostic Library. NHS 9. Text
    edited by Carl Schmidt. Translation and notes by Violet
    MacDermot. Leiden: E. J. Brill, 1978.

Polotsky, H. J. "Nominalsatz und Cleft Sentence im Koptischen."
    Orientalia 31 (1962) 413-30. Reprinted in *Collected
    Papers*. Jerusalem: Magnes Press, 1971.

Puech, Henri-Charles. "Découverte d'une bibliothèque gnostique
    en Haute-Egypte." *Encyclopédie Française*. Tome 19: *Philo-
    sophie, Religion*. Paris: Société Nouvelle de l'Encyclo-
    pédie Française, 1957.

_____. "Les nouveaux écrits gnostiques découverts en Haute-
    Egypte (premier inventaire et essai d'identification)."
    Coptic Studies in Honor of Walter Ewing Crum. Boston:
    Byzantine Institute, 1950.

Robinson, James M. "The Construction of the Nag Hammadi
    Codices." *Essays on the Nag Hammadi Texts in Honour of
    Pahor Labib*. NHS 6. Ed. Martin Krause. Leiden: E. J.
    Brill, 1975.

_____. "The Coptic Gnostic Library Today." *New Testament
    Studies* 14 (1968) 356-401.

_____. "The Jung Codex: The Rise and Fall of a Monopoly."
    Religious Studies Review 3 (1977) 17-30.

_____. "*Logoi Sophon:* on the *Gattung* of Q." *The Future of
    Our Religious Past: Essays in Honour of Rudolf Bultmann*.
    Trans. Charles E. Carlston and Robert P. Scharlemann.
    Ed. James M. Robinson. New York: Harper & Row, 1971.

_____. *The Nag Hammadi Codices: A general introduction to
    the nature and significance of the Coptic Gnostic Library
    from Nag Hammadi*. 2nd ed. Claremont, CA: Institute for
    Antiquity and Christianity, 1977.

Robinson, James M. "On the Codicology of the Nag Hammadi
    Codices." *Les Textes de Nag Hammadi: Colloque du Centre
    d'Histoire des Religions (Strasbourg, 23-25 octobre 1974)*.
    NHS 7. Ed. Jacques-E. Ménard. Leiden: E. J. Brill, 1975.

_____. "The Three Steles of Seth and the Gnostics of
    Plotinus." *Proceedings of the International Colloquium
    on Gnosticism*. Ed. Geo Widengren. Stockholm: Almquist &
    Wiksell, 1977.

Rudolph, Kurt. "Der gnostische 'Dialog' als literarisches
    Genus." *Probleme der koptischen Literatur*. Wissen-
    schaftliche Beiträge, K2. Halle-Wittenberg: Martin-
    Luther-Universität, 1968.

Sanders, Jack T. "The Transition from Opening Epistolary
    Thanksgiving to Body in the Letters of the Pauline
    Corpus." *Journal of Biblical Literature* 81 (1962) 348-62.

Schenke, Hans-Martin. "On the Middle Egyptian Dialect of the
    Coptic Language." *Enchoria* 8 (1978, Sonderband) 43*(89)-
    58*(104).

Scholer, David M. *Nag Hammadi Bibliography 1948-1969*. NHS 1.
    Leiden: Brill, 1971. Supplemented annually in the autumn
    issue of *Novum Testamentum*.

Sell, Jesse Jeremiah. "A Note on a Striking Johannine Motif
    Found at CG VI:6,19." *Novum Testamentum* 20 (1978) 232-
    40.

_____. "A Study of the Self-Predication Statements Attribu-
    ted to 'Jesus Christ' in the Naga-Hammadi Coptic 'Gnostic'
    Corpus." Ph.D. dissertation, Duke University, 1976.

Sieber, John H. "An Introduction to the Tractate Zostrianos
    from Nag Hammadi." *Novum Testamentum* 15 (1973) 233-40.

Smith, Jonathan Z. "The Garments of Shame." *History of
    Religions* 5 (1966) 217-38.

Stead, G. C. "The Valentinian Myth of Sophia." *Journal of
    Theological Studies* 20 n.s. (1969) 75-104.

Stein, Robert H. "Is the Transfiguration (Mark 9:2-8) a Mis-
    placed Resurrection-Account?" *Journal of Biblical
    Literature* 95 (1976) 79-96.

Talbert, Charles H. *Literary Patterns, Theological Themes,
    and the Genre of Luke-Acts*. SBLMS 20. Missoula, MT:
    Society of Biblical Literature, 1974.

_____. *Luke and the Gnostics: An Examination of the Lucan
    Purpose*. Nashville: Abingdon, 1966.

Theological Dictionary of the New Testament. 10 vols.
    Ed. Gerhard Kittel and Gerhard Friedrich. Trans. Geoffrey
    W. Bromiley. Grand Rapids, MI: Wm. B. Eerdmans, 1964-76.

Till, Walter C., ed. *Die gnostischen Schriften des koptischen
    Papyrus Berolinensis 8502.* TU 60/5/5. Berlin: Akademie,
    1955.

_____. *Koptische Dialektgrammatik.* 2. Aufl. Munich:
    C. H. Beck, 1961.

_____. *Koptische Grammatik (Saïdischer Dialekt).* 3. Aufl.
    Lehrbücher für das Studium der orientalischen und afri-
    kanischen Sprachen, Band 1. Leipzig: VEB, 1966.

Tröger, Karl Wolfgang. "Doketistische Christologie in Nag-
    Hammadi-Texten: Ein Beitrag zum Doketismus in früh-
    christlicher Zeit." *Kairos* 19 (1977) 45-52.

Turner, Eric G. *Greek Manuscripts of the Ancient World.*
    Oxford: Clarendon, 1971.

Vielhauer, Philipp. "ΑΝΑΠΑΥΣΙΣ: Zum gnostischen Hintergrund
    des Thomasevangeliums." *Apophoreta: Festschrift für Ernst
    Haenchen zu seinem siebzigsten Geburtstag am 10. Dezember
    1964.* BZNW 30. Ed. Walther Eltester and Franz Heinrich
    Kettler. Berlin: Alfred Töpelmann, 1964.

Walters, C. C. *An Elementary Coptic Grammar of the Sahidic
    Dialect.* Oxford: B. H. Blackwell, 1972.

Wilson, Marvin R. *Coptic Future Tenses: Syntactical Studies
    in Sahidic.* Janua Linguarum: Studia Memoriae Nicolai Van
    Wijk Dedicata; Series Practica 64. Ed. C. H. Van Schoone-
    veld. The Hague: Mouton, 1970.

Wintermute, Orval. "Coptic Grammar to the Gospel of Thomas."
    Unpublished typescript, on file in the Nag Hammadi Archive
    of the Institute for Antiquity and Christianity. (Mimeo-
    graphed)

_____. "The Verbal System of VIII,2." Unpublished type-
    script, on file in the Nag Hammadi Archive of the Institute
    for Antiquity and Christianity.

Wisse, Frederik. *"The Letter of Peter to Philip* (VIII,2)."
    Typescript of a portion of a book on Gnosticism and the
    Nag Hammadi codices, to be published.

_____. Unpublished transcription and notes to *The Letter of
    Peter to Philip,* on file in the Nag Hammadi Archive of the
    Institute for Antiquity and Christianity.

Zehnle, Richard F. *Peter's Pentecost Discourse: Tradition and
    Lukan Reinterpretation in Peter's Speeches of Acts 2 and 3.*
    SBLMS 15. Nashville: Abingdon, 1971.

INDEX OF ANCIENT SOURCES

211